CASEY AND KYLE

Something Sticky This Way Comes!!!

HAPPY READING!

A Casey and Kyle Collection by Will Robertson

CASEY AND KYLE: Something Sticky This Way Comes!!!

Printed in the United States of America.

For more information, Will Robertson can be reached online at www.caseyandkylecomics.com

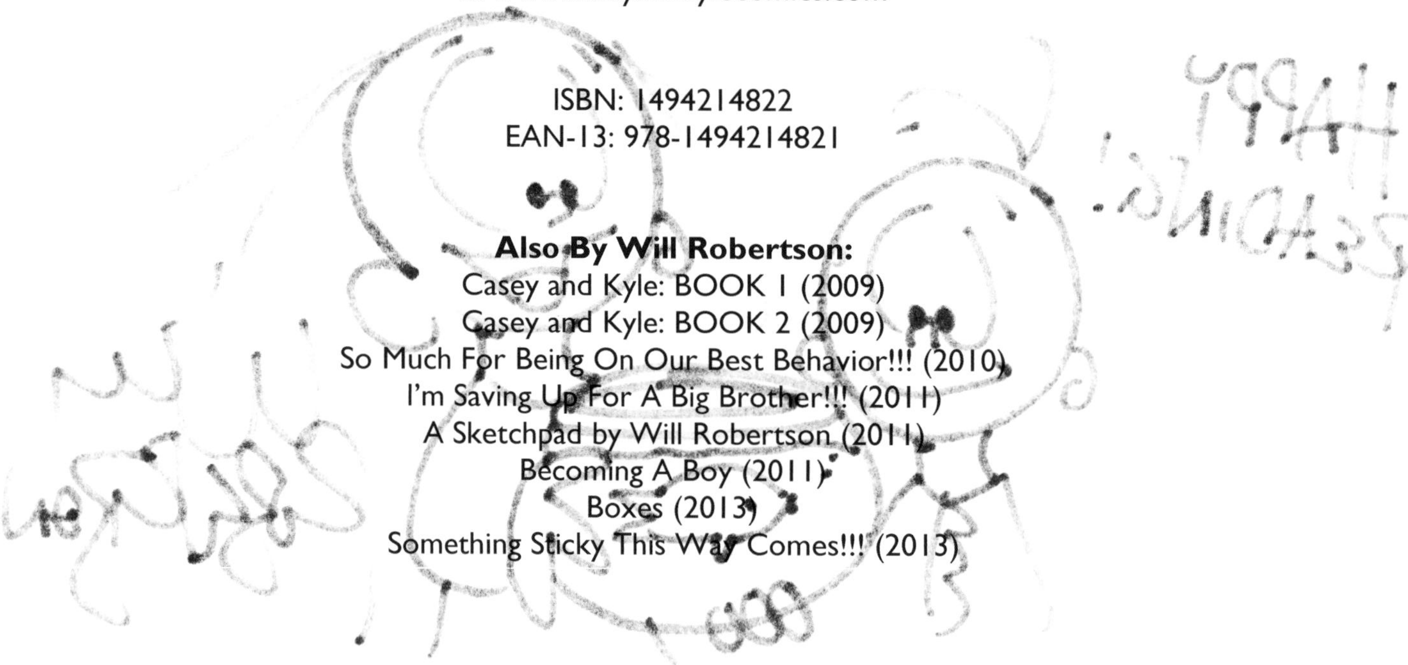
HAPPY READING!

ISBN: 1494214822
EAN-13: 978-1494214821

Also By Will Robertson:

Casey and Kyle: BOOK 1 (2009)
Casey and Kyle: BOOK 2 (2009)
So Much For Being On Our Best Behavior!!! (2010)
I'm Saving Up For A Big Brother!!! (2011)
A Sketchpad by Will Robertson (2011)
Becoming A Boy (2011)
Boxes (2013)
Something Sticky This Way Comes!!! (2013)

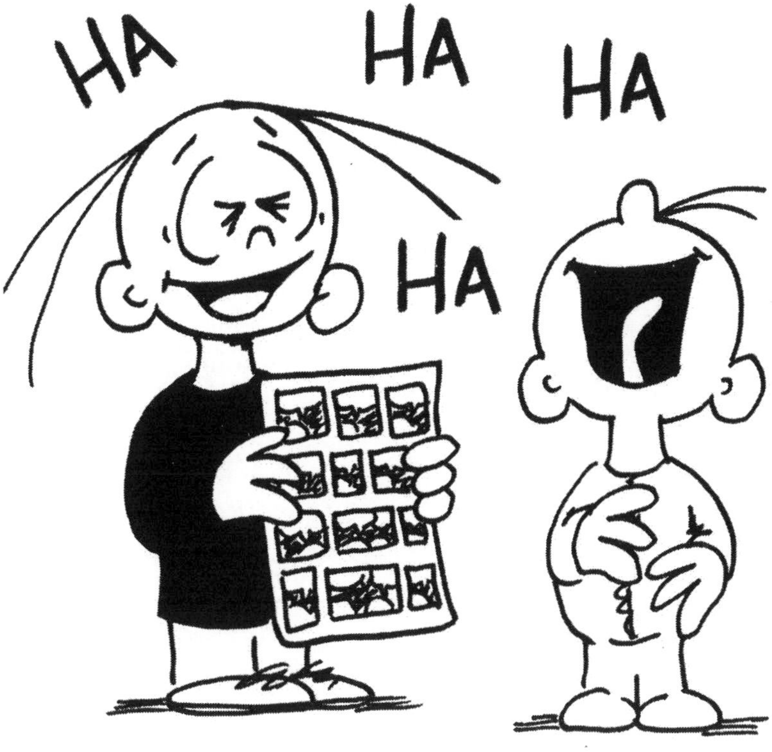
HA
HA
HA
HA

TO MIKE
AND SMALL FRY
FOR MAKING LIFE
MORE FUN

— THE CAST —

Casey and Kyle

CASEY is a fun-loving four year old. He's smart for his age and has a sarcastic side that can get him in trouble. He's a good kid, but finds that he has a lot of learning to do as he grows.

KYLE is a toddler, and is often at the mercy of his energetic older brother. He is just learning to talk and loves to have fun. Casey has a different idea of what fun is, so they clash.

Carter and Zachary

CARTER is Casey's best friend and lives on his street. He is shy and somewhat naïve, and although he doesn't intentionally cause problems, he often falls victim to Casey's agenda.

ZACHARY is several years older than the other kids and is the street's mean kid, causing problems and taking advantage of anyone he can.

Mom and Dad

MOM is the glue that holds the family together. She's a loving mother, but sometimes her sarcastic side comes out and she'll make jokes at the kids' expense.

DAD enjoys roughhousing with the kids and often creates chaos when his idea of good fun is not what Mom has in mind.

Pudding and Rock

JONATHAN PUDDING loves the army... He digs foxholes in the yard and drills his plastic army men. At night, he keeps watch, making sure the enemy doesn't invade.

ROCK is Casey's beloved pet fish. Every so often Casey's parents have to pick up a new "Rock" at the pet store. Don't tell Casey!

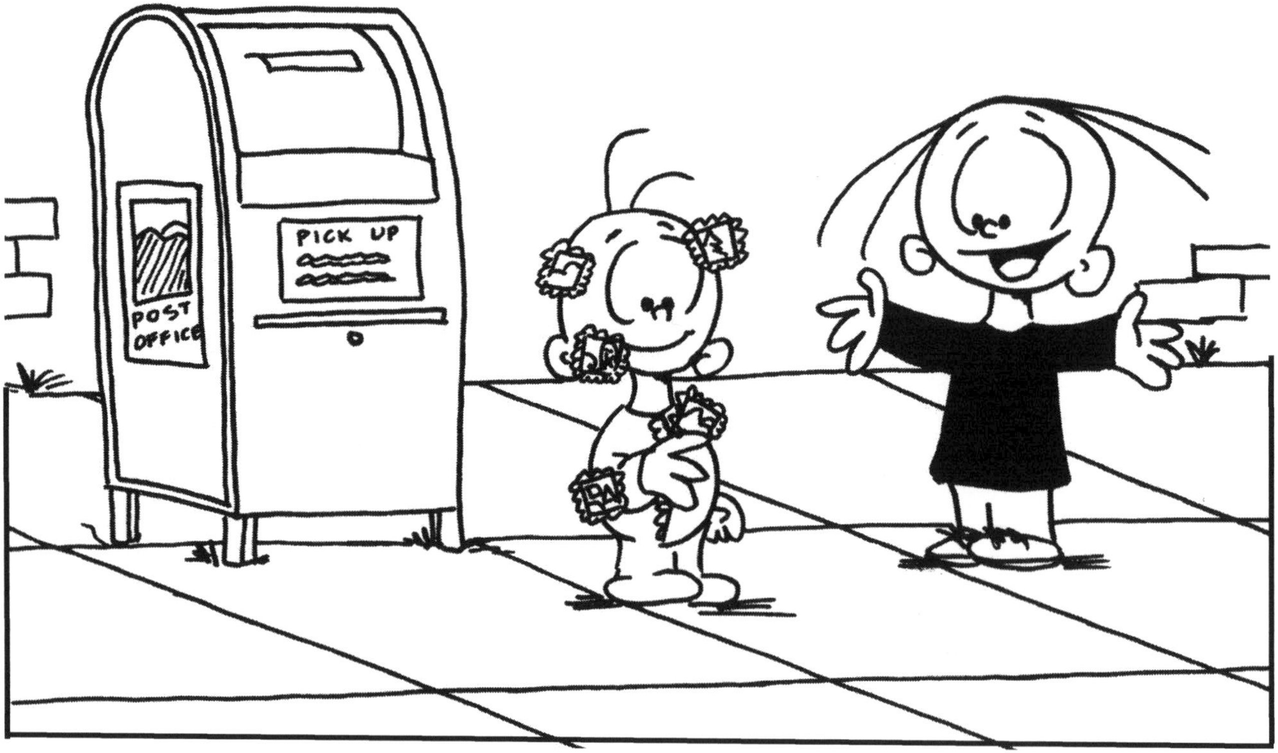
PICK UP
POST OFFICE

JOIN THE FAN CLUB!

SIGN UP FOR FREE AT:
WWW.CASEYANDKYLECOMICS.COM

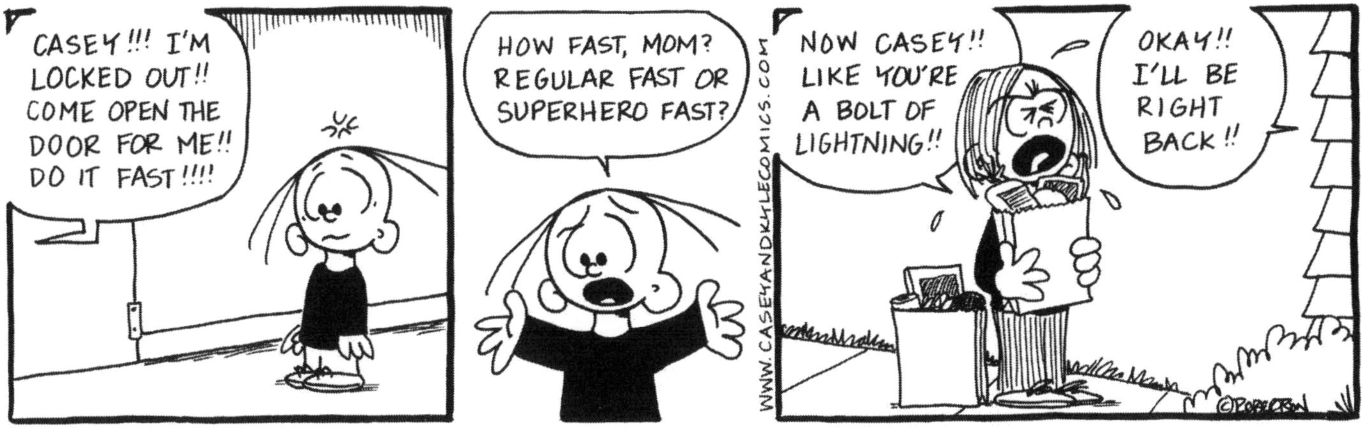
CASEY!!! I'M LOCKED OUT!! COME OPEN THE DOOR FOR ME!! DO IT FAST!!!!
HOW FAST, MOM? REGULAR FAST OR SUPERHERO FAST?
WWW.CASEYANDKYLECOMICS.COM
NOW CASEY!! LIKE YOU'RE A BOLT OF LIGHTNING!!
OKAY!! I'LL BE RIGHT BACK!!
©ROBERTSON

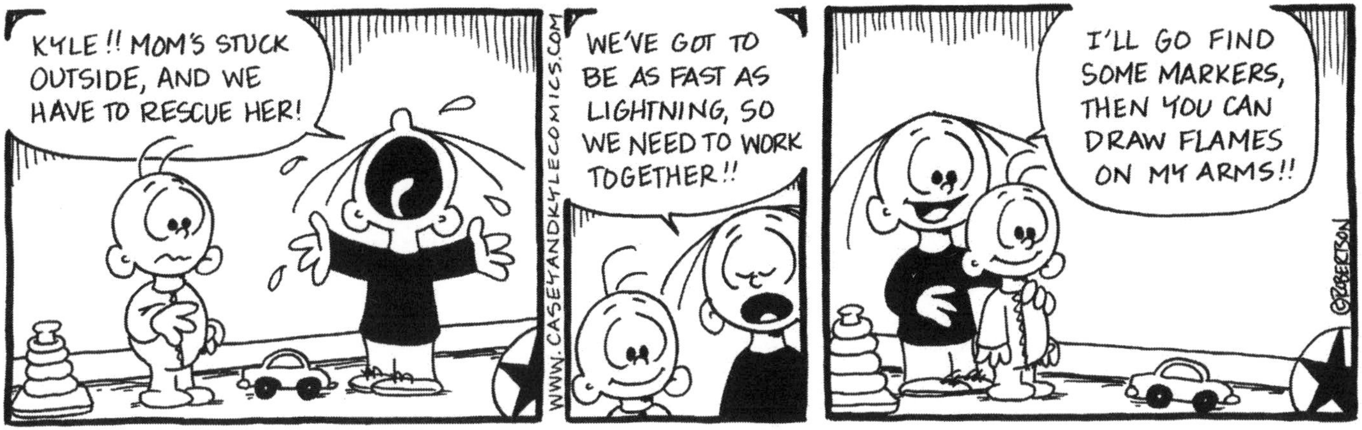
KYLE!! MOM'S STUCK OUTSIDE, AND WE HAVE TO RESCUE HER!
WWW.CASEYANDKYLECOMICS.COM
WE'VE GOT TO BE AS FAST AS LIGHTNING, SO WE NEED TO WORK TOGETHER!!
I'LL GO FIND SOME MARKERS, THEN YOU CAN DRAW FLAMES ON MY ARMS!!
©ROBERTSON

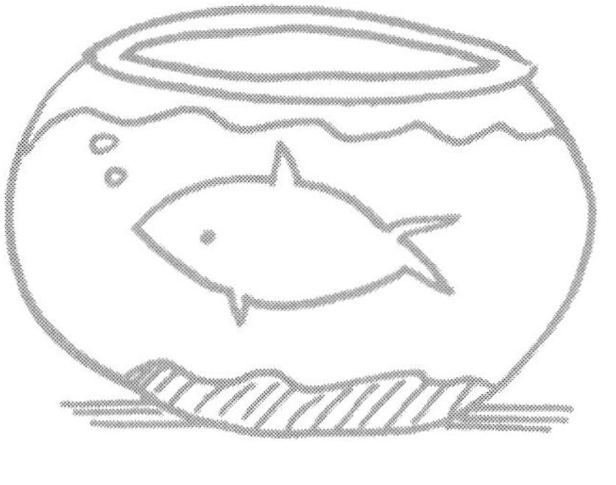

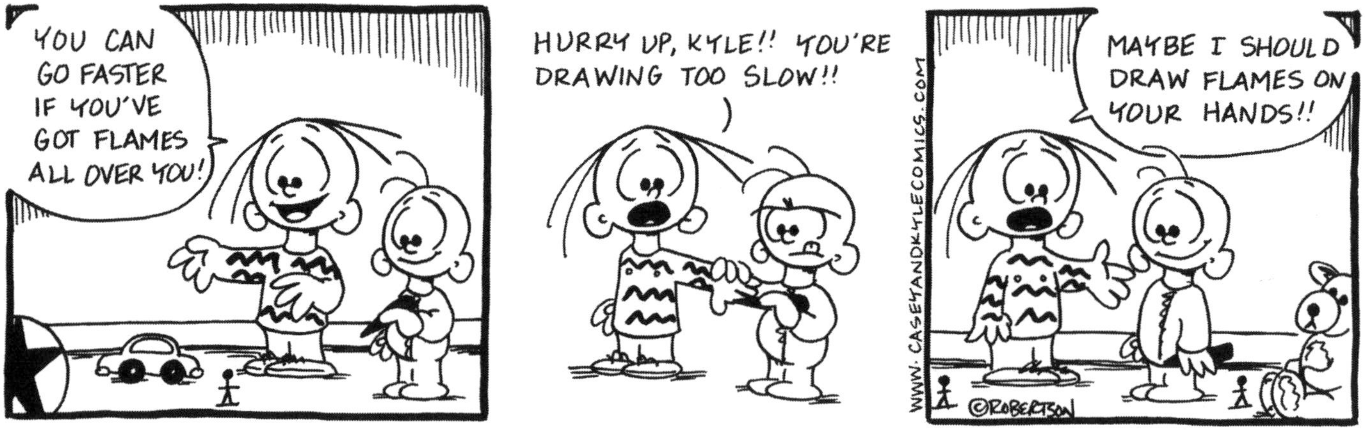
YOU CAN GO FASTER IF YOU'VE GOT FLAMES ALL OVER YOU!
HURRY UP, KYLE!! YOU'RE DRAWING TOO SLOW!!
MAYBE I SHOULD DRAW FLAMES ON YOUR HANDS!!
WWW.CASEYANDKYLECOMICS.COM
©ROBERTSON

8

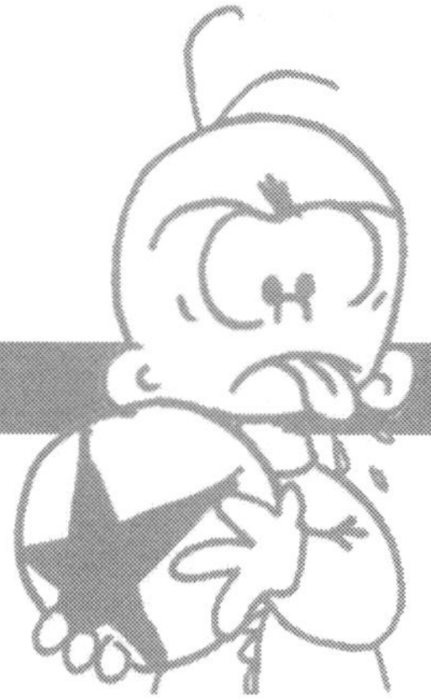

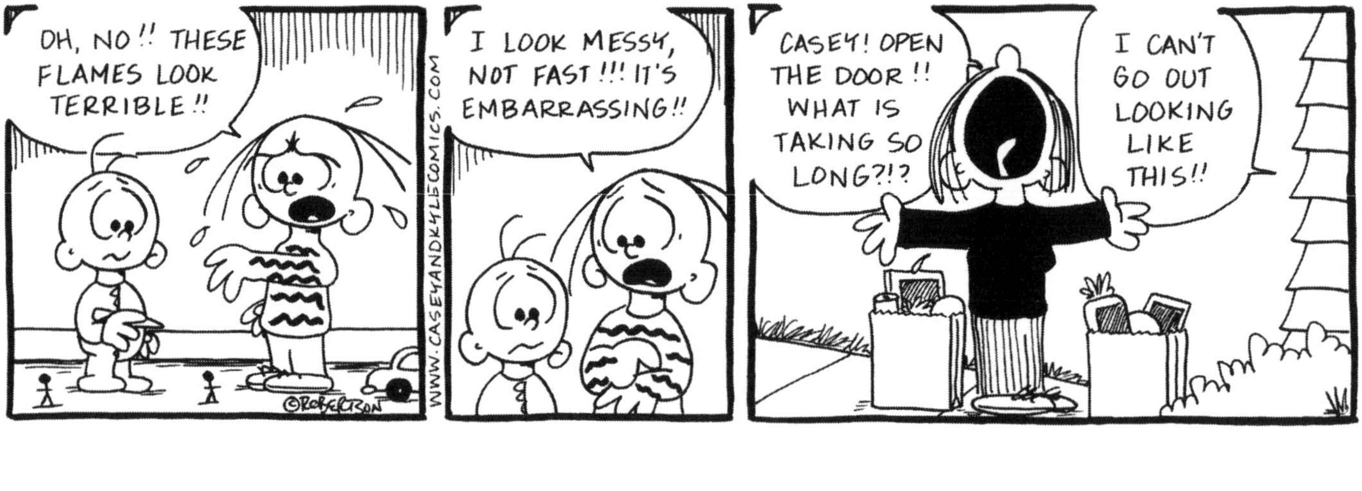
OH, NO!! THESE FLAMES LOOK TERRIBLE!!
©ROBERTSON
WWW.CASEYANDKYLECOMICS.COM
I LOOK MESSY, NOT FAST!!! IT'S EMBARRASSING!!
CASEY! OPEN THE DOOR!! WHAT IS TAKING SO LONG?!?
I CAN'T GO OUT LOOKING LIKE THIS!!

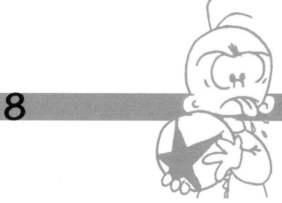

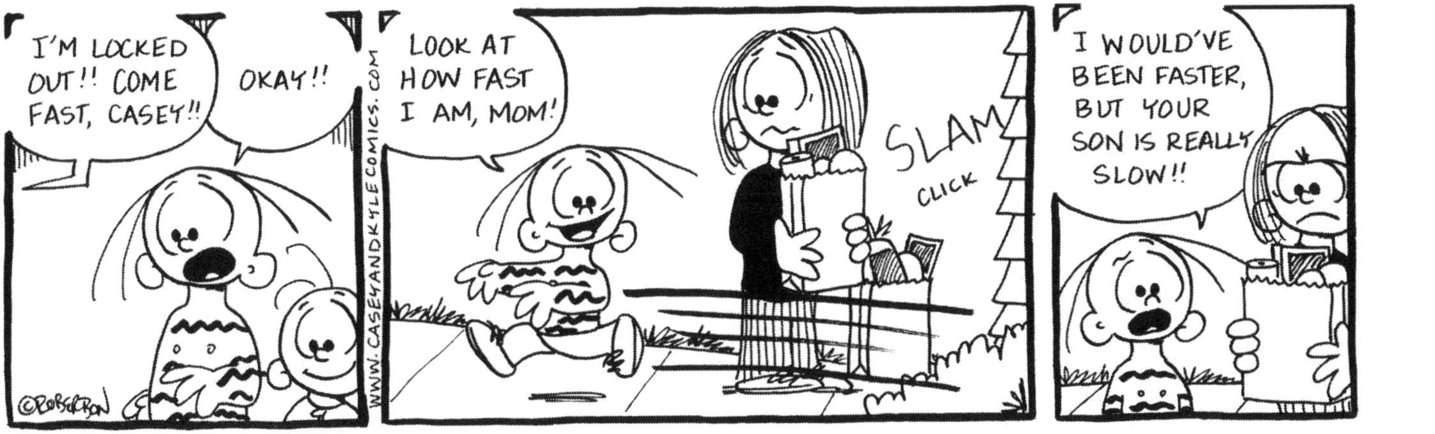
I'M LOCKED OUT!! COME FAST, CASEY!!
OKAY!!
WWW.CASEYANDKYLECOMICS.COM
LOOK AT HOW FAST I AM, MOM!
SLAM
CLICK
I WOULD'VE BEEN FASTER, BUT YOUR SON IS REALLY SLOW!!

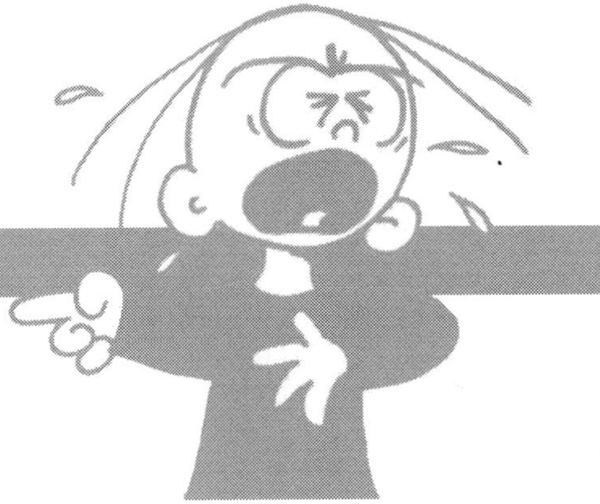

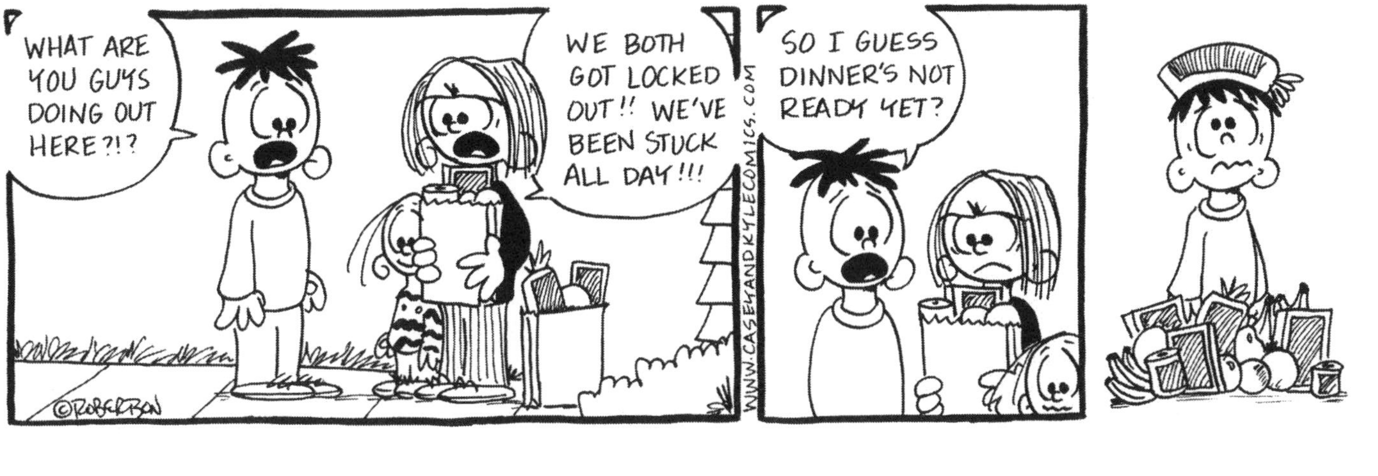
WHAT ARE YOU GUYS DOING OUT HERE?!?
WE BOTH GOT LOCKED OUT!! WE'VE BEEN STUCK ALL DAY!!!
WWW.CASEYANDKYLECOMICS.COM
SO I GUESS DINNER'S NOT READY YET?

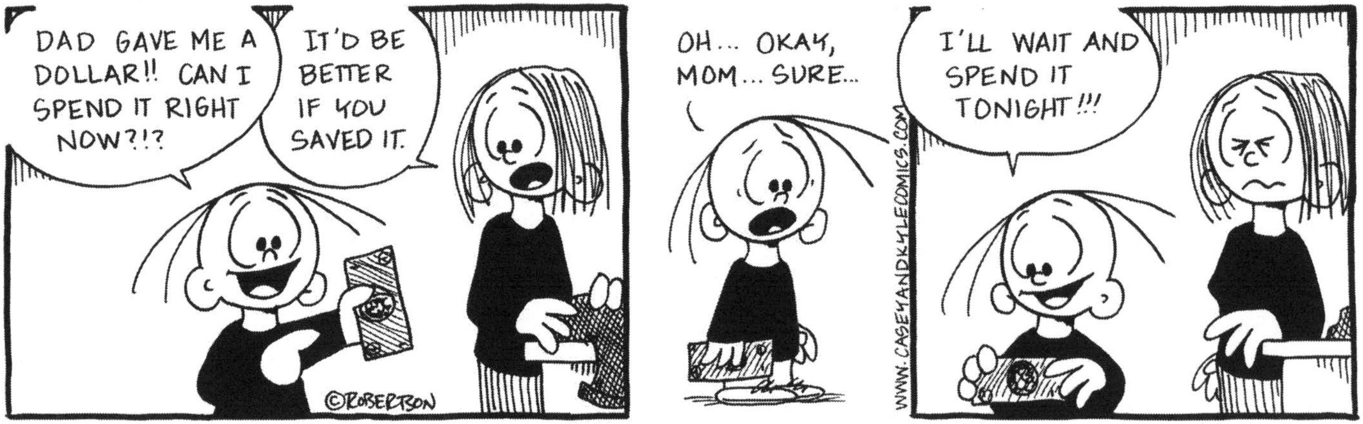
DAD GAVE ME A DOLLAR!! CAN I SPEND IT RIGHT NOW?!?
IT'D BE BETTER IF YOU SAVED IT.
©ROBERTSON
OH... OKAY, MOM... SURE...
WWW.CASEYANDKYLECOMICS.COM
I'LL WAIT AND SPEND IT TONIGHT!!!

10

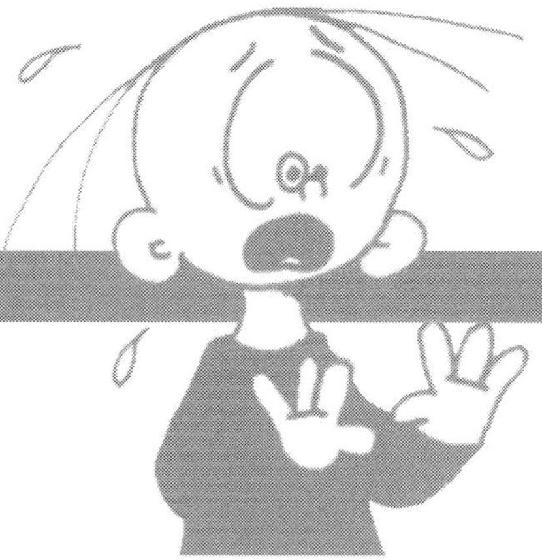

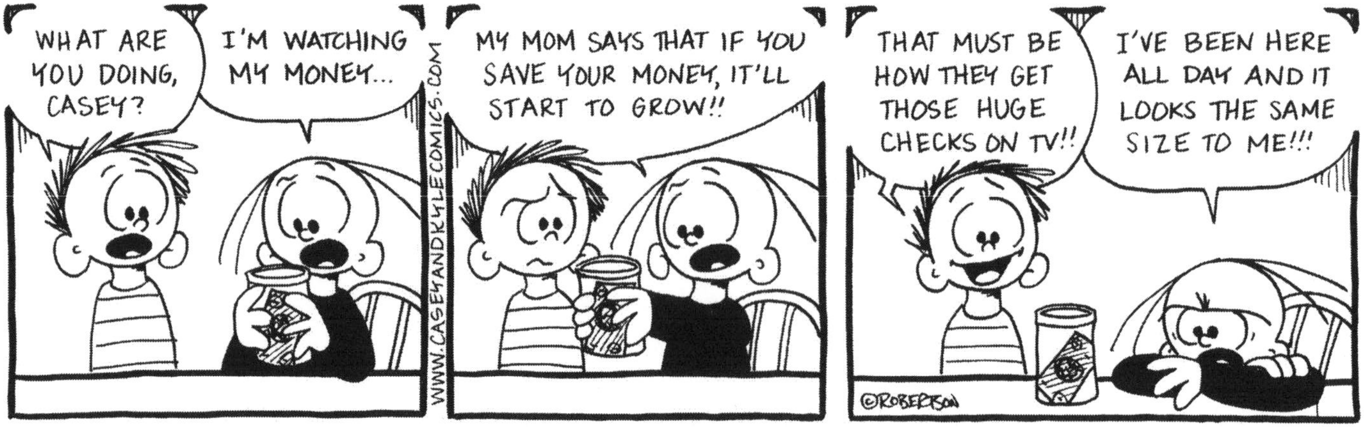
WHAT ARE YOU DOING, CASEY?
I'M WATCHING MY MONEY...
WWW.CASEYANDKYLECOMICS.COM
MY MOM SAYS THAT IF YOU SAVE YOUR MONEY, IT'LL START TO GROW!!
THAT MUST BE HOW THEY GET THOSE HUGE CHECKS ON TV!!
I'VE BEEN HERE ALL DAY AND IT LOOKS THE SAME SIZE TO ME!!!
©ROBERTSON

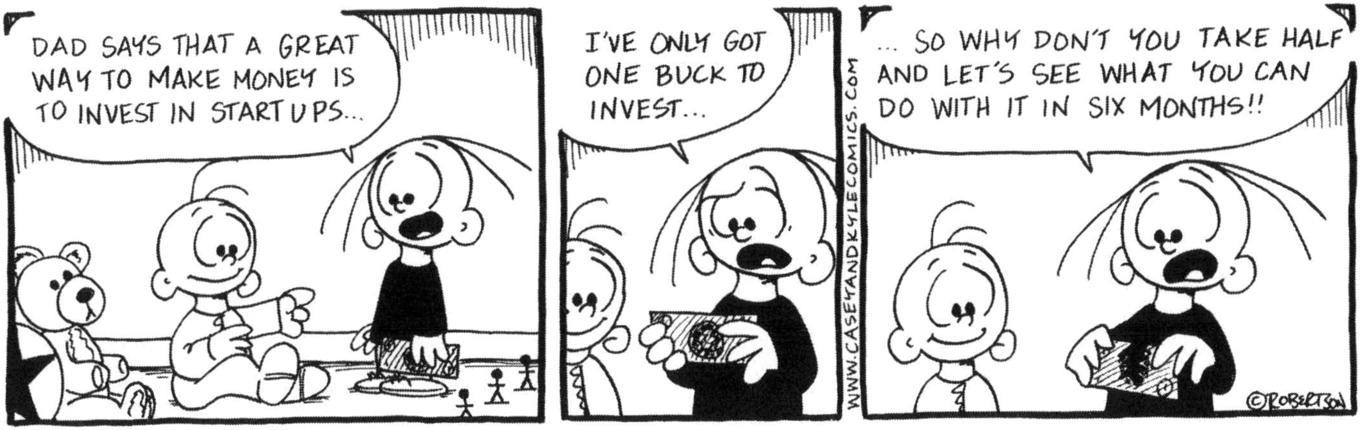
DAD SAYS THAT A GREAT WAY TO MAKE MONEY IS TO INVEST IN START UPS...
I'VE ONLY GOT ONE BUCK TO INVEST...
... SO WHY DON'T YOU TAKE HALF AND LET'S SEE WHAT YOU CAN DO WITH IT IN SIX MONTHS!!
WWW.CASEYANDKYLECOMICS.COM
©ROBERTSON

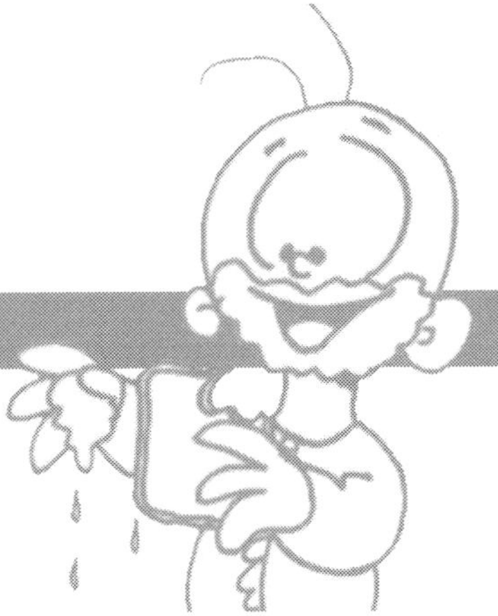

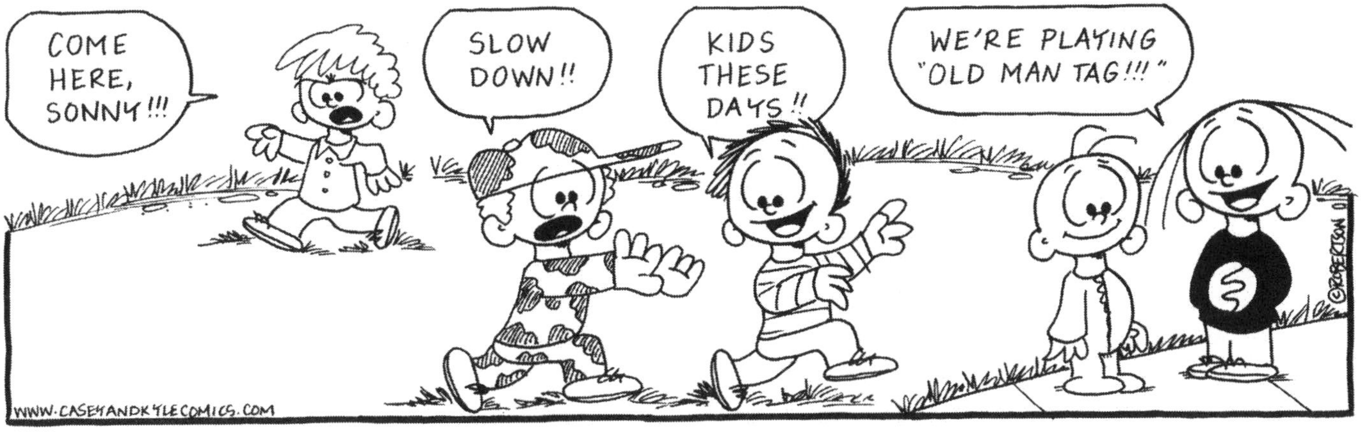
COME HERE, SONNY!!!
SLOW DOWN!!
KIDS THESE DAYS!!
WE'RE PLAYING "OLD MAN TAG!!!"
©ROBERTSON
WWW.CASEYANDKYLECOMICS.COM

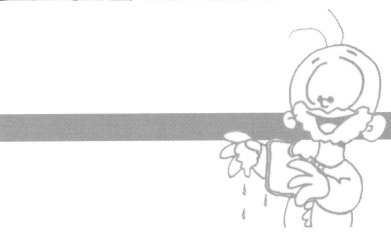

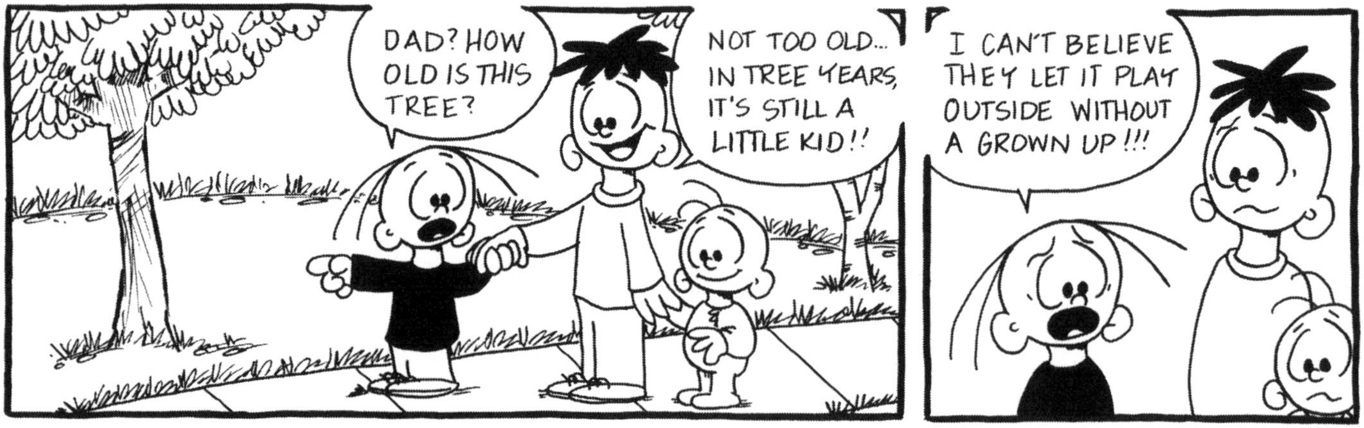
DAD? HOW OLD IS THIS TREE?
NOT TOO OLD... IN TREE YEARS, IT'S STILL A LITTLE KID!!
I CAN'T BELIEVE THEY LET IT PLAY OUTSIDE WITHOUT A GROWN UP!!!

12

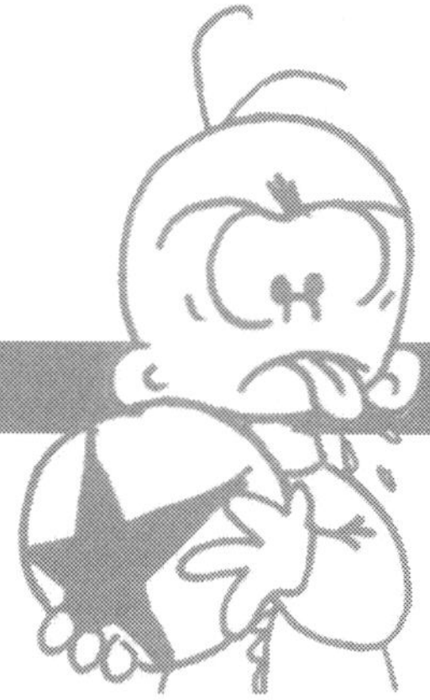

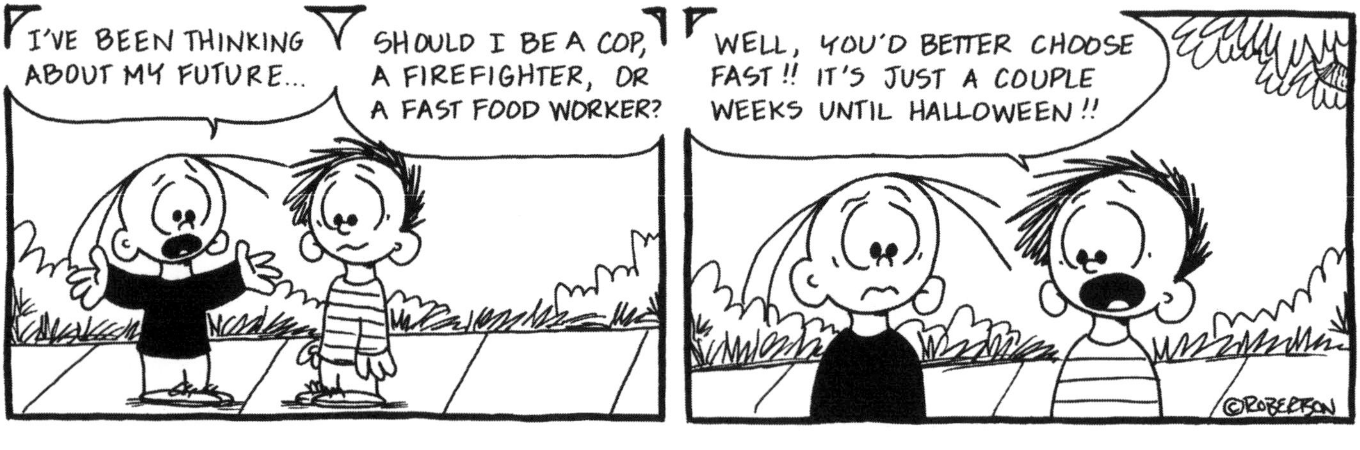
I'VE BEEN THINKING ABOUT MY FUTURE...
SHOULD I BE A COP, A FIREFIGHTER, OR A FAST FOOD WORKER?
WELL, YOU'D BETTER CHOOSE FAST!! IT'S JUST A COUPLE WEEKS UNTIL HALLOWEEN!!
©ROBERTSON

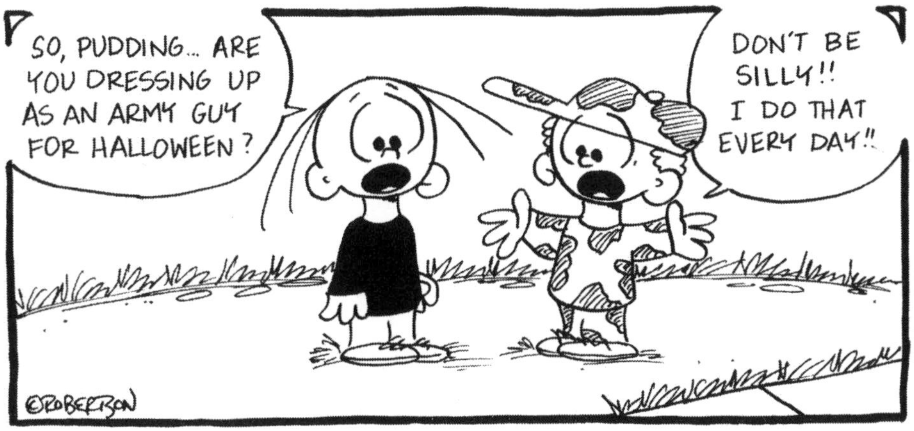
SO, PUDDING... ARE YOU DRESSING UP AS AN ARMY GUY FOR HALLOWEEN?
DON'T BE SILLY!! I DO THAT EVERY DAY!!
FOR HALLOWEEN, I'M GOING AS A MARINE!!
©ROBERTSON

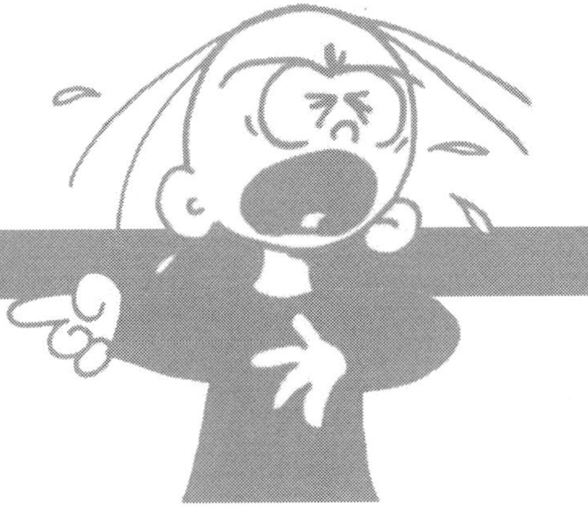

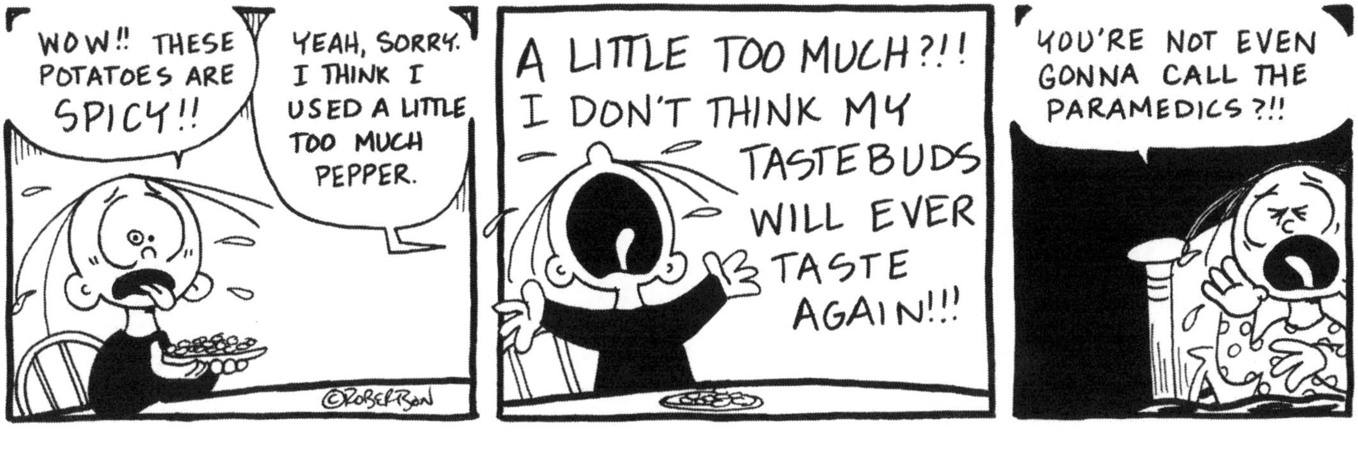
WOW!! THESE POTATOES ARE SPICY!!
YEAH, SORRY. I THINK I USED A LITTLE TOO MUCH PEPPER.
©ROBERTSON
A LITTLE TOO MUCH?!! I DON'T THINK MY TASTEBUDS WILL EVER TASTE AGAIN!!!
YOU'RE NOT EVEN GONNA CALL THE PARAMEDICS?!!

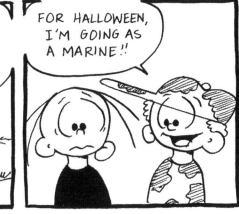

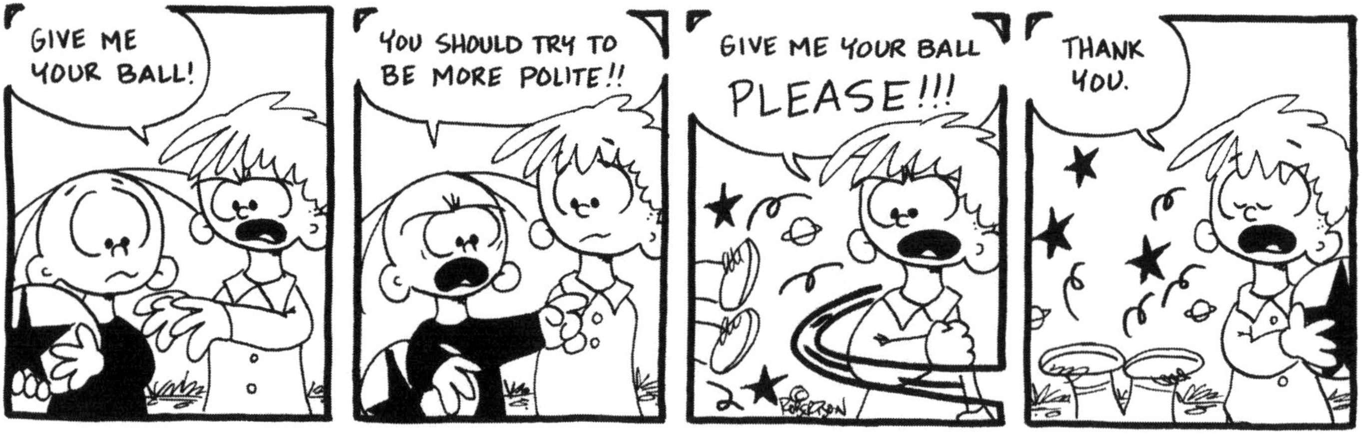
GIVE ME YOUR BALL!
YOU SHOULD TRY TO BE MORE POLITE!!
GIVE ME YOUR BALL PLEASE!!!
THANK YOU.
©ROBERTSON

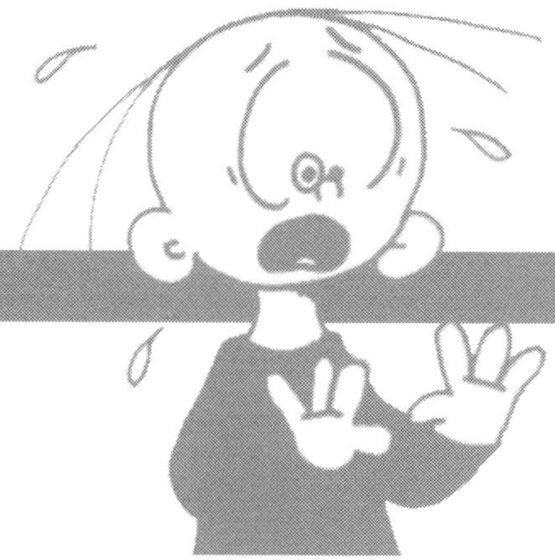

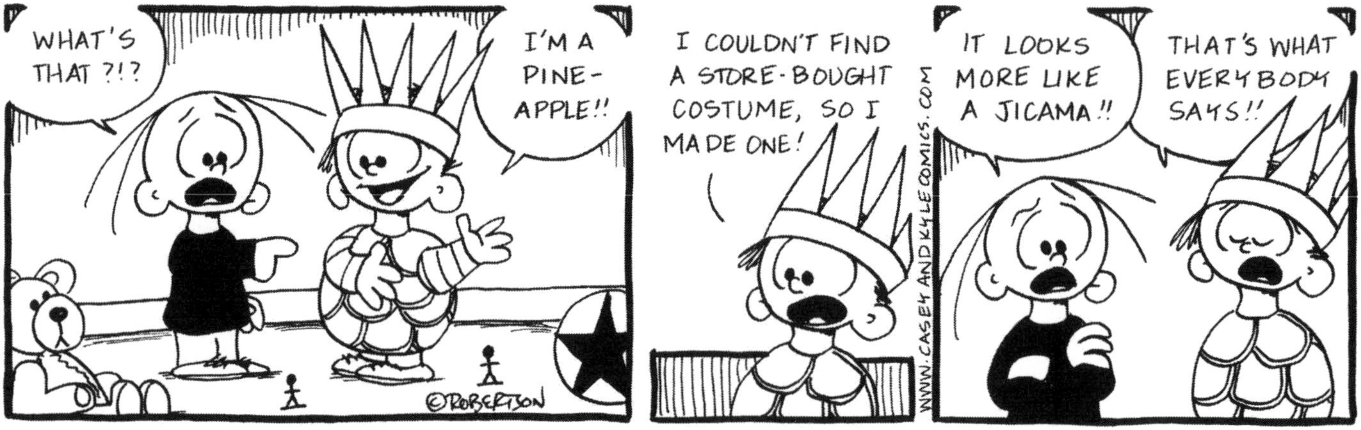
WHAT'S THAT ?!?
I'M A PINE-APPLE!!
I COULDN'T FIND A STORE-BOUGHT COSTUME, SO I MADE ONE!
IT LOOKS MORE LIKE A JICAMA!!
THAT'S WHAT EVERYBODY SAYS!!
©ROBERTSON
WWW.CASEYANDKYLECOMICS.COM

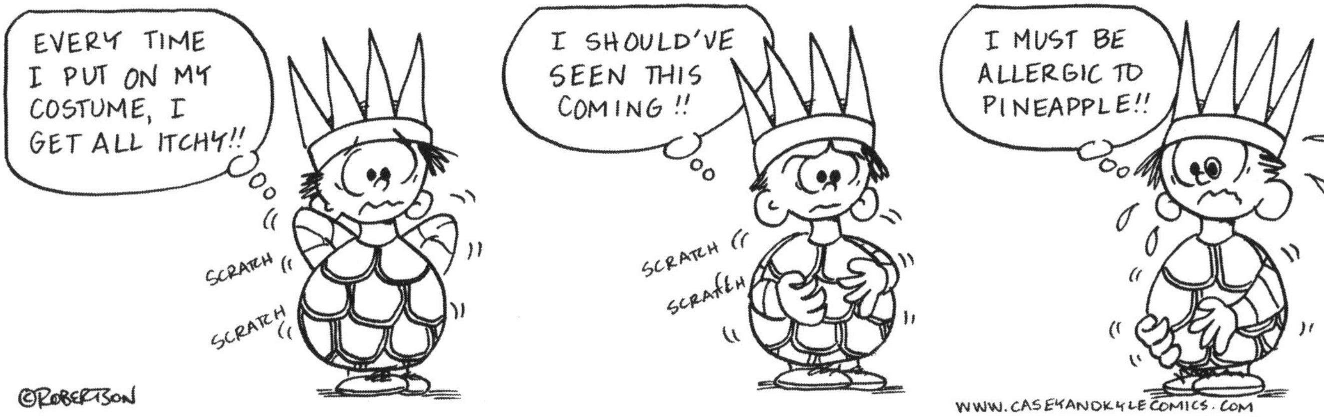
EVERY TIME I PUT ON MY COSTUME, I GET ALL ITCHY!!
SCRATCH
SCRATCH
I SHOULD'VE SEEN THIS COMING!!
SCRATCH
SCRATCH
I MUST BE ALLERGIC TO PINEAPPLE!!
©ROBERTSON
WWW.CASEYANDKYLECOMICS.COM

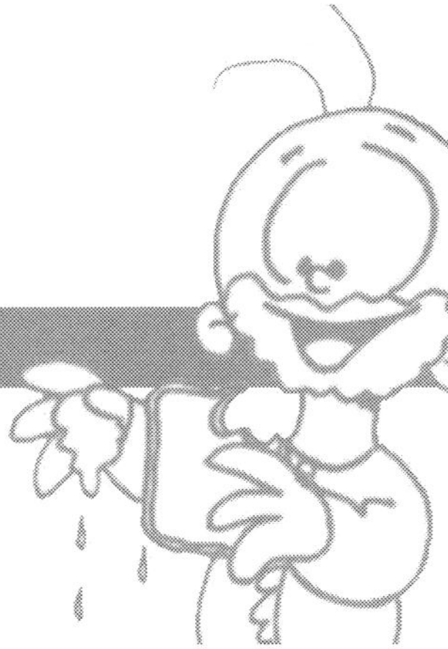

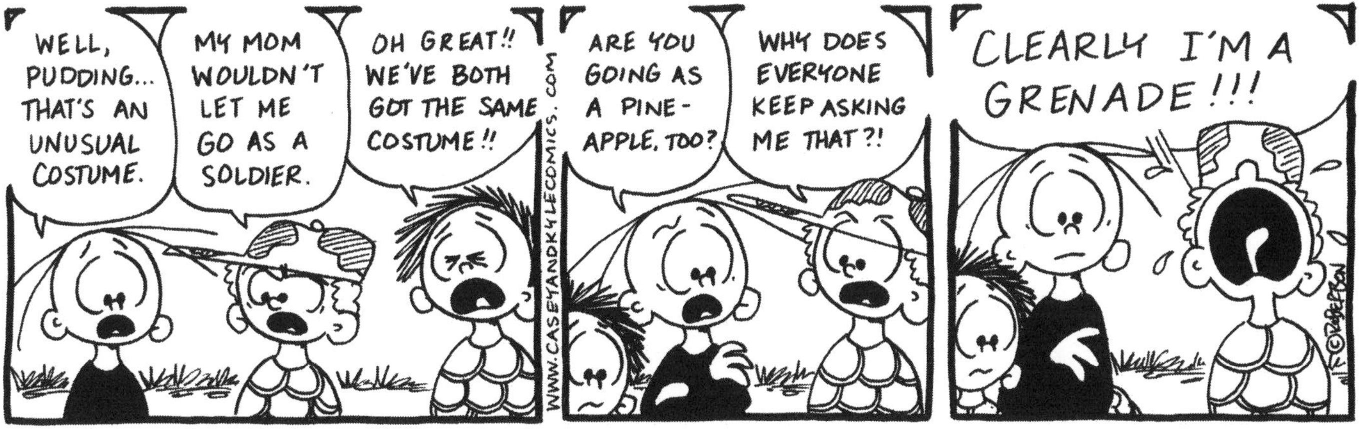
WELL, PUDDING... THAT'S AN UNUSUAL COSTUME.
MY MOM WOULDN'T LET ME GO AS A SOLDIER.
OH GREAT!! WE'VE BOTH GOT THE SAME COSTUME!!
WWW.CASEYANDKYLECOMICS.COM
ARE YOU GOING AS A PINE-APPLE, TOO?
WHY DOES EVERYONE KEEP ASKING ME THAT?!
CLEARLY I'M A GRENADE!!!
©ROBERTSON

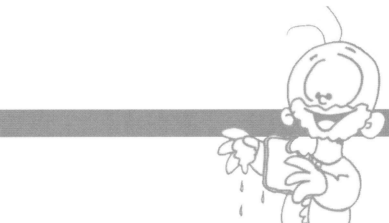

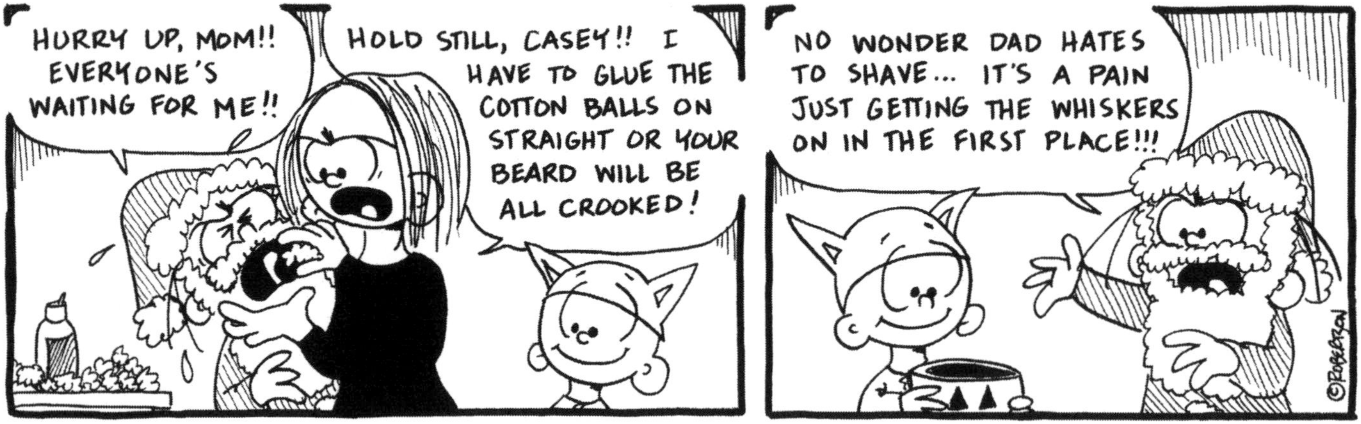
HURRY UP, MOM!! EVERYONE'S WAITING FOR ME!!
HOLD STILL, CASEY!! I HAVE TO GLUE THE COTTON BALLS ON STRAIGHT OR YOUR BEARD WILL BE ALL CROOKED!
NO WONDER DAD HATES TO SHAVE... IT'S A PAIN JUST GETTING THE WHISKERS ON IN THE FIRST PLACE!!!
©ROBERSON

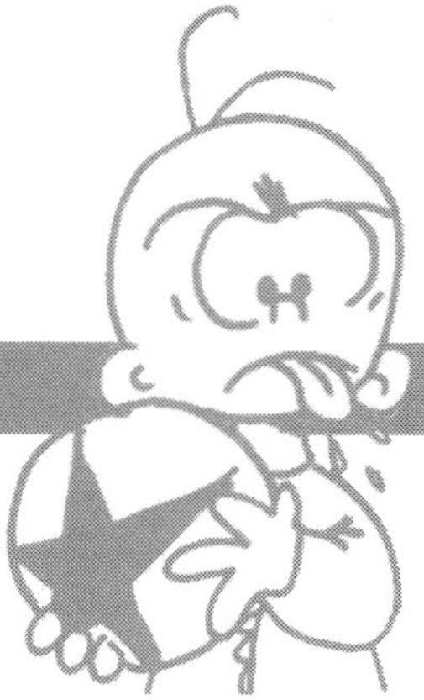

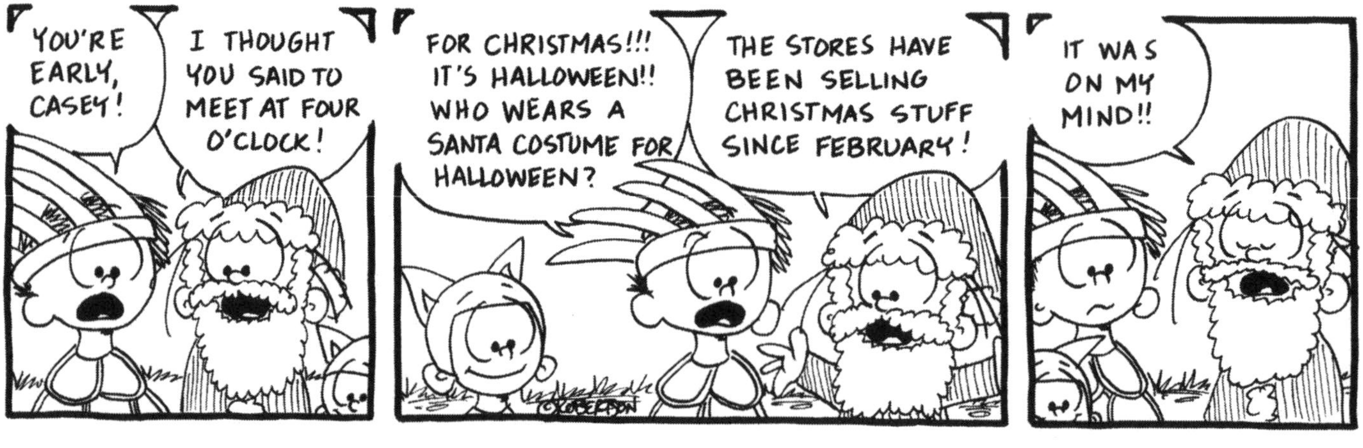
YOU'RE EARLY, CASEY!
I THOUGHT YOU SAID TO MEET AT FOUR O'CLOCK!
FOR CHRISTMAS!!! IT'S HALLOWEEN!! WHO WEARS A SANTA COSTUME FOR HALLOWEEN?
THE STORES HAVE BEEN SELLING CHRISTMAS STUFF SINCE FEBRUARY!
IT WAS ON MY MIND!!
©ROBERSON

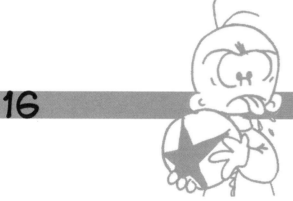

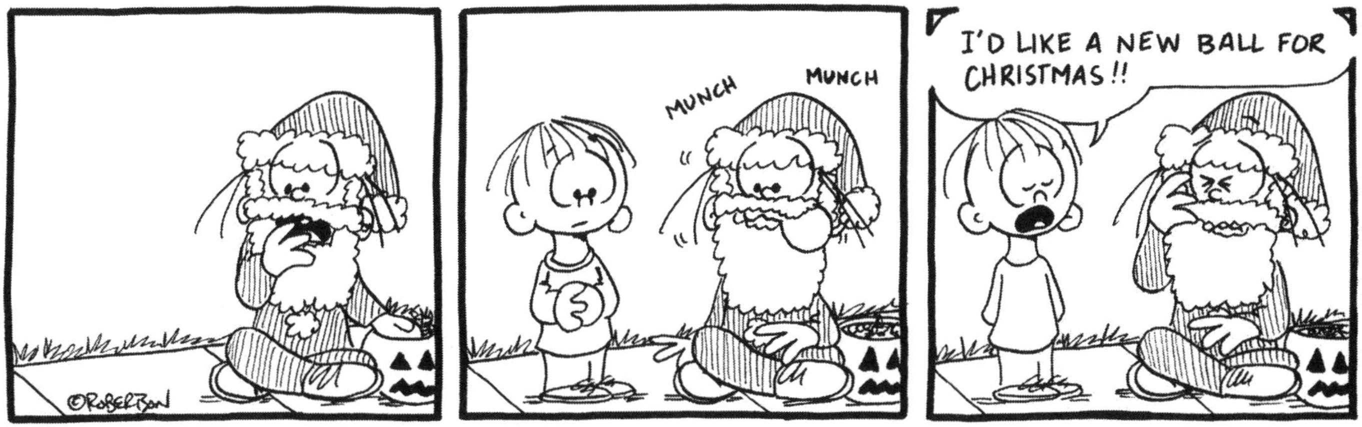
©ROBERTSON
MUNCH
MUNCH
I'D LIKE A NEW BALL FOR CHRISTMAS!!

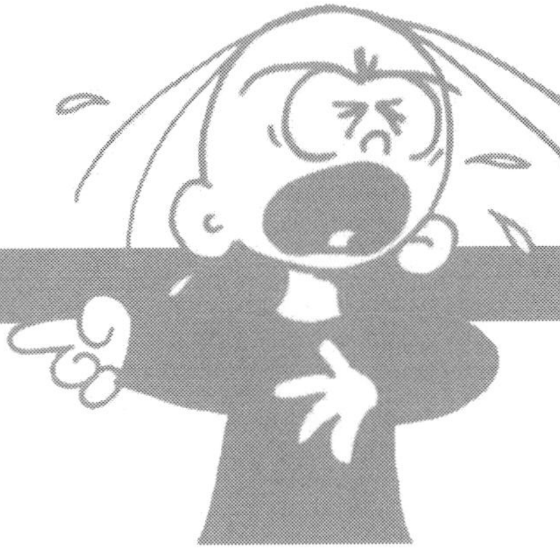

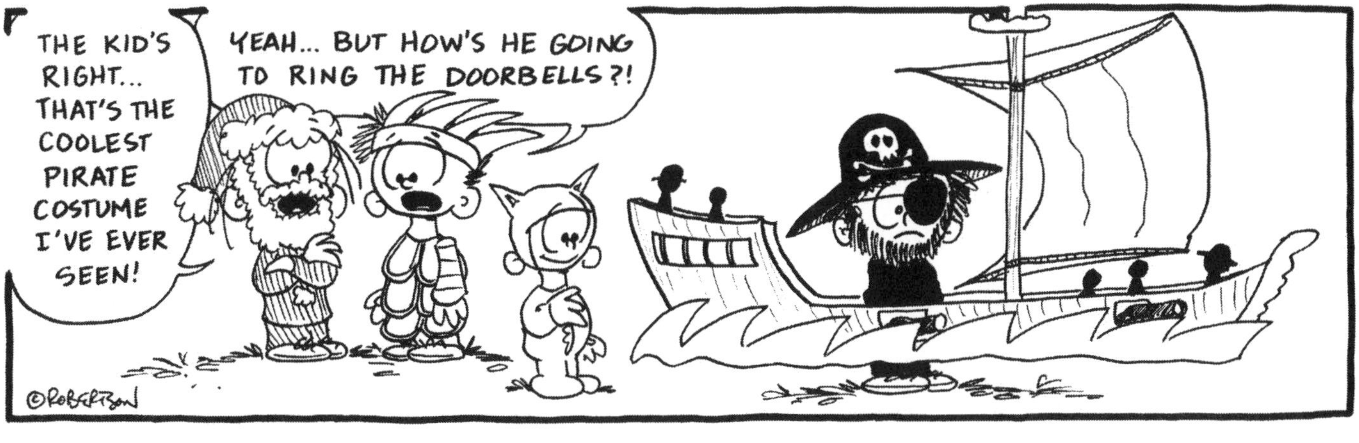
THE KID'S RIGHT... THAT'S THE COOLEST PIRATE COSTUME I'VE EVER SEEN!
YEAH... BUT HOW'S HE GOING TO RING THE DOORBELLS?!
©ROBERTSON

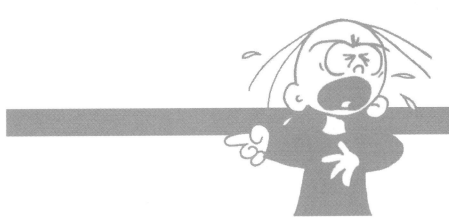

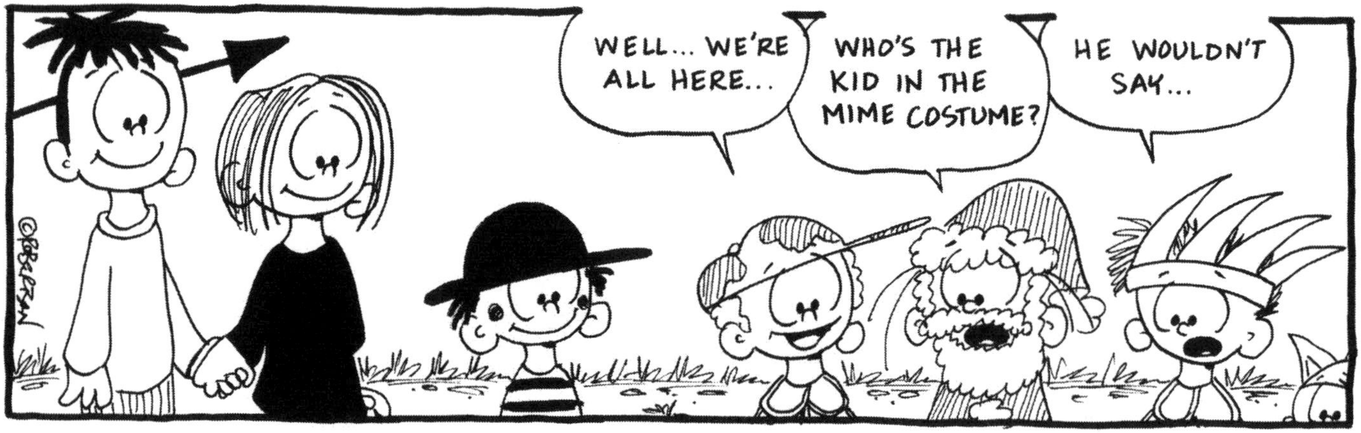
©ROBERTSON
WELL... WE'RE ALL HERE...
WHO'S THE KID IN THE MIME COSTUME?
HE WOULDN'T SAY...

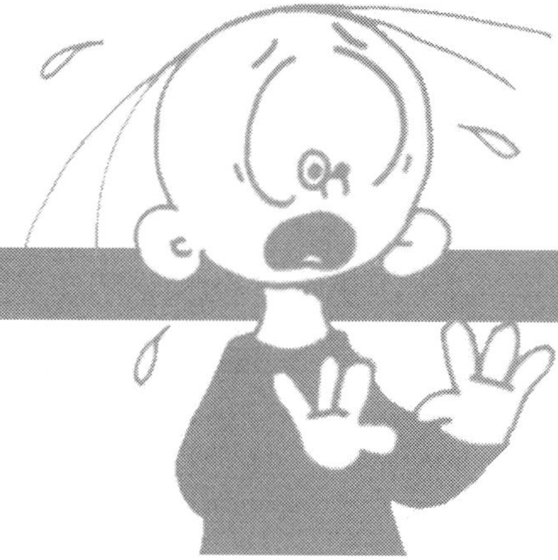

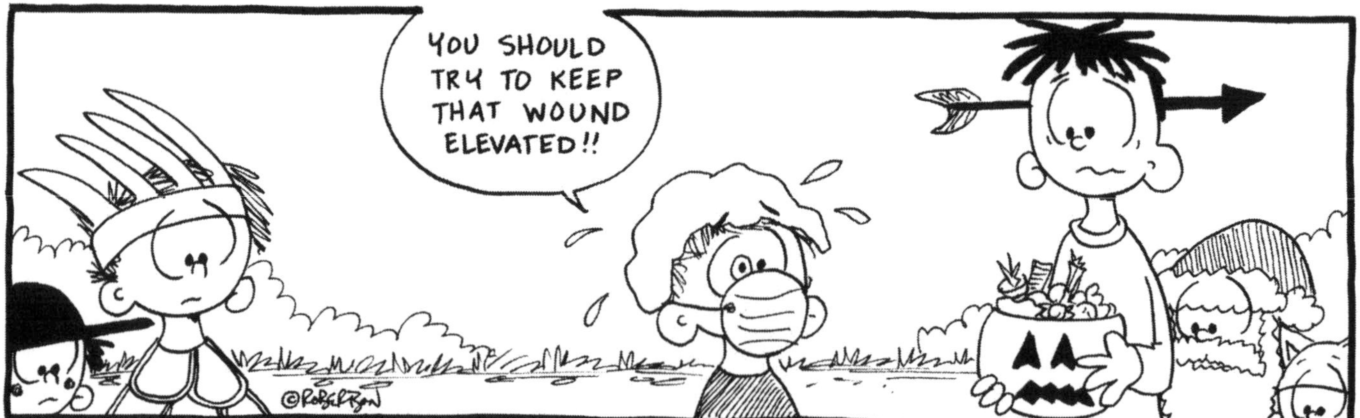
YOU SHOULD TRY TO KEEP THAT WOUND ELEVATED!!
©ROBERTSON

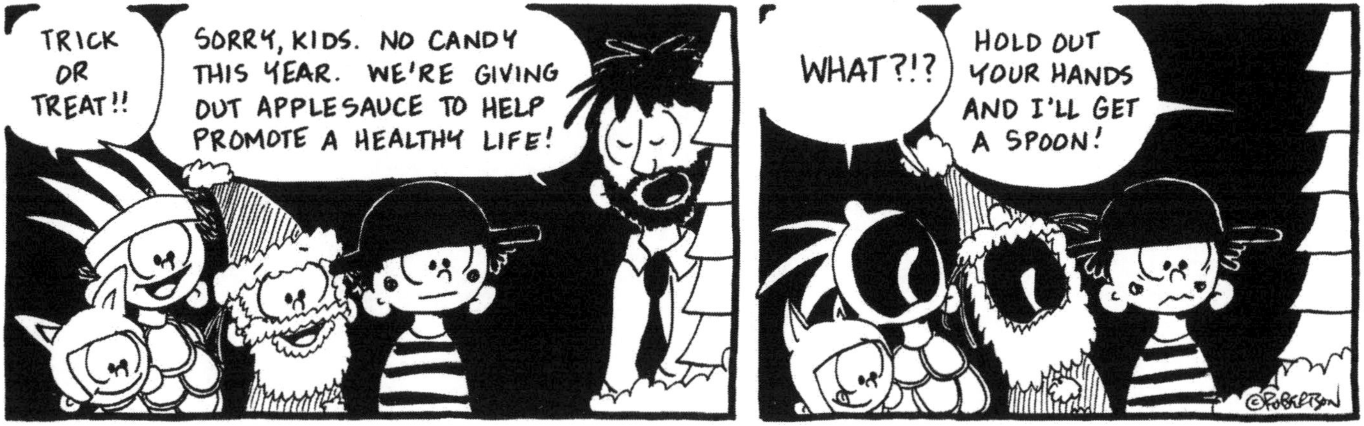
TRICK OR TREAT!!
SORRY, KIDS. NO CANDY THIS YEAR. WE'RE GIVING OUT APPLESAUCE TO HELP PROMOTE A HEALTHY LIFE!
WHAT?!?
HOLD OUT YOUR HANDS AND I'LL GET A SPOON!
©ROBERTSON

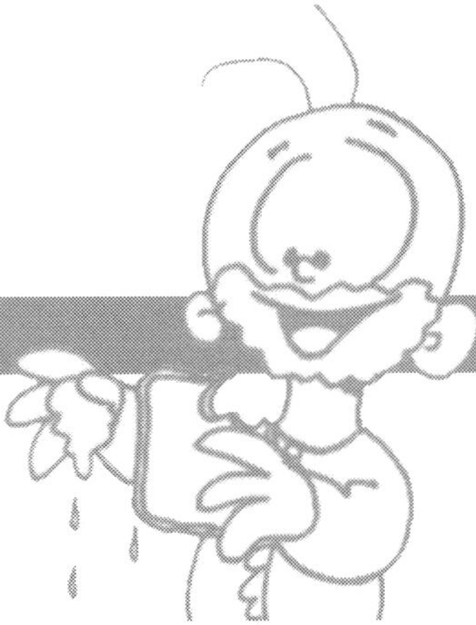

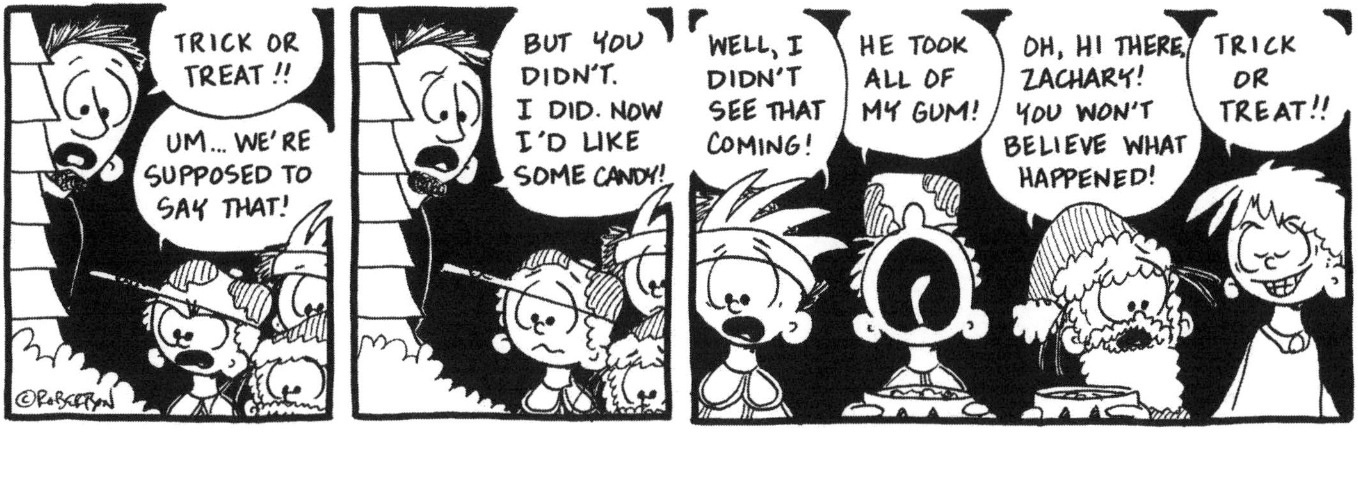
TRICK OR TREAT!!
UM... WE'RE SUPPOSED TO SAY THAT!
©ROBERTSON
BUT YOU DIDN'T. I DID. NOW I'D LIKE SOME CANDY!
WELL, I DIDN'T SEE THAT COMING!
HE TOOK ALL OF MY GUM!
OH, HI THERE, ZACHARY! YOU WON'T BELIEVE WHAT HAPPENED!
TRICK OR TREAT!!

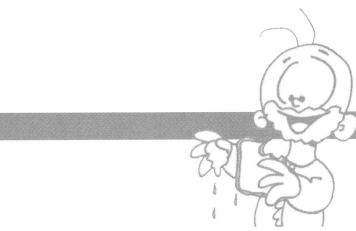

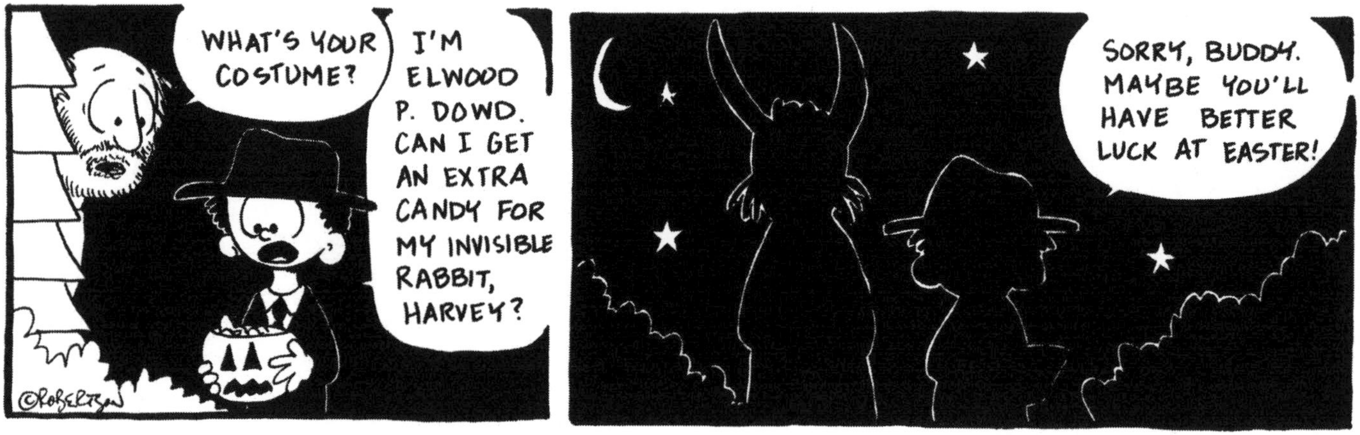
WHAT'S YOUR COSTUME?
I'M ELWOOD P. DOWD. CAN I GET AN EXTRA CANDY FOR MY INVISIBLE RABBIT, HARVEY?
©ROBERTSON
SORRY, BUDDY. MAYBE YOU'LL HAVE BETTER LUCK AT EASTER!

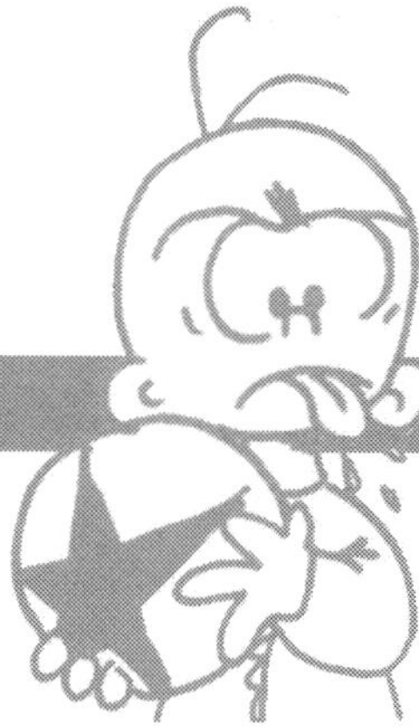

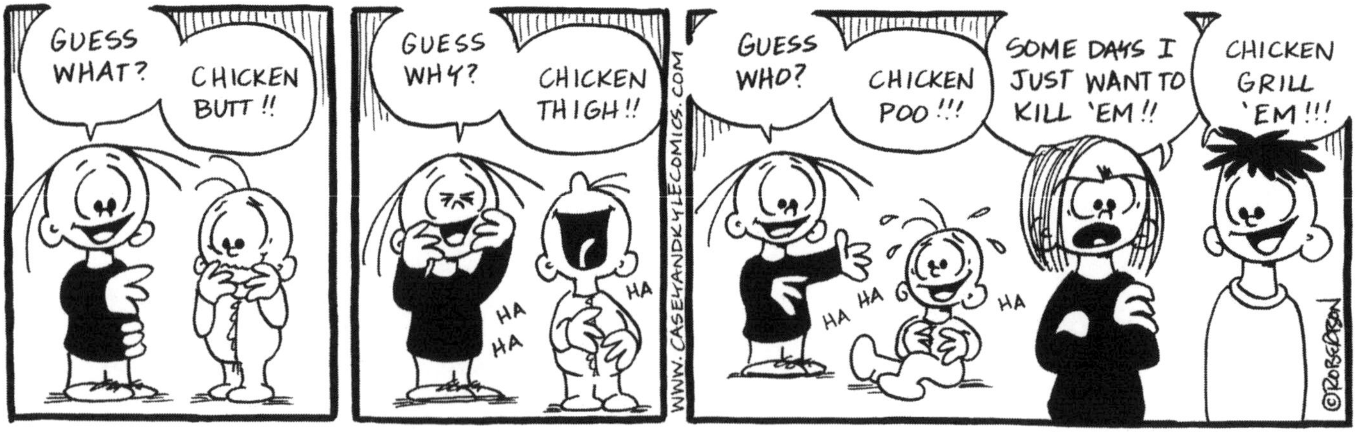
GUESS WHAT?
CHICKEN BUTT!!
GUESS WHY?
CHICKEN THIGH!!
HA HA
HA
WWW.CASEYANDKYLECOMICS.COM
GUESS WHO?
CHICKEN POO!!!
HA HA
HA
SOME DAYS I JUST WANT TO KILL 'EM!!
CHICKEN GRILL 'EM!!!
©ROBERTSON

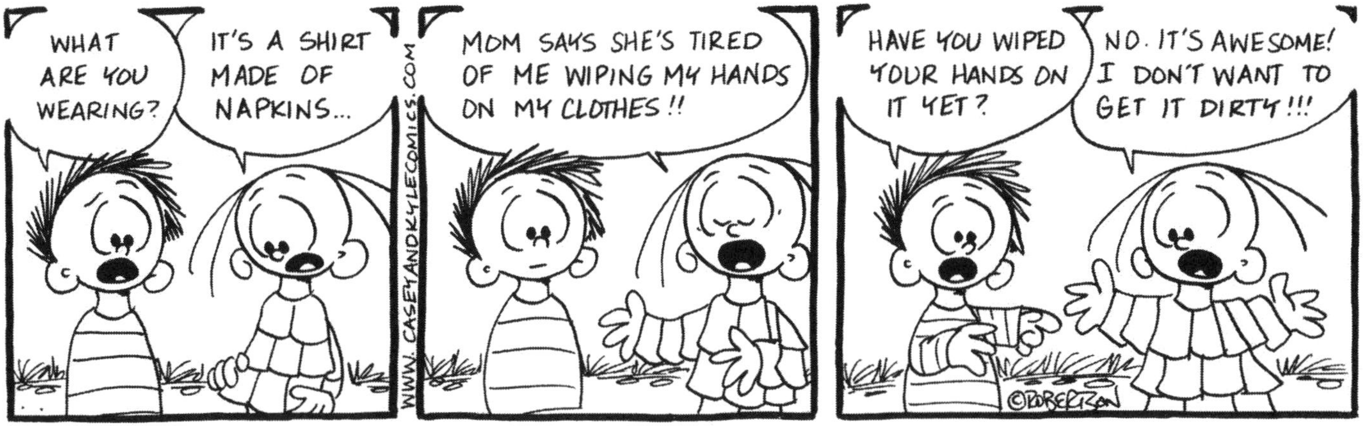
WHAT ARE YOU WEARING?
IT'S A SHIRT MADE OF NAPKINS...
WWW.CASEYANDKYLECOMICS.COM
MOM SAYS SHE'S TIRED OF ME WIPING MY HANDS ON MY CLOTHES!!
HAVE YOU WIPED YOUR HANDS ON IT YET?
NO. IT'S AWESOME! I DON'T WANT TO GET IT DIRTY!!!
©ROBERTSON

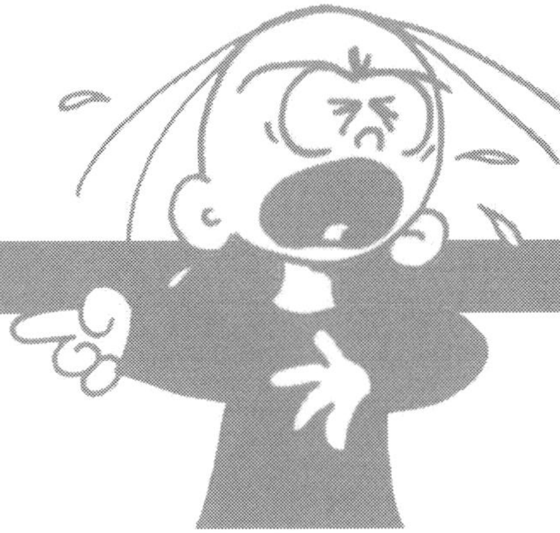

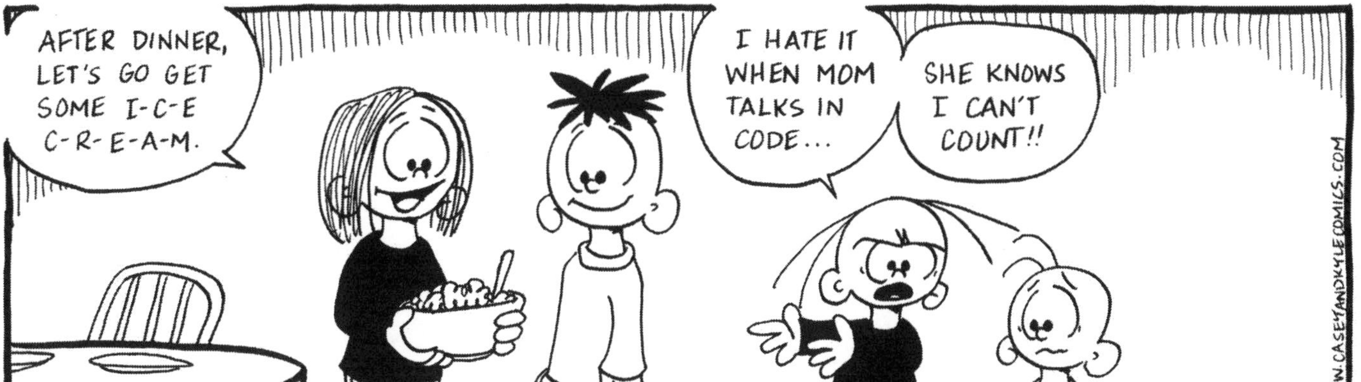
AFTER DINNER, LET'S GO GET SOME I-C-E C-R-E-A-M.
I HATE IT WHEN MOM TALKS IN CODE...
SHE KNOWS I CAN'T COUNT!!
©ROBERTSON
WWW.CASEYANDKYLECOMICS.COM

GO FISH!!!
©ROBERTSON
WWW.CASEYANDKYLECOMICS.COM

22

THAT'S NO SLUG BUG!! YOU'RE A CHEATER!! I GET TO HIT YOU TEN TIMES!
WWW.CASEYANDKYLECOMICS.COM
CASEY!! DON'T YOU DARE HIT YOUR BROTHER!!
KICK
©ROBERTSON

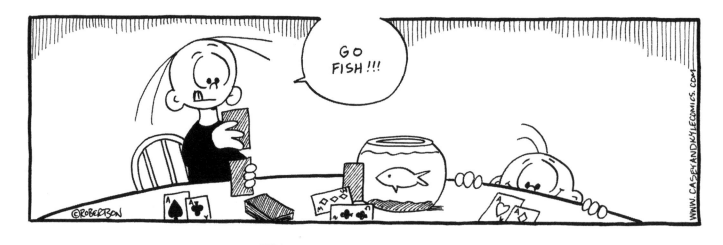

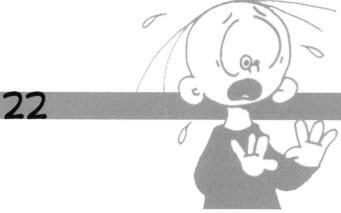

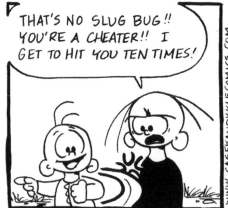

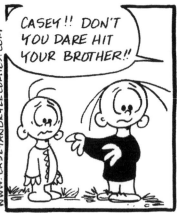

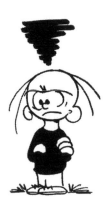

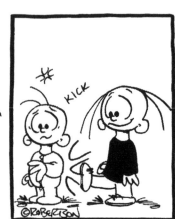

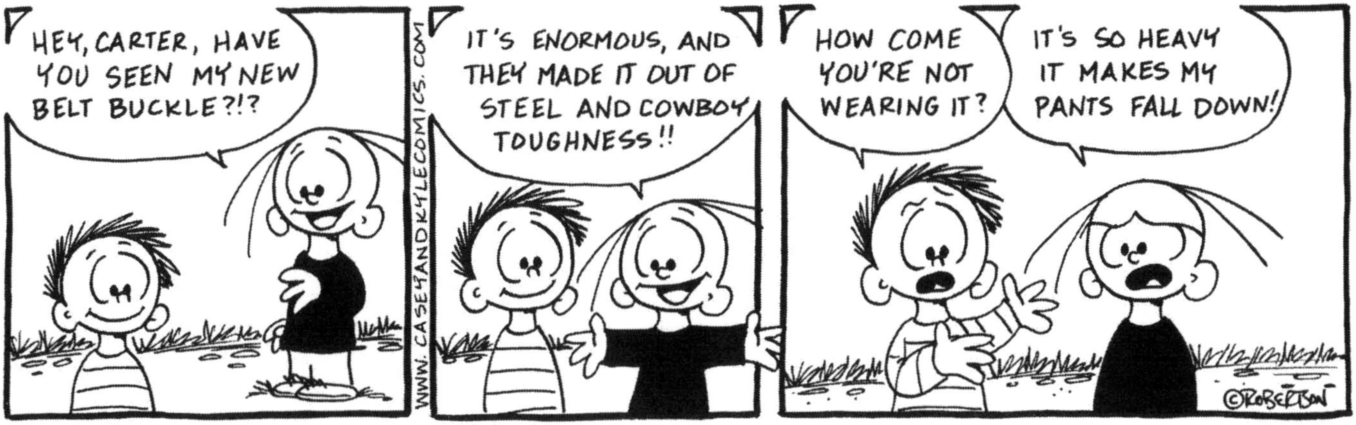
HEY, CARTER, HAVE YOU SEEN MY NEW BELT BUCKLE?!?
WWW.CASEYANDKYLECOMICS.COM
IT'S ENORMOUS, AND THEY MADE IT OUT OF STEEL AND COWBOY TOUGHNESS!!
HOW COME YOU'RE NOT WEARING IT?
IT'S SO HEAVY IT MAKES MY PANTS FALL DOWN!
©ROBERTSON

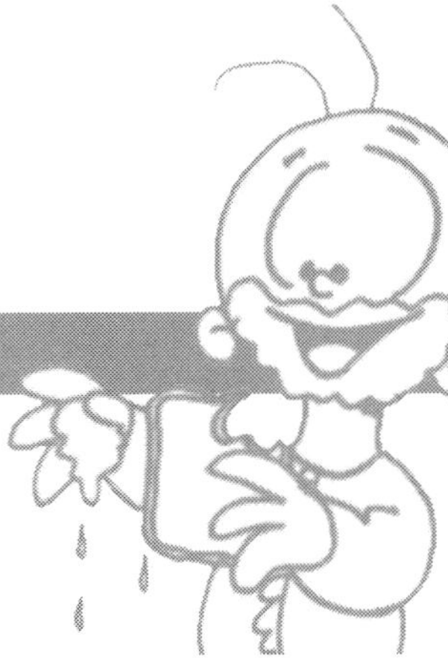

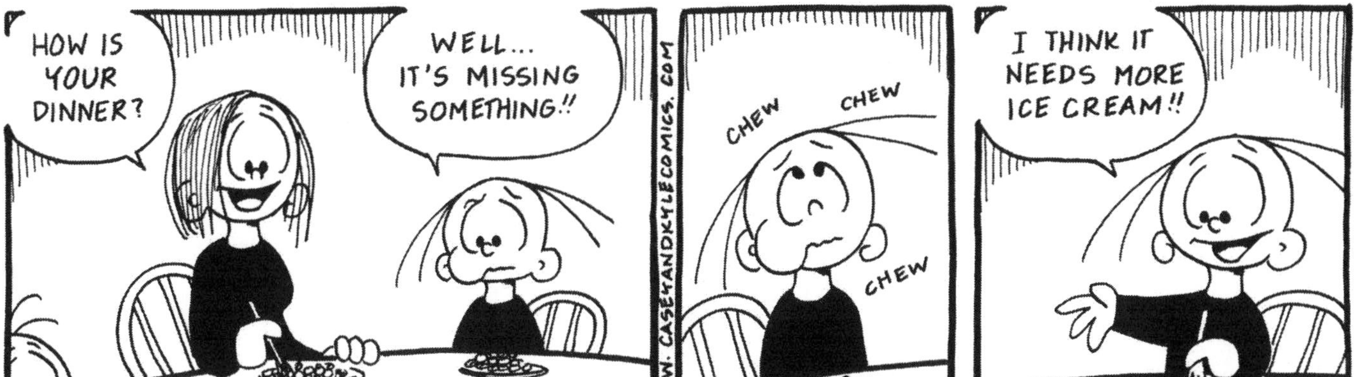
HOW IS YOUR DINNER?
WELL... IT'S MISSING SOMETHING!!
WWW.CASEYANDKYLECOMICS.COM
CHEW
CHEW
CHEW
I THINK IT NEEDS MORE ICE CREAM!!
©ROBERTSON

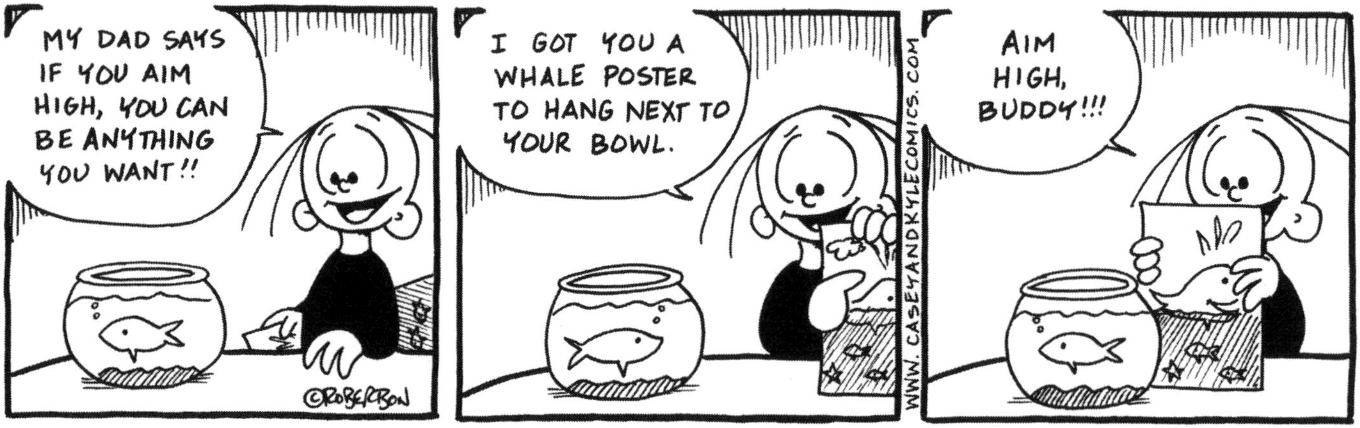
MY DAD SAYS IF YOU AIM HIGH, YOU CAN BE ANYTHING YOU WANT!!
©ROBERSON
I GOT YOU A WHALE POSTER TO HANG NEXT TO YOUR BOWL.
WWW.CASEYANDKYLECOMICS.COM
AIM HIGH, BUDDY!!!

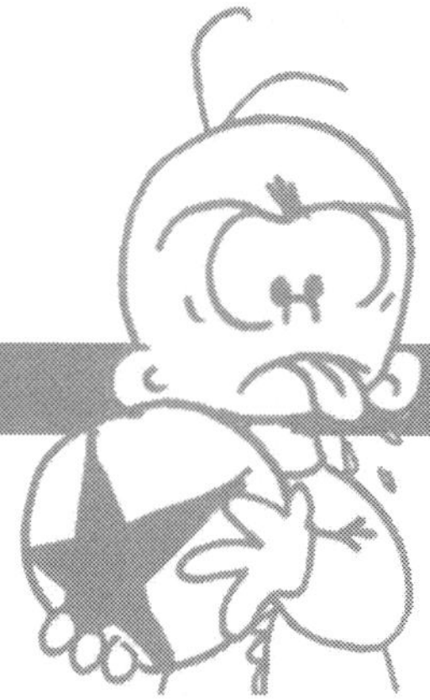

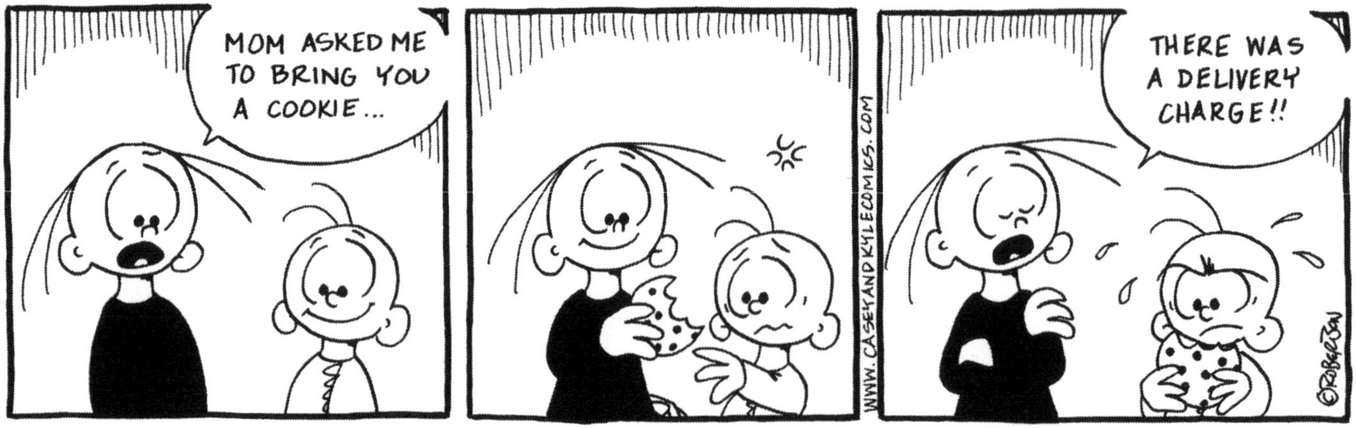
MOM ASKED ME TO BRING YOU A COOKIE...
WWW.CASEYANDKYLECOMICS.COM
THERE WAS A DELIVERY CHARGE!!
©ROBERSON

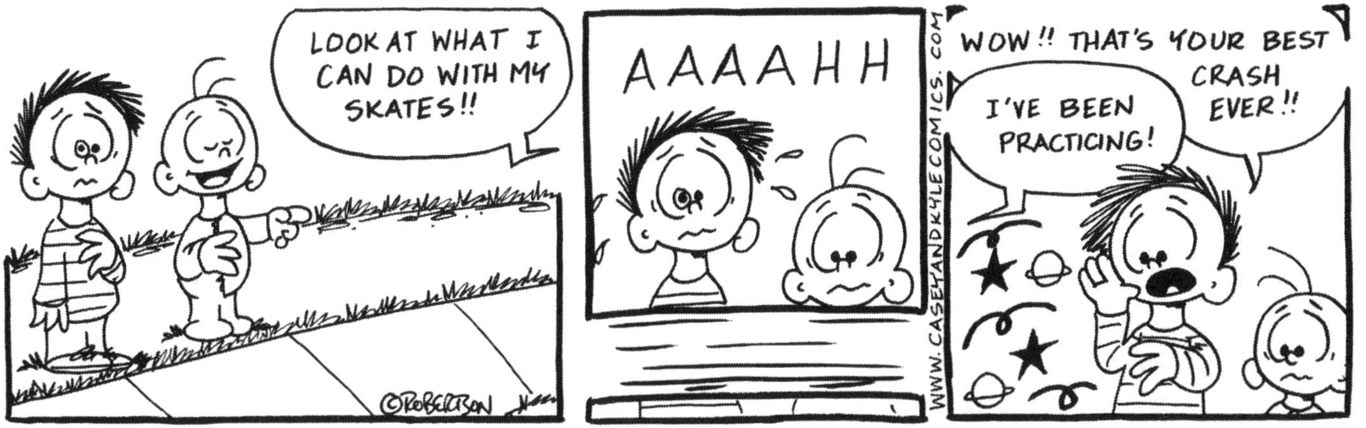
LOOK AT WHAT I CAN DO WITH MY SKATES!!
©ROBERTSON
AAAAHH
WWW.CASEYANDKYLECOMICS.COM
WOW!! THAT'S YOUR BEST CRASH EVER!!
I'VE BEEN PRACTICING!

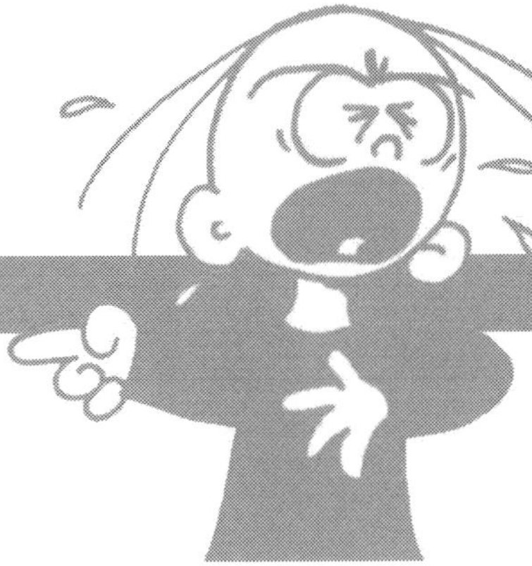

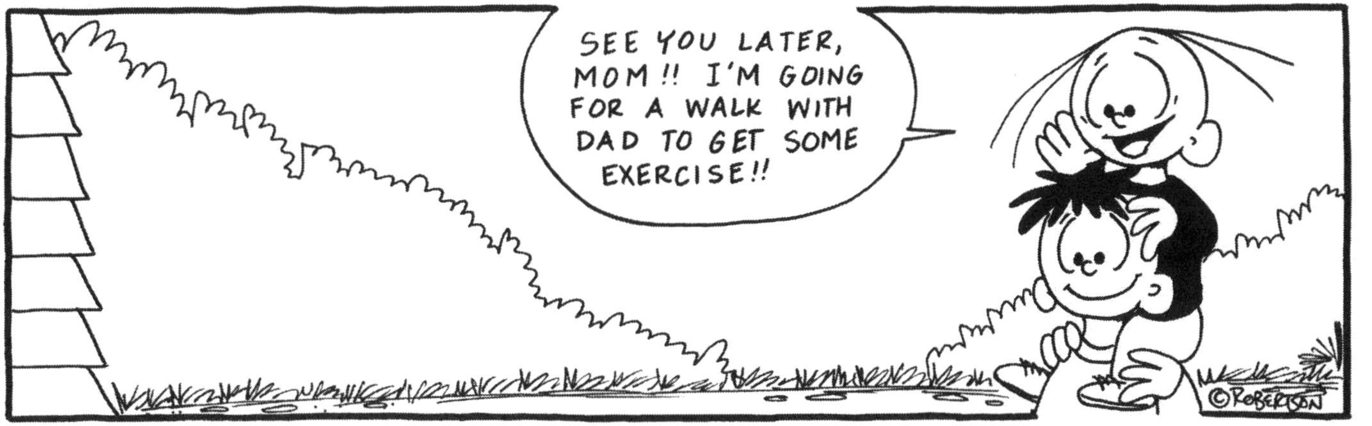
SEE YOU LATER, MOM!! I'M GOING FOR A WALK WITH DAD TO GET SOME EXERCISE!!
©ROBERTSON

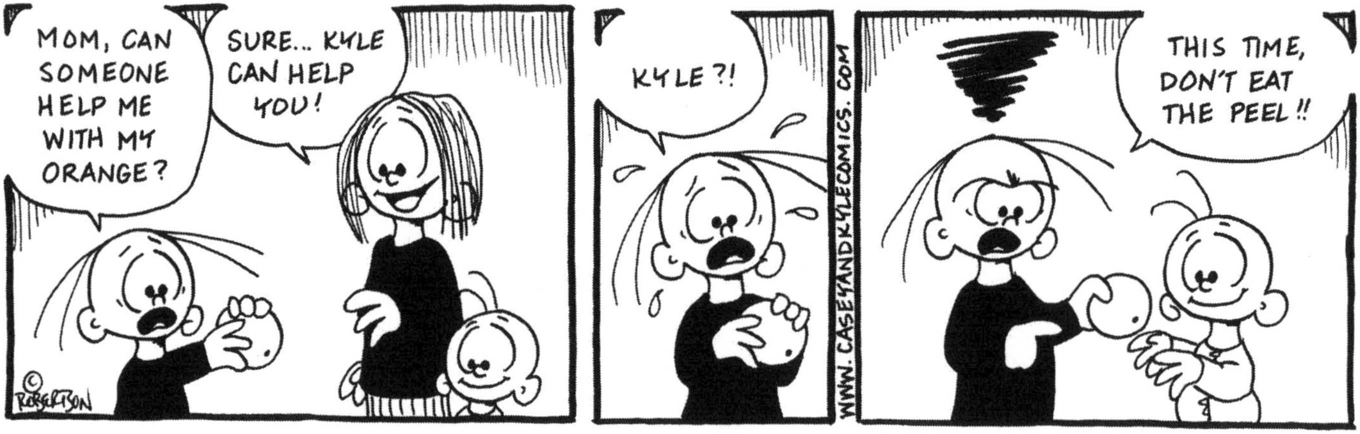
MOM, CAN SOMEONE HELP ME WITH MY ORANGE?
SURE... KYLE CAN HELP YOU!
KYLE?!
THIS TIME, DON'T EAT THE PEEL!!
© ROBERTSON
WWW.CASEYANDKYLECOMICS.COM

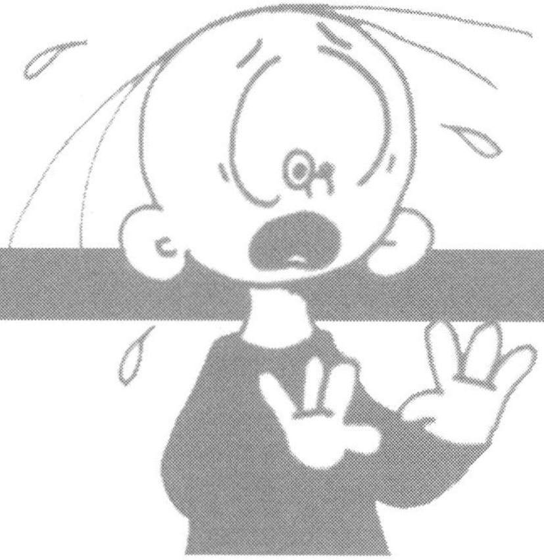

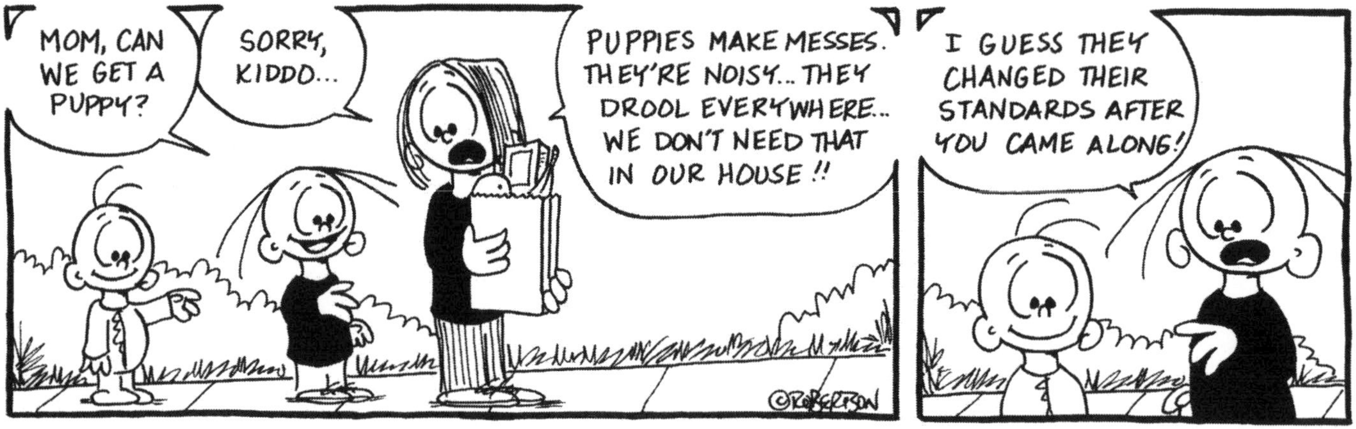
MOM, CAN WE GET A PUPPY?
SORRY, KIDDO...
PUPPIES MAKE MESSES. THEY'RE NOISY... THEY DROOL EVERYWHERE... WE DON'T NEED THAT IN OUR HOUSE!!
I GUESS THEY CHANGED THEIR STANDARDS AFTER YOU CAME ALONG!
©ROBERTSON

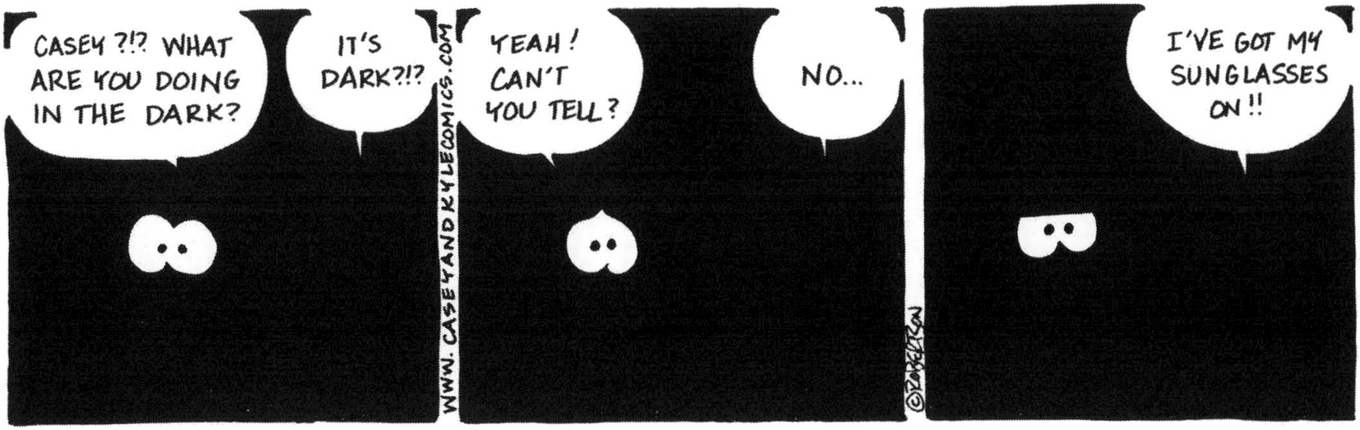
CASEY ?!? WHAT ARE YOU DOING IN THE DARK?
IT'S DARK?!?
YEAH! CAN'T YOU TELL?
NO...
I'VE GOT MY SUNGLASSES ON!!
WWW.CASEYANDKYLECOMICS.COM
©ROBERTSON

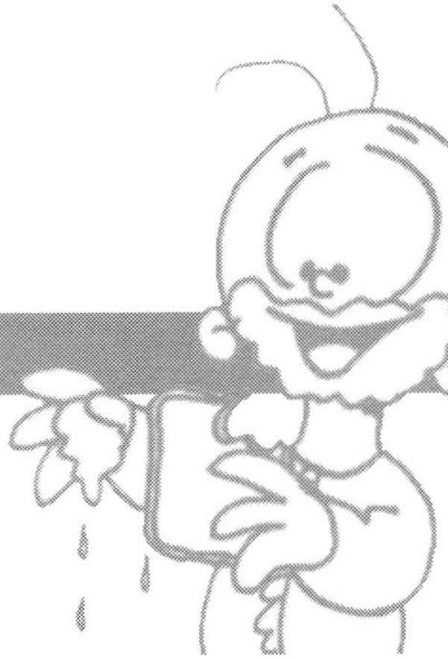

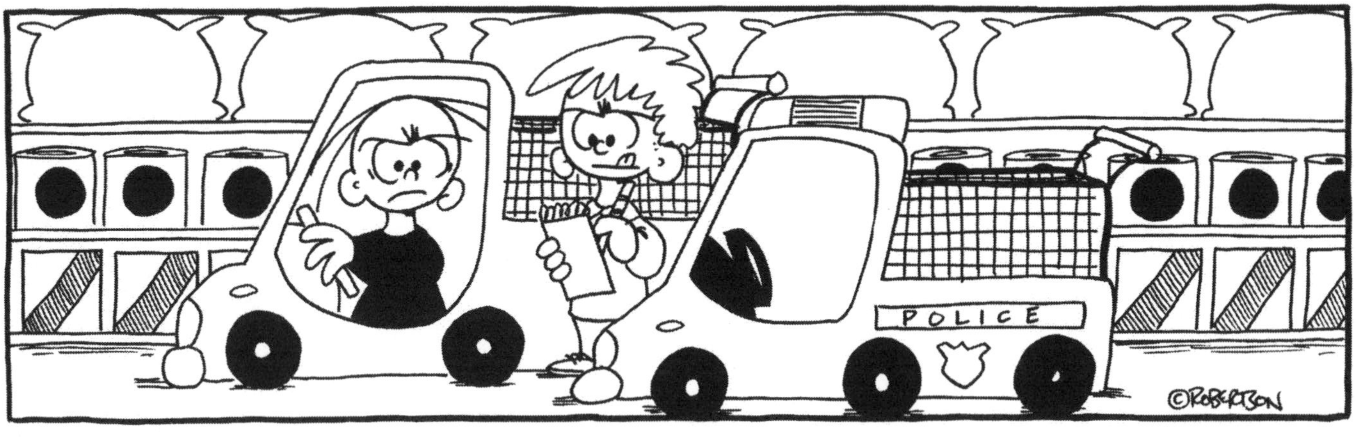
POLICE
©ROBERTSON

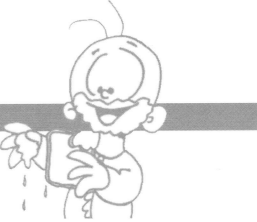

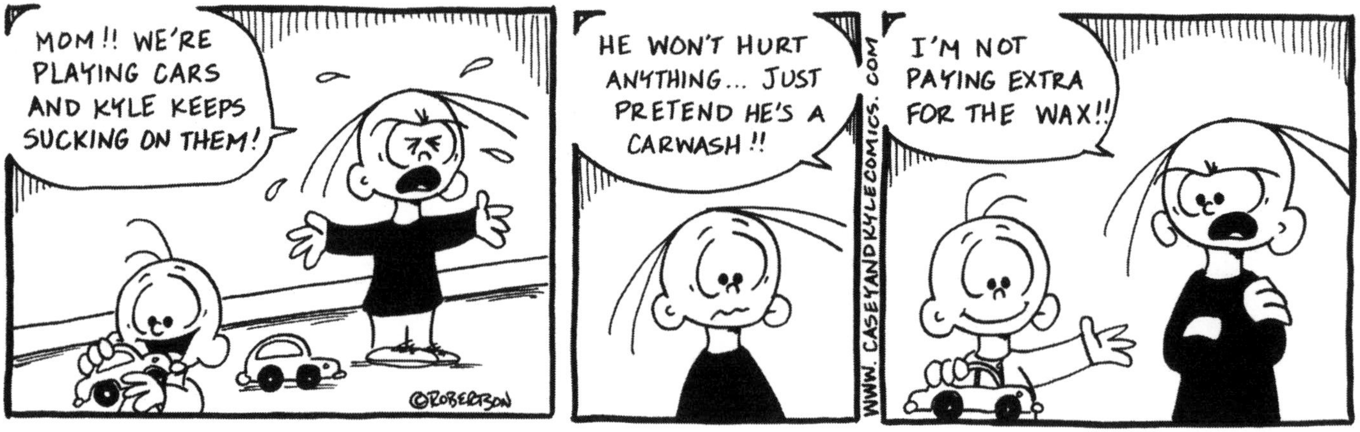
MOM!! WE'RE PLAYING CARS AND KYLE KEEPS SUCKING ON THEM!
©ROBERTSON
HE WON'T HURT ANYTHING... JUST PRETEND HE'S A CARWASH!!
WWW.CASEYANDKYLECOMICS.COM
I'M NOT PAYING EXTRA FOR THE WAX!!

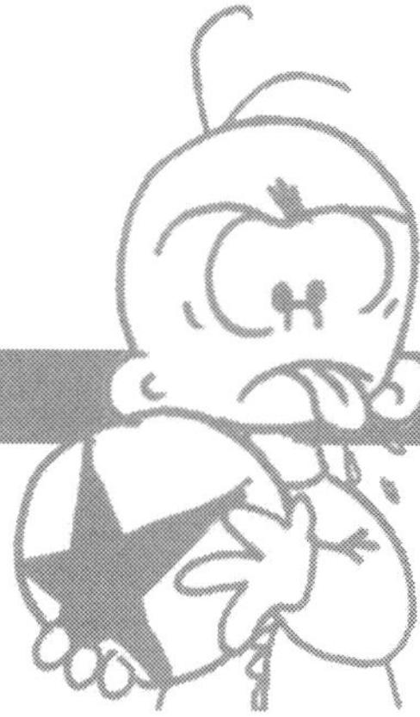

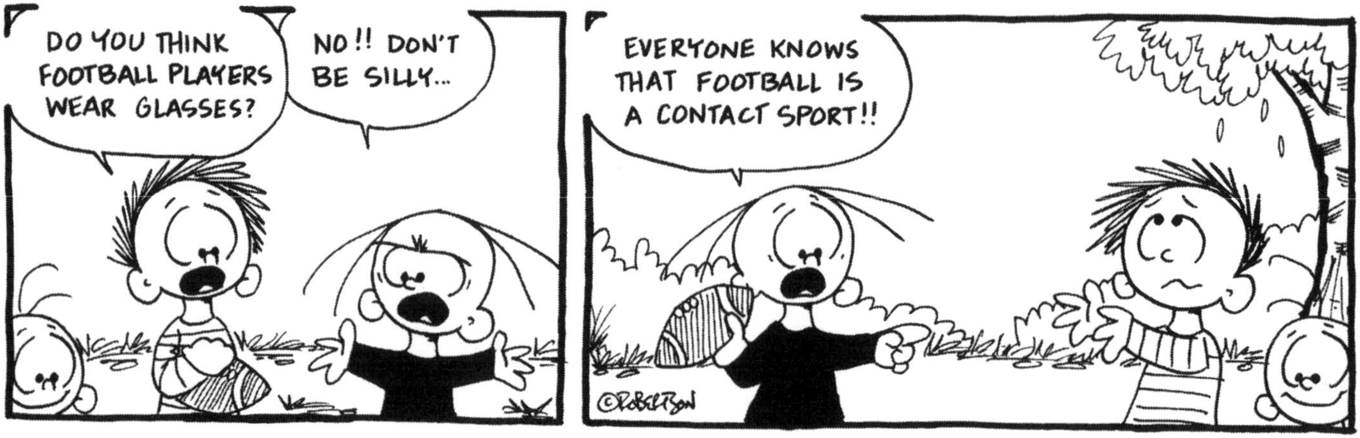
DO YOU THINK FOOTBALL PLAYERS WEAR GLASSES?
NO!! DON'T BE SILLY...
EVERYONE KNOWS THAT FOOTBALL IS A CONTACT SPORT!!
©ROBERTSON

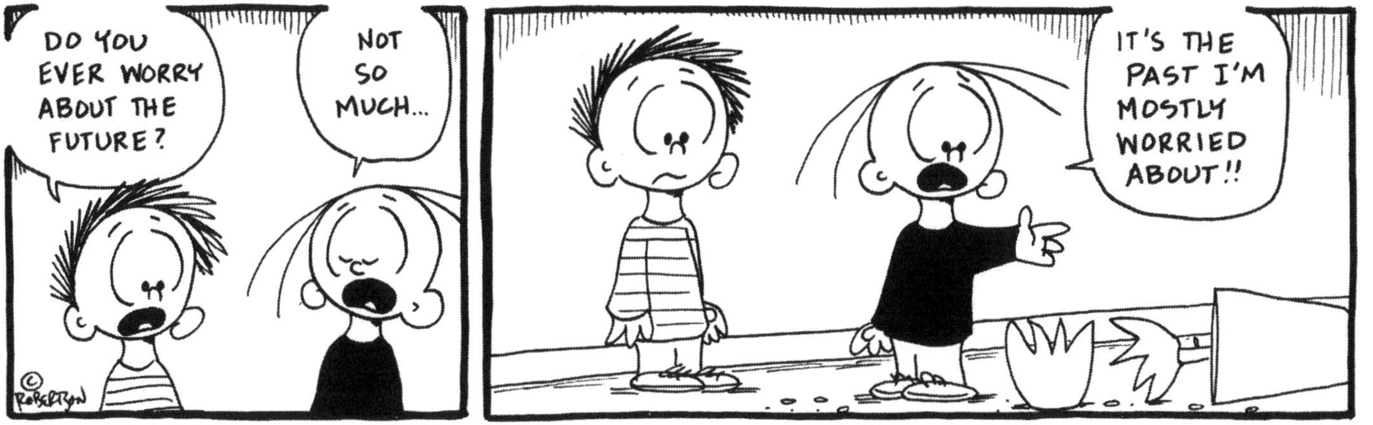
DO YOU EVER WORRY ABOUT THE FUTURE?
NOT SO MUCH...
© ROBERTSON
IT'S THE PAST I'M MOSTLY WORRIED ABOUT!!

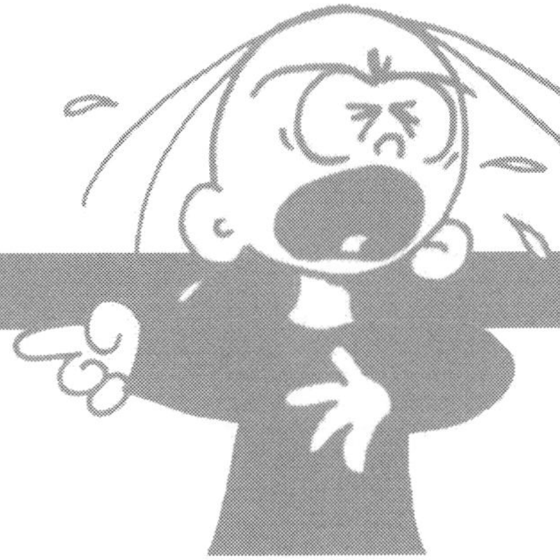

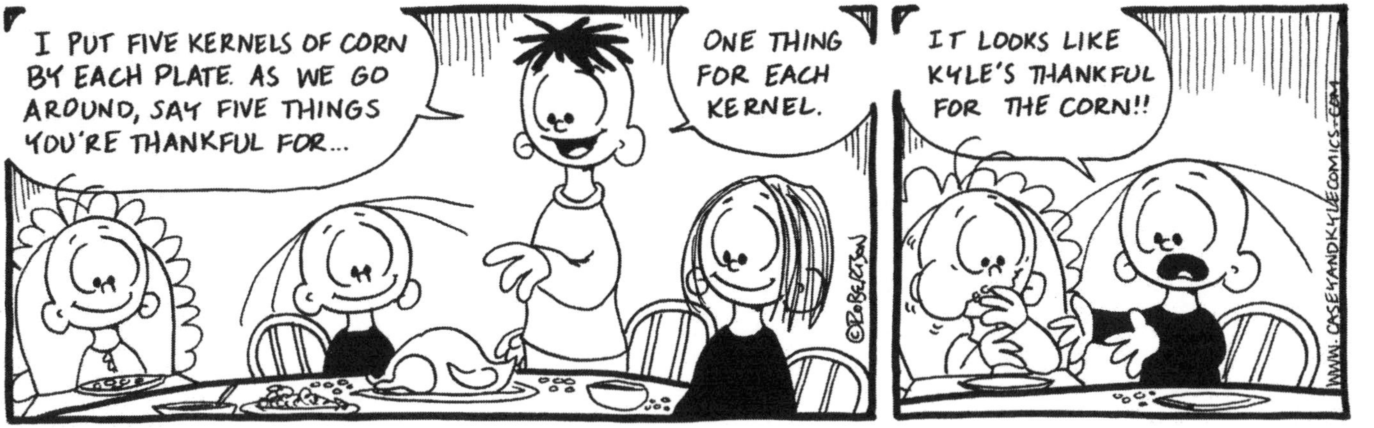
I PUT FIVE KERNELS OF CORN BY EACH PLATE. AS WE GO AROUND, SAY FIVE THINGS YOU'RE THANKFUL FOR...
ONE THING FOR EACH KERNEL.
©ROBERTSON
IT LOOKS LIKE KYLE'S THANKFUL FOR THE CORN!!
WWW.CASEYANDKYLECOMICS.COM

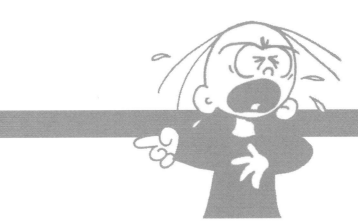

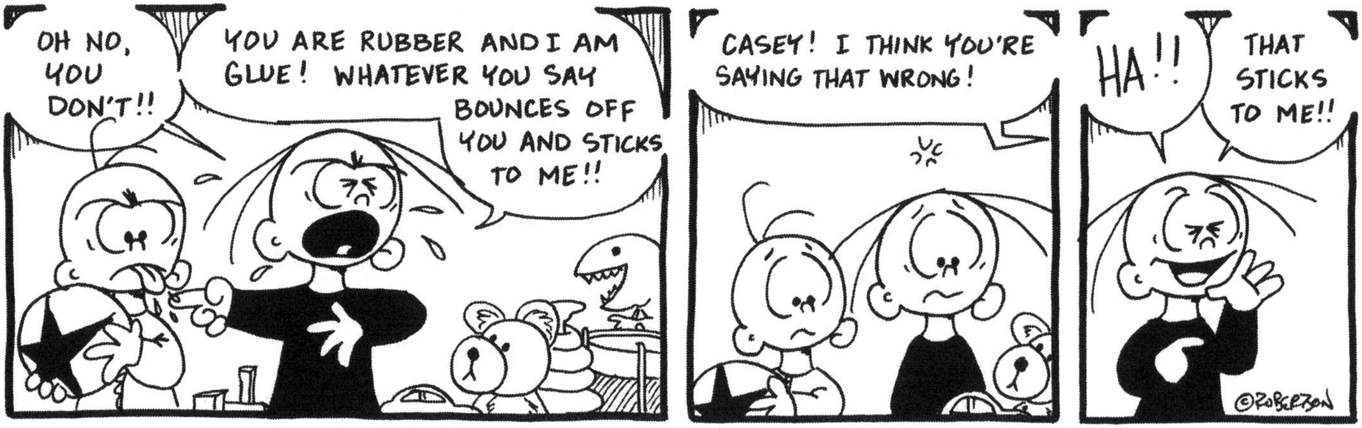
OH NO, YOU DON'T!!
YOU ARE RUBBER AND I AM GLUE! WHATEVER YOU SAY BOUNCES OFF YOU AND STICKS TO ME!!
CASEY! I THINK YOU'RE SAYING THAT WRONG!
HA!!
THAT STICKS TO ME!!
©ROBERTSON

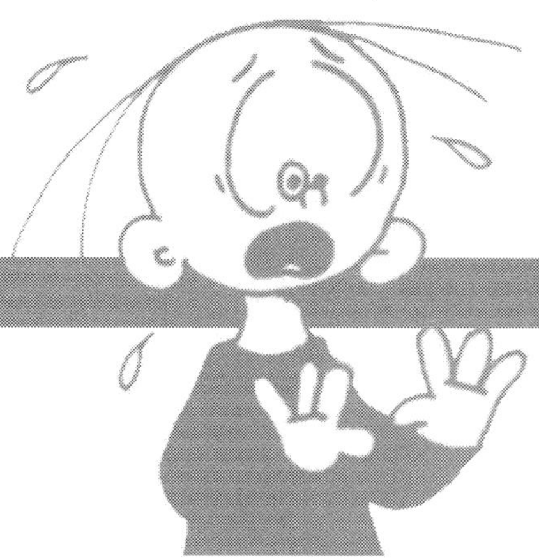

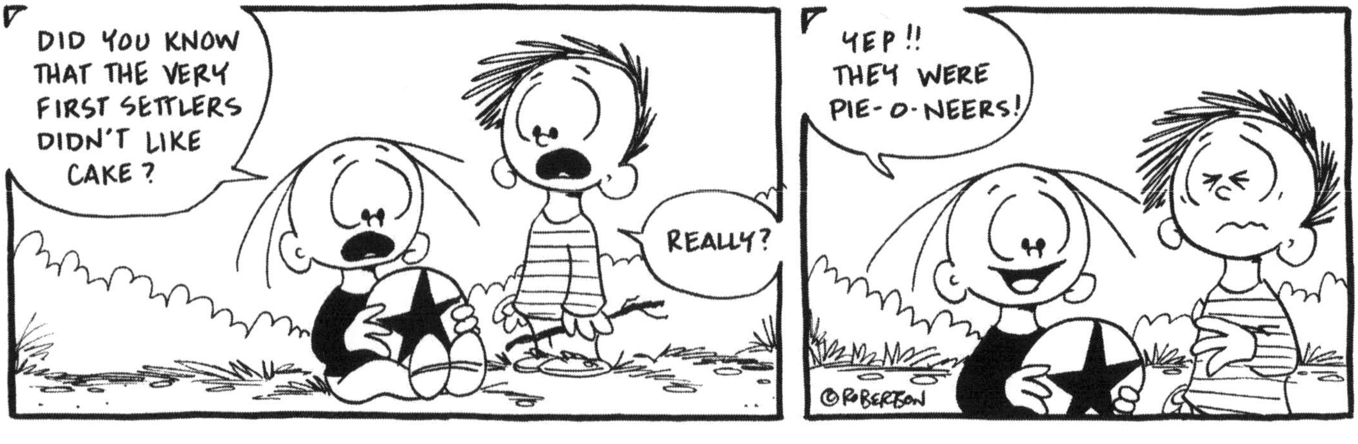
DID YOU KNOW THAT THE VERY FIRST SETTLERS DIDN'T LIKE CAKE?
REALLY?
YEP!! THEY WERE PIE-O-NEERS!
©ROBERTSON

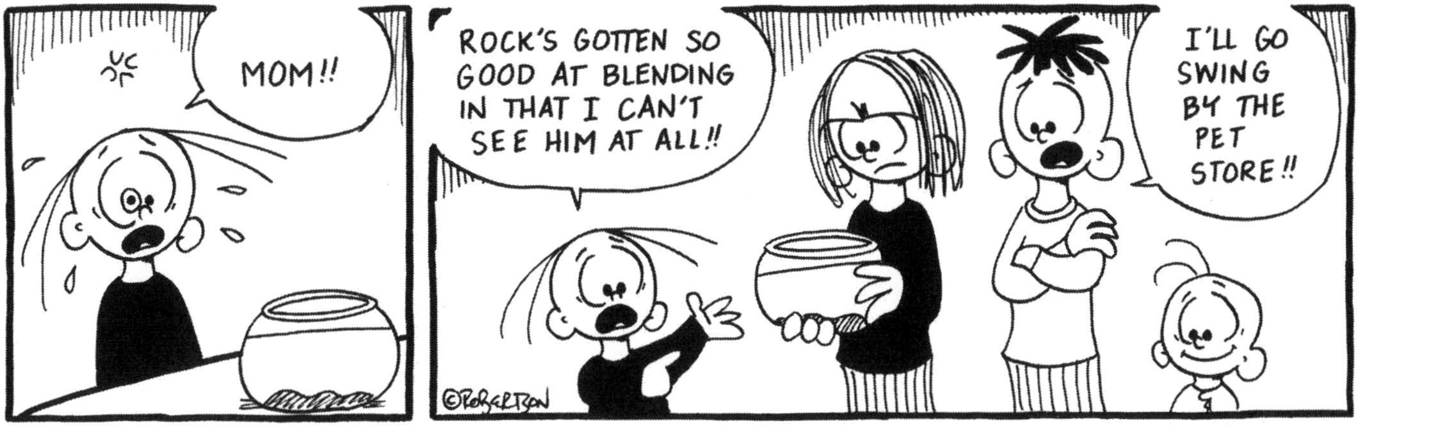
MOM!!
ROCK'S GOTTEN SO GOOD AT BLENDING IN THAT I CAN'T SEE HIM AT ALL!!
I'LL GO SWING BY THE PET STORE!!
©ROBERTSON

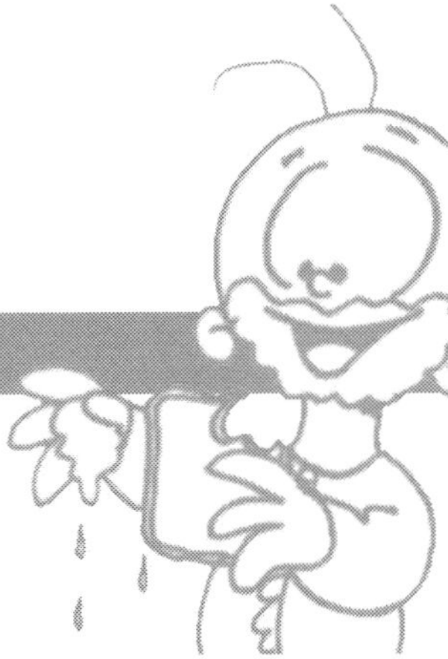

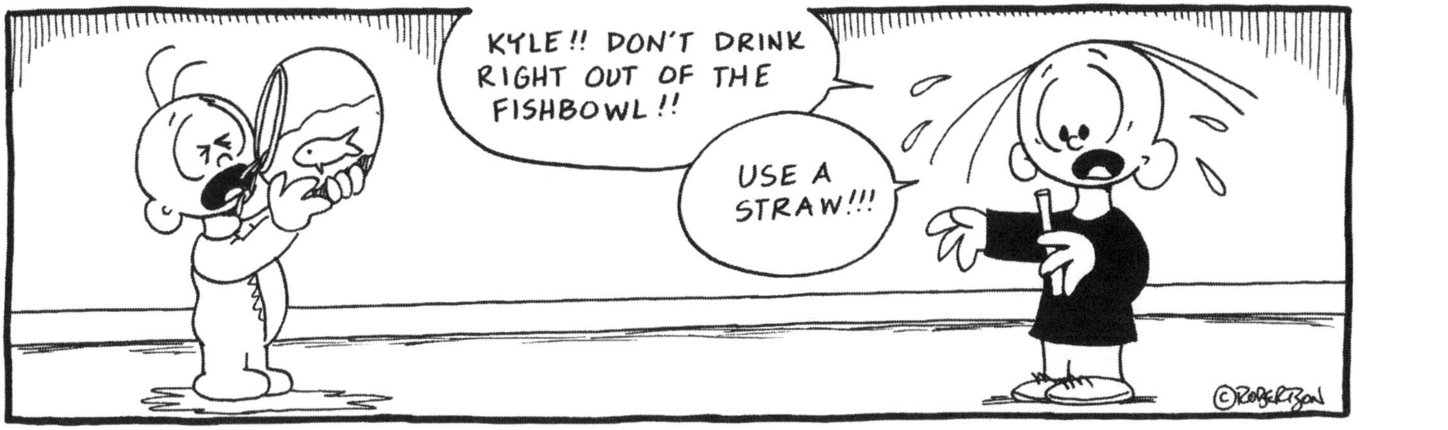
KYLE!! DON'T DRINK RIGHT OUT OF THE FISHBOWL!!
USE A STRAW!!!
©ROBERTSON

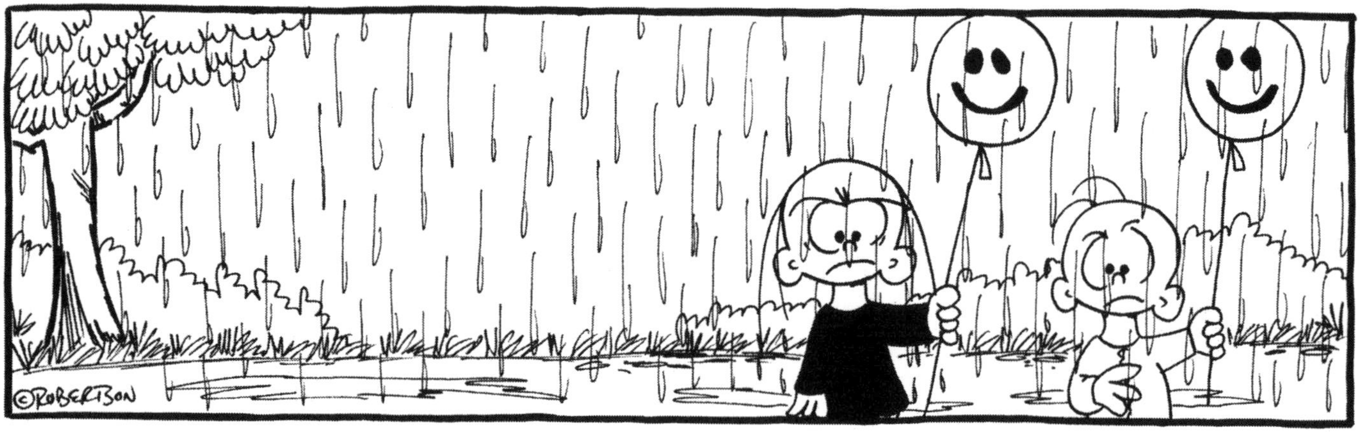
©ROBERTSON

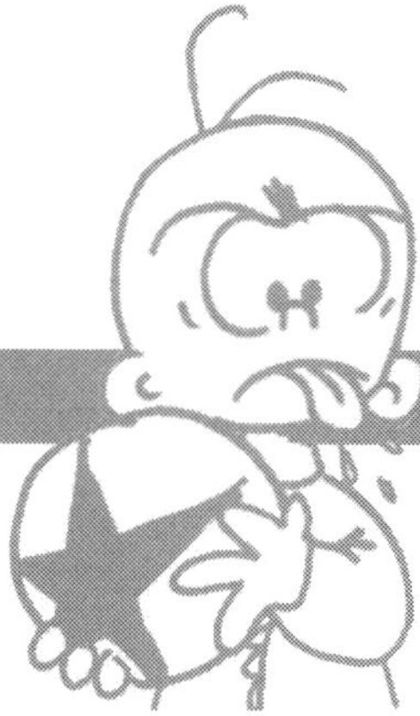

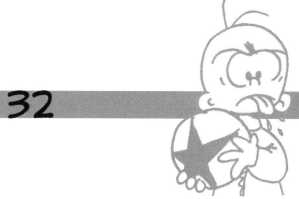

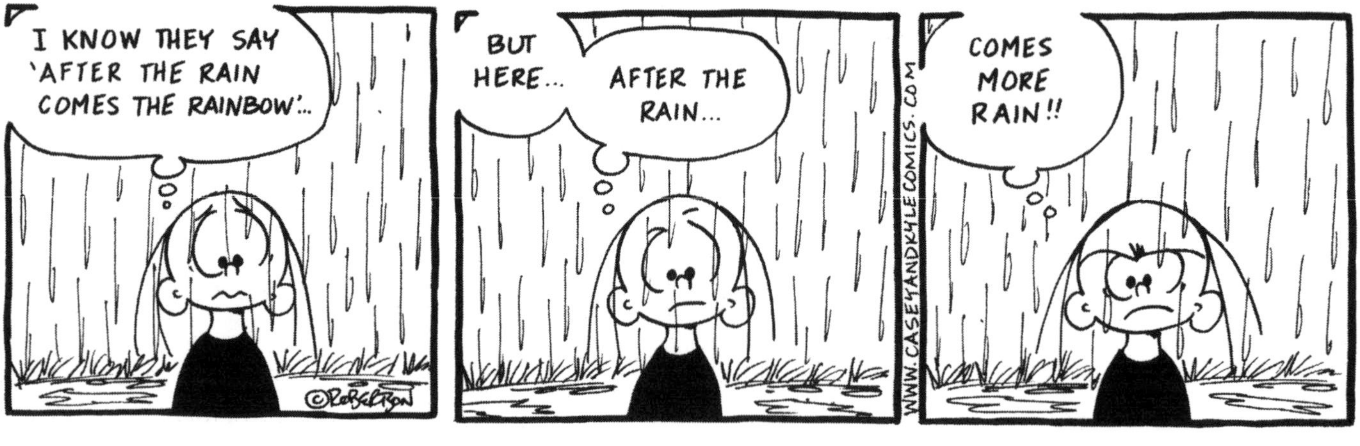
I KNOW THEY SAY 'AFTER THE RAIN COMES THE RAINBOW'...
©ROBERTSON
BUT HERE...
AFTER THE RAIN...
WWW.CASEYANDKYLECOMICS.COM
COMES MORE RAIN!!

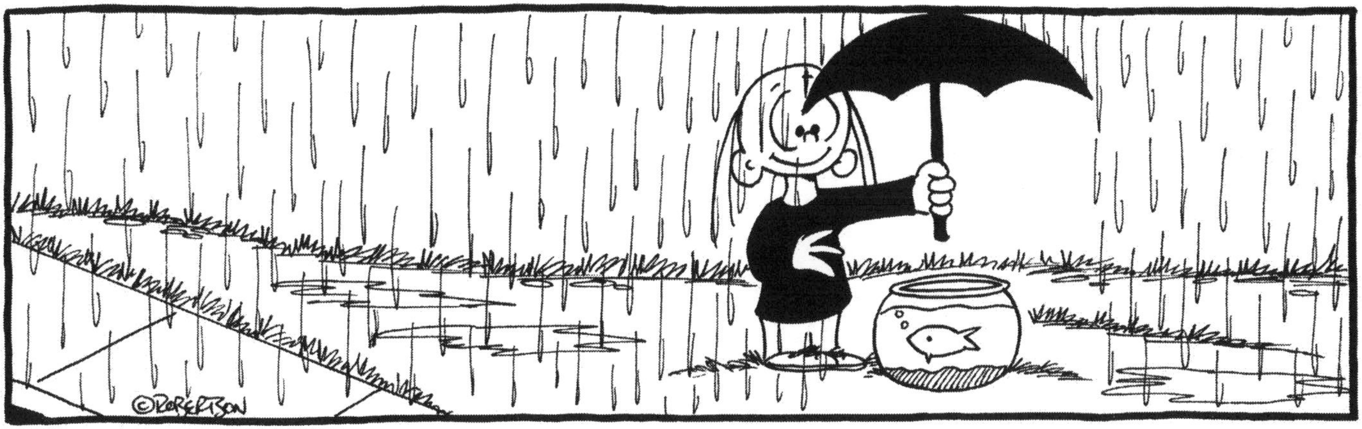

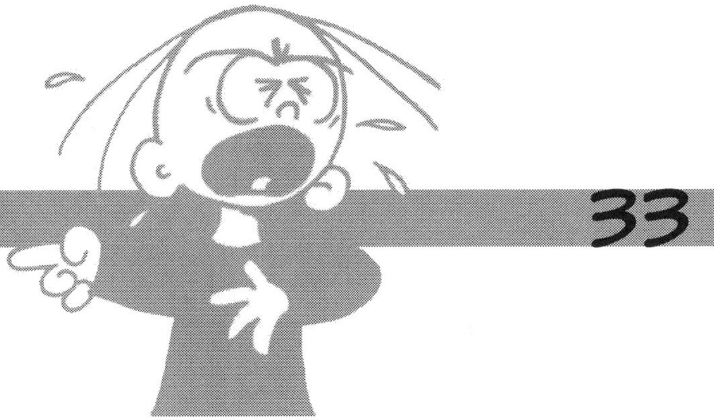

33

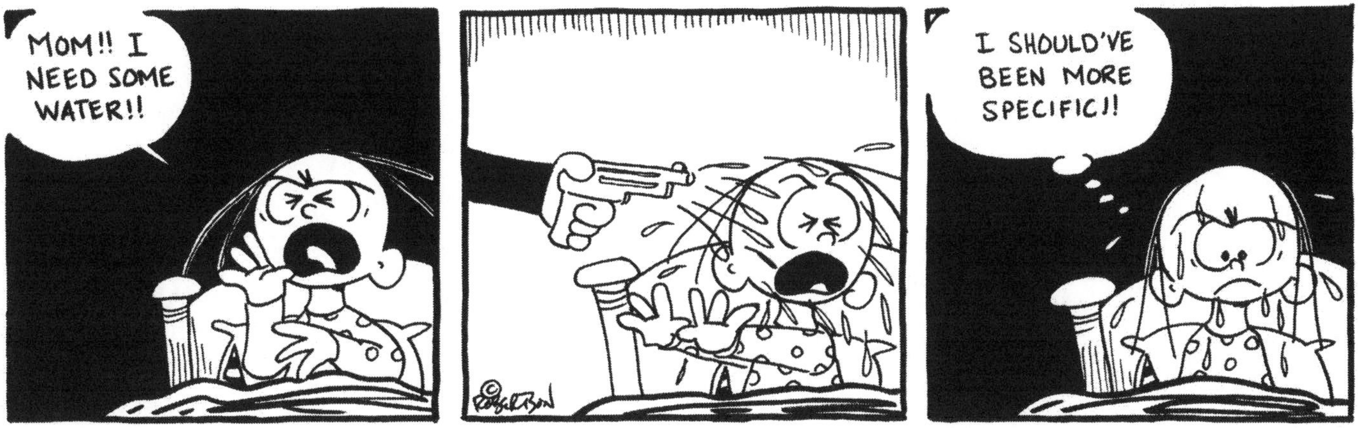
MOM!! I NEED SOME WATER!!
I SHOULD'VE BEEN MORE SPECIFIC!!

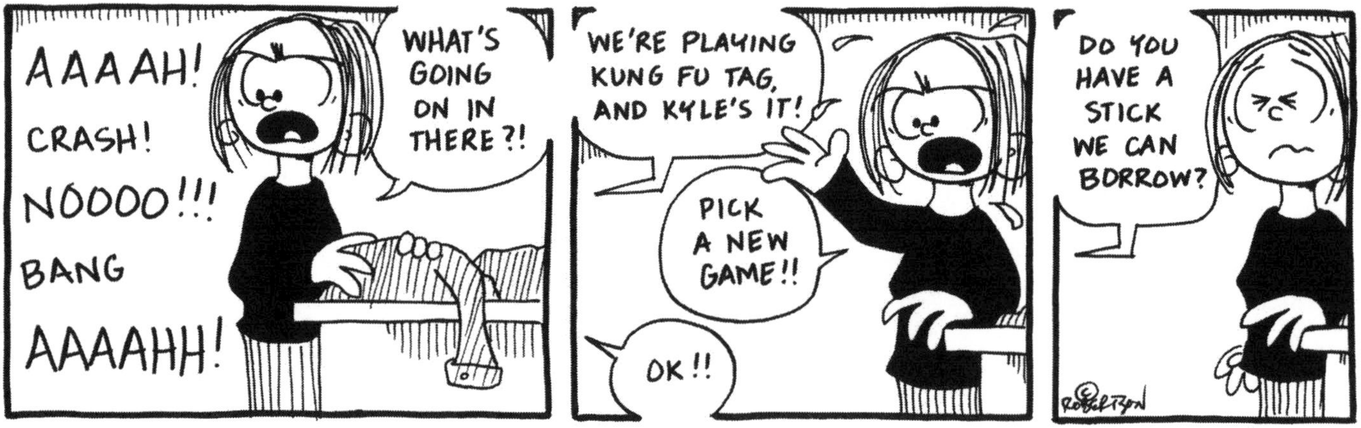
AAAAH!
CRASH!
NOOOO!!!
BANG
AAAAHH!
WHAT'S GOING ON IN THERE?!
WE'RE PLAYING KUNG FU TAG, AND KYLE'S IT!
PICK A NEW GAME!!
OK!!
DO YOU HAVE A STICK WE CAN BORROW?
©ROBERTSON

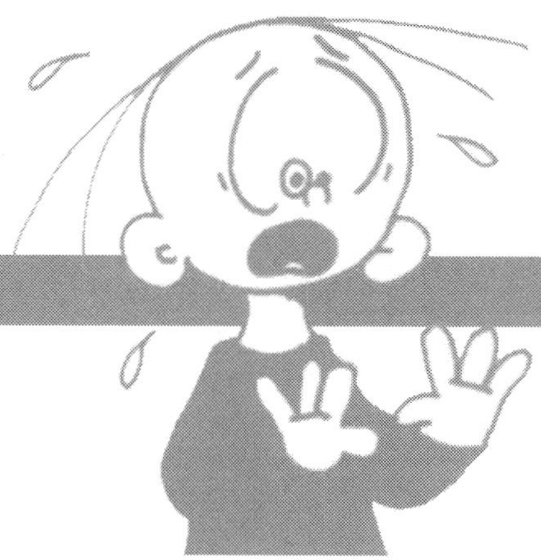

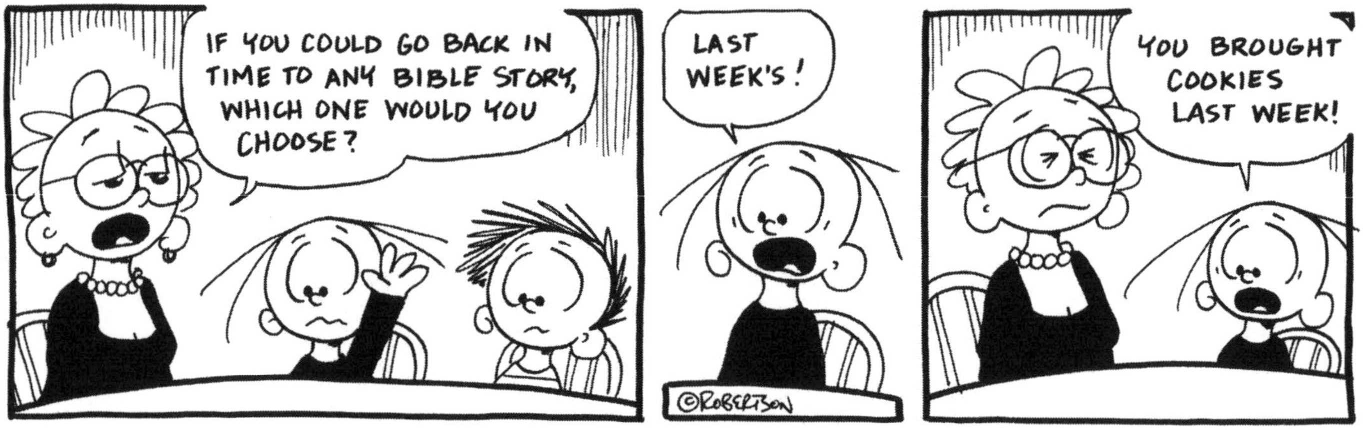
IF YOU COULD GO BACK IN TIME TO ANY BIBLE STORY, WHICH ONE WOULD YOU CHOOSE?
LAST WEEK'S!
©ROBERTSON
YOU BROUGHT COOKIES LAST WEEK!

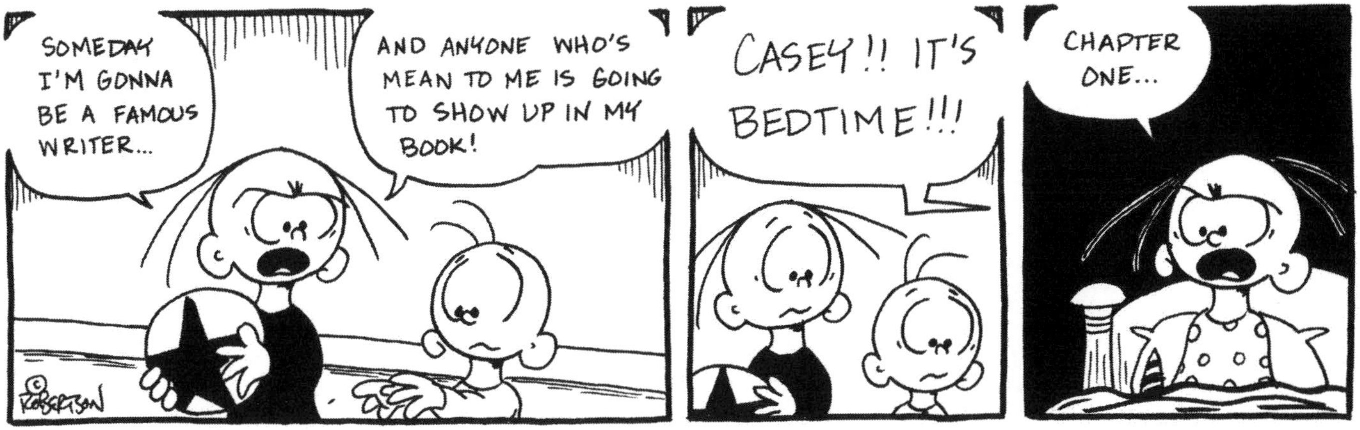
SOMEDAY I'M GONNA BE A FAMOUS WRITER...
AND ANYONE WHO'S MEAN TO ME IS GOING TO SHOW UP IN MY BOOK!
CASEY!! IT'S BEDTIME!!!
CHAPTER ONE...
© ROBERTSON

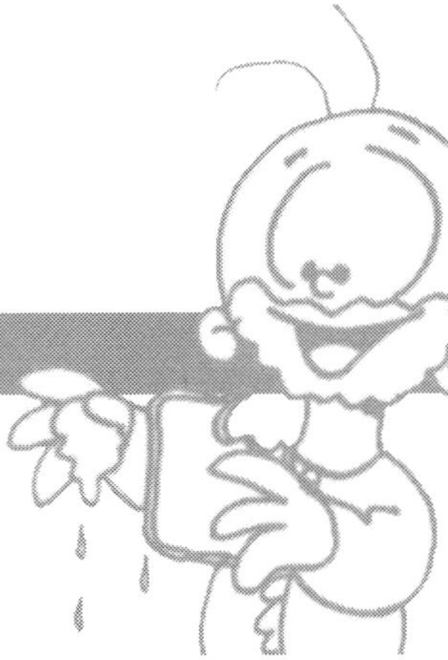

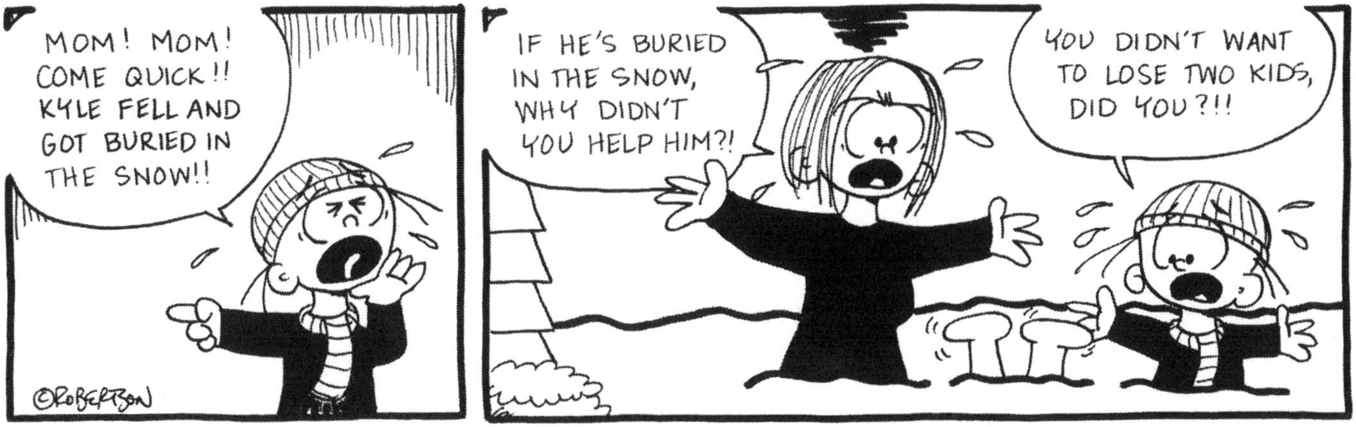
MOM! MOM! COME QUICK!! KYLE FELL AND GOT BURIED IN THE SNOW!!
IF HE'S BURIED IN THE SNOW, WHY DIDN'T YOU HELP HIM?!
YOU DIDN'T WANT TO LOSE TWO KIDS, DID YOU?!!
©ROBERTSON

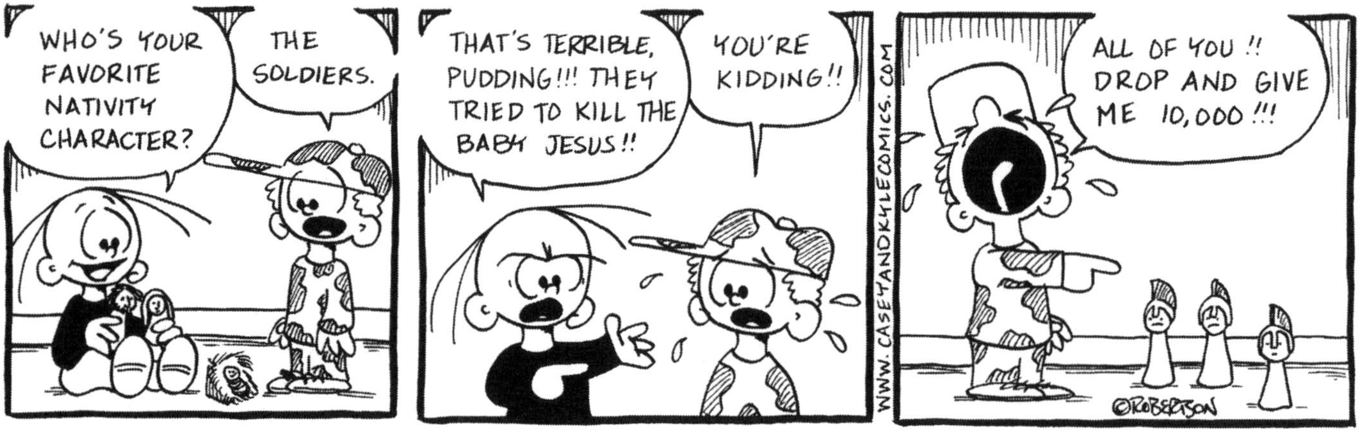
WHO'S YOUR FAVORITE NATIVITY CHARACTER?
THE SOLDIERS.
THAT'S TERRIBLE, PUDDING!!! THEY TRIED TO KILL THE BABY JESUS!!
YOU'RE KIDDING!!
WWW.CASEYANDKYLECOMICS.COM
ALL OF YOU!! DROP AND GIVE ME 10,000!!!
©ROBERTSON

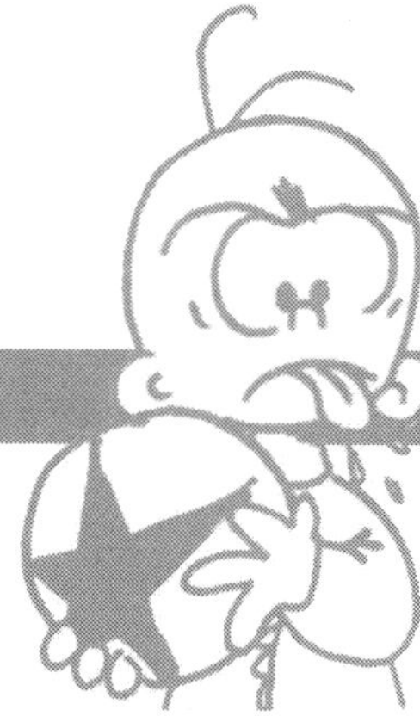

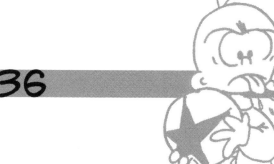

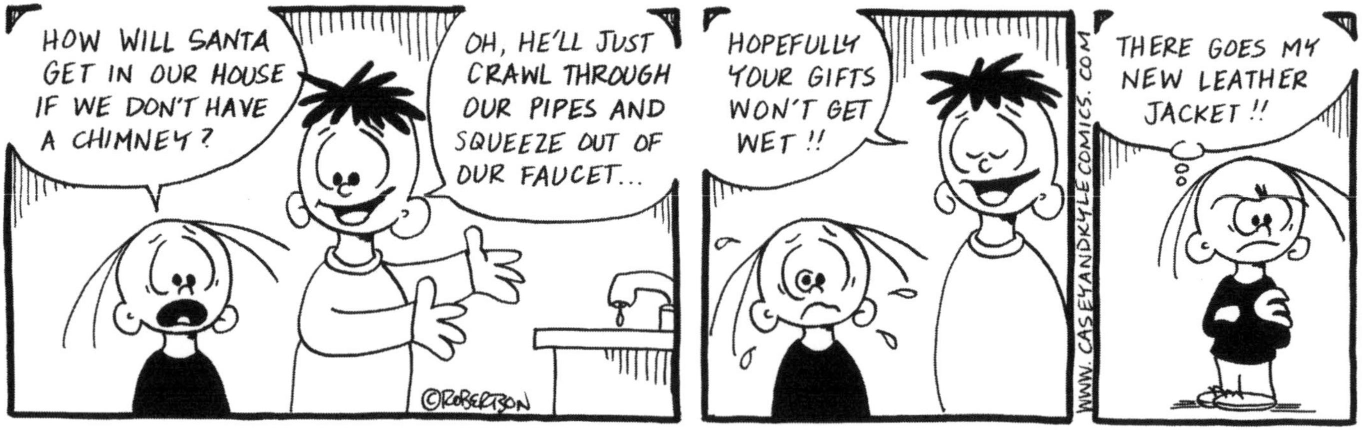
HOW WILL SANTA GET IN OUR HOUSE IF WE DON'T HAVE A CHIMNEY?
OH, HE'LL JUST CRAWL THROUGH OUR PIPES AND SQUEEZE OUT OF OUR FAUCET...
©ROBERTSON
HOPEFULLY YOUR GIFTS WON'T GET WET!!
WWW.CASEYANDKYLECOMICS.COM
THERE GOES MY NEW LEATHER JACKET!!

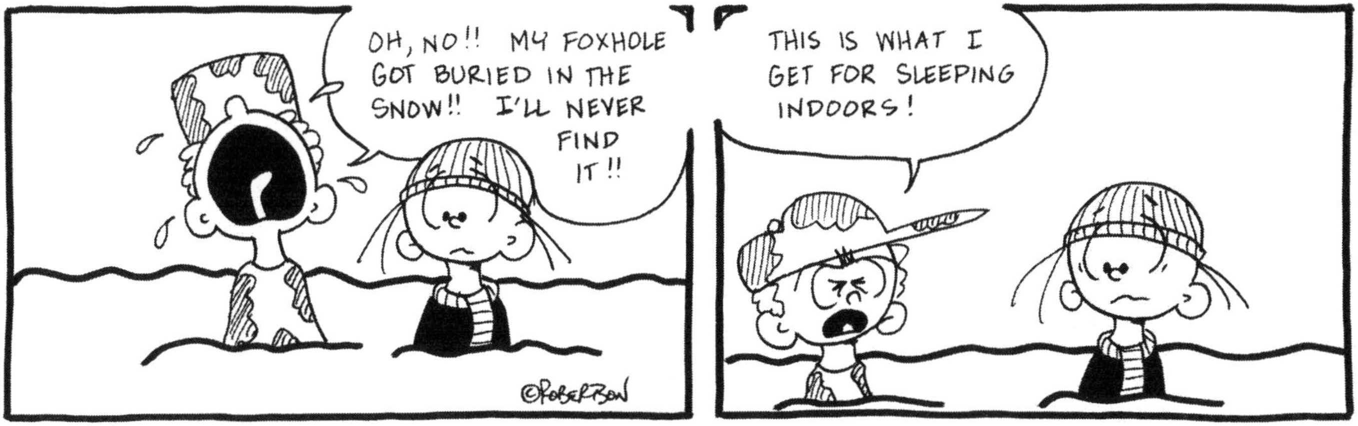
OH, NO!! MY FOXHOLE GOT BURIED IN THE SNOW!! I'LL NEVER FIND IT!!
©ROBERTSON
THIS IS WHAT I GET FOR SLEEPING INDOORS!

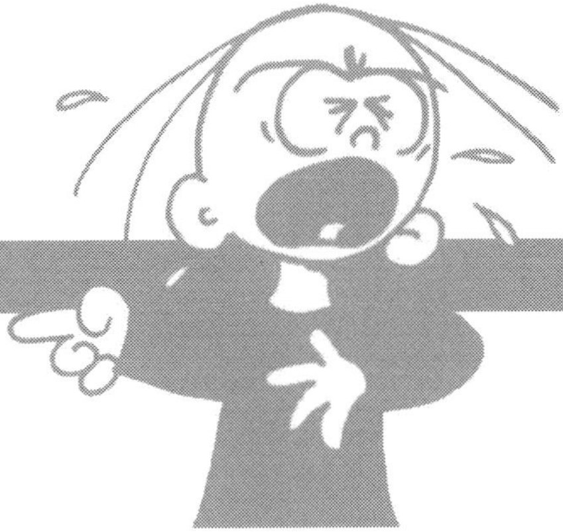

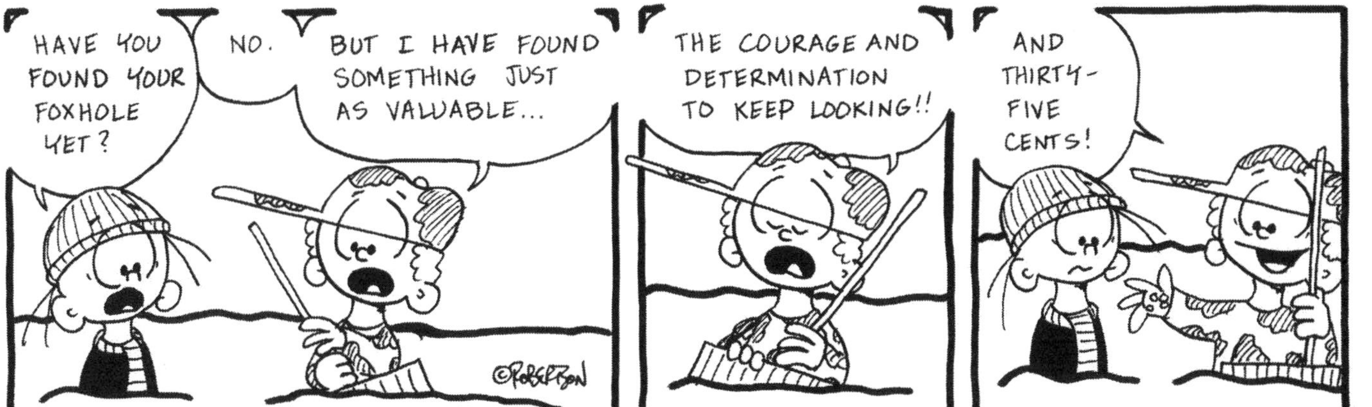
HAVE YOU FOUND YOUR FOXHOLE YET?
NO.
BUT I HAVE FOUND SOMETHING JUST AS VALUABLE...
©ROBERTSON
THE COURAGE AND DETERMINATION TO KEEP LOOKING!!
AND THIRTY-FIVE CENTS!

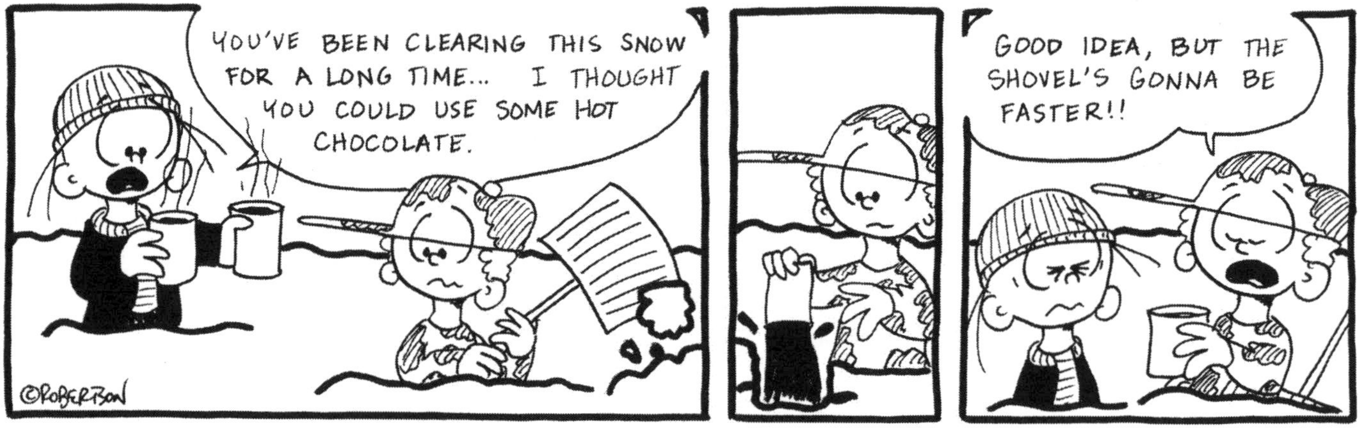
YOU'VE BEEN CLEARING THIS SNOW FOR A LONG TIME... I THOUGHT YOU COULD USE SOME HOT CHOCOLATE.
GOOD IDEA, BUT THE SHOVEL'S GONNA BE FASTER!!
©ROBERTSON

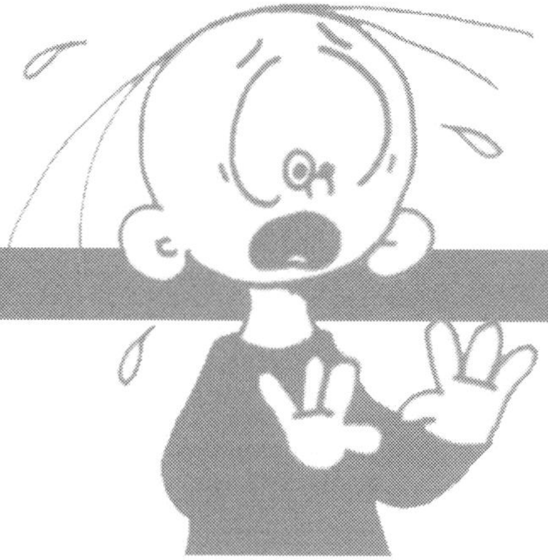

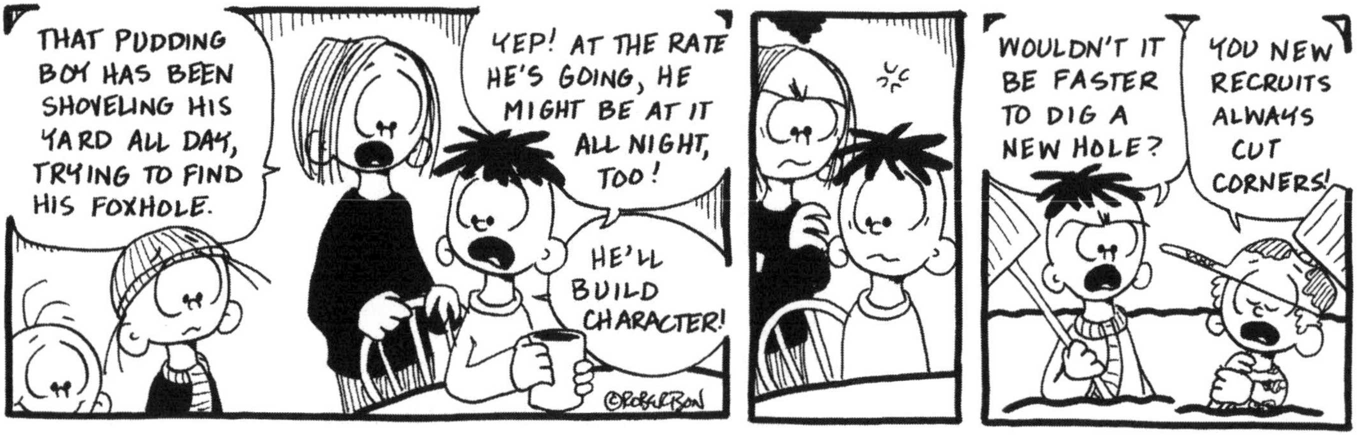
THAT PUDDING BOY HAS BEEN SHOVELING HIS YARD ALL DAY, TRYING TO FIND HIS FOXHOLE.
YEP! AT THE RATE HE'S GOING, HE MIGHT BE AT IT ALL NIGHT, TOO!
HE'LL BUILD CHARACTER!
©ROBERTSON
WOULDN'T IT BE FASTER TO DIG A NEW HOLE?
YOU NEW RECRUITS ALWAYS CUT CORNERS!

WELL... THE YARD IS FINALLY CLEARED, AND ALL THE SNOW IS PILED UP. WHERE'S YOUR FOXHOLE?

THIS IS ODD! PERHAPS IT IS BURIED UNDER THE PILE OF SNOW!!

TELL YOUR MOM I'M GONNA BE AWHILE!!

IF IT'S NOT THERE, I GUESS WE CHECK THE NEIGHBOR'S YARD!

WELL, PUDDING, WE FINALLY FOUND YOUR FOXHOLE.

YES! YOUR DEDICATION TO DUTY AND DEVOTION TO YOUR FRIEND WARMS MY HEART.

IT WARMS MY HEART, TOO...

BUT I'M GOING IN NOW. THE REST OF ME IS FREEZING!!

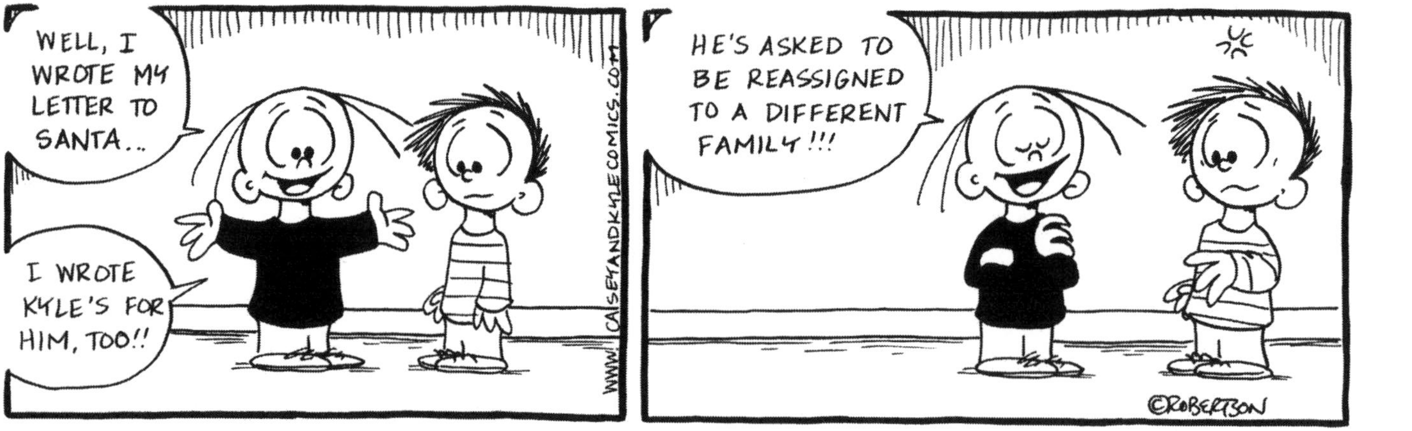
WELL, I WROTE MY LETTER TO SANTA...
I WROTE KYLE'S FOR HIM, TOO!!
WWW.CASEYANDKYLECOMICS.COM
HE'S ASKED TO BE REASSIGNED TO A DIFFERENT FAMILY!!!
©ROBERTSON

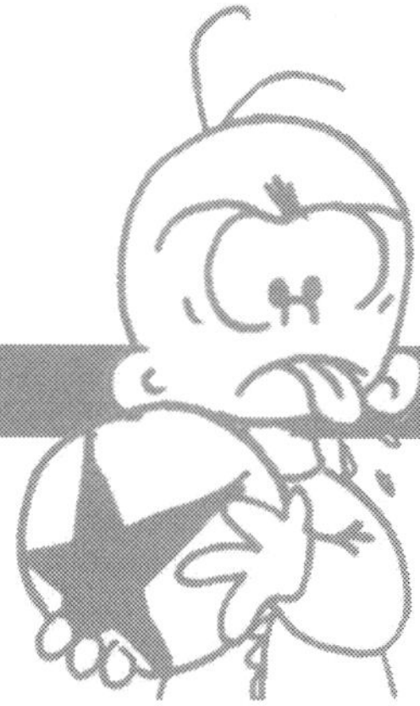

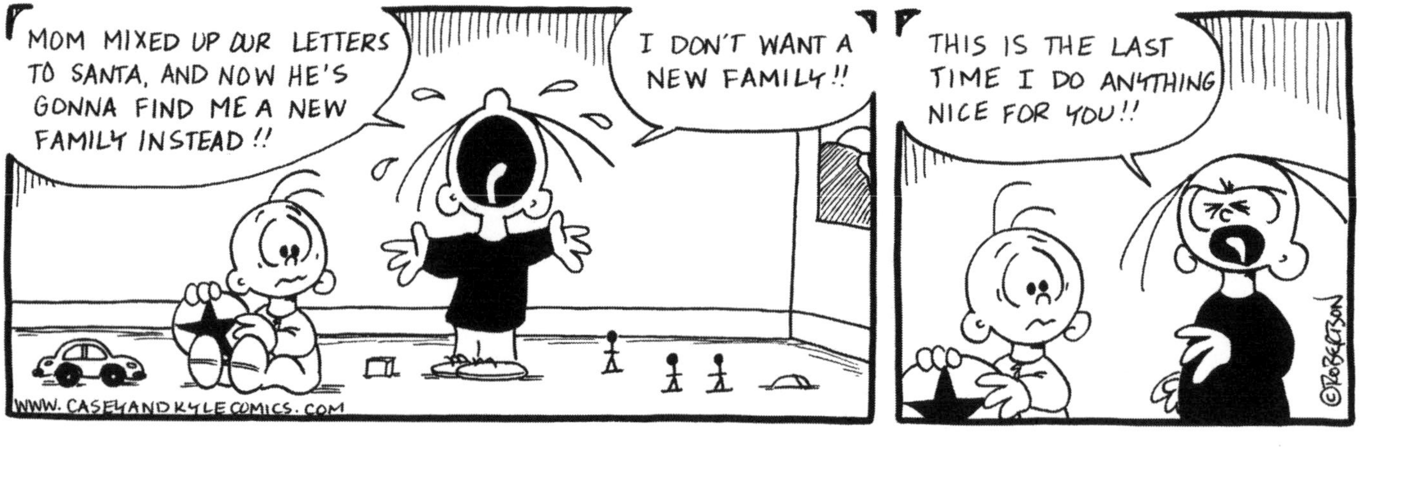
MOM MIXED UP OUR LETTERS TO SANTA, AND NOW HE'S GONNA FIND ME A NEW FAMILY INSTEAD!!
I DON'T WANT A NEW FAMILY!!
WWW.CASEYANDKYLECOMICS.COM
THIS IS THE LAST TIME I DO ANYTHING NICE FOR YOU!!
©ROBERTSON

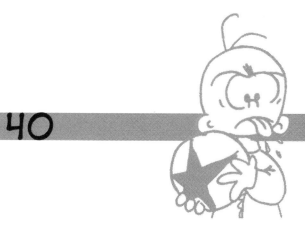

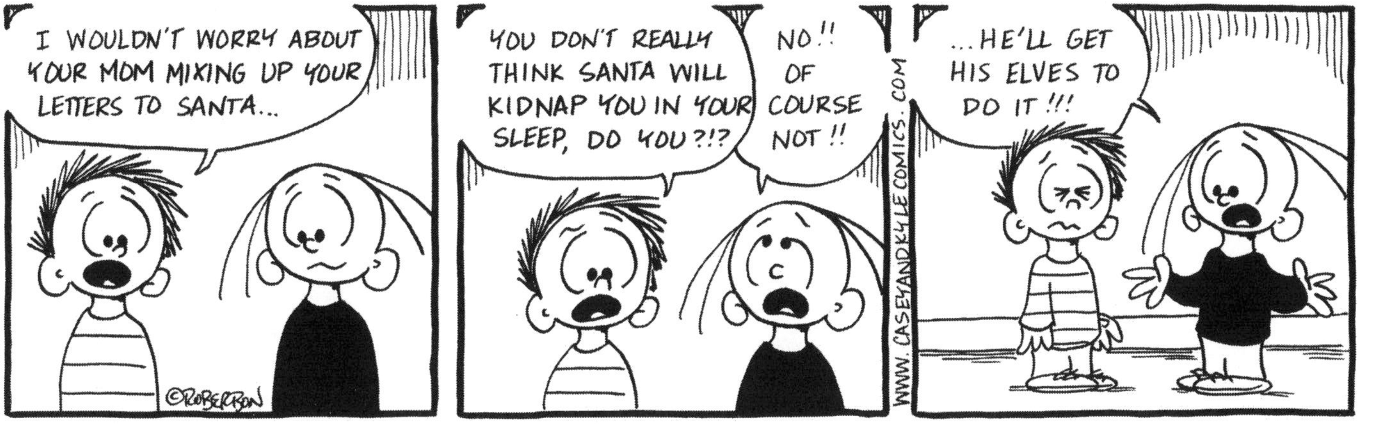

I WOULDN'T WORRY ABOUT YOUR MOM MIXING UP YOUR LETTERS TO SANTA...
©ROBERTSON
YOU DON'T REALLY THINK SANTA WILL KIDNAP YOU IN YOUR SLEEP, DO YOU?!?
NO!! OF COURSE NOT!!
WWW.CASEYANDKYLECOMICS.COM
...HE'LL GET HIS ELVES TO DO IT!!!

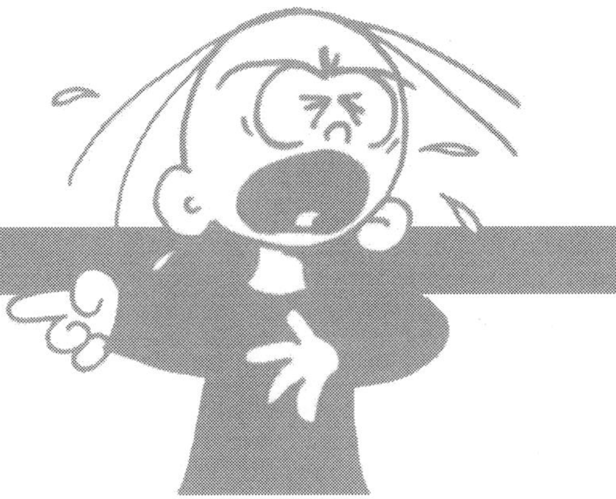

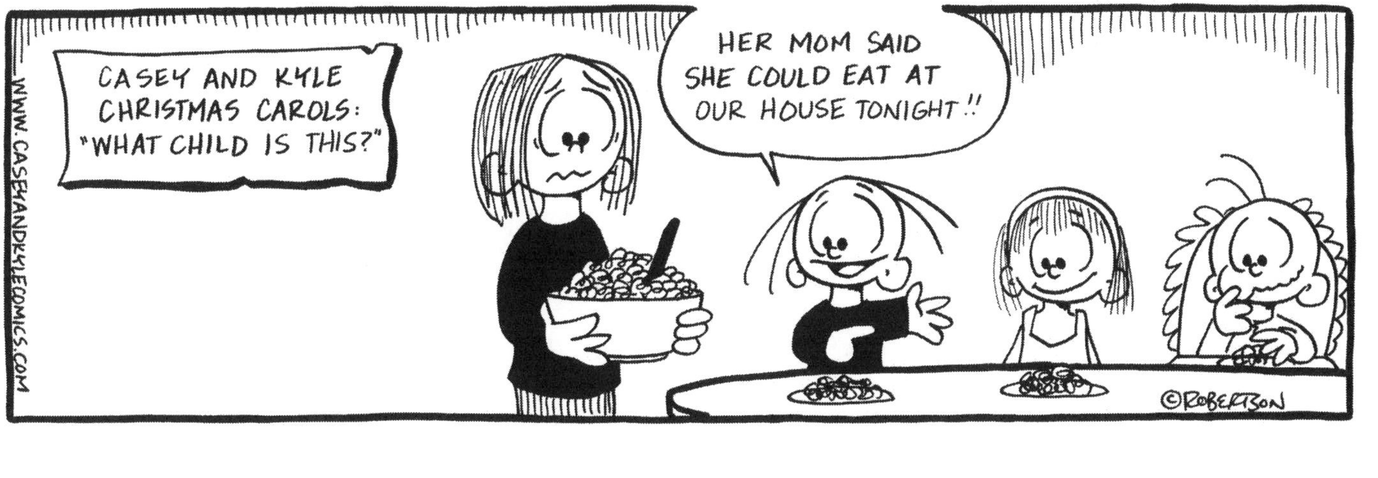

WWW.CASEYANDKYLECOMICS.COM
CASEY AND KYLE CHRISTMAS CAROLS: "WHAT CHILD IS THIS?"
HER MOM SAID SHE COULD EAT AT OUR HOUSE TONIGHT!!
©ROBERTSON

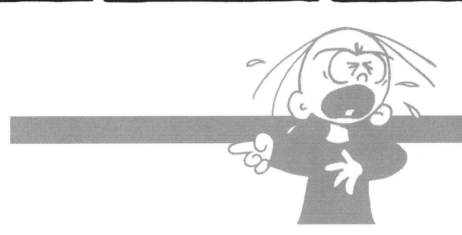

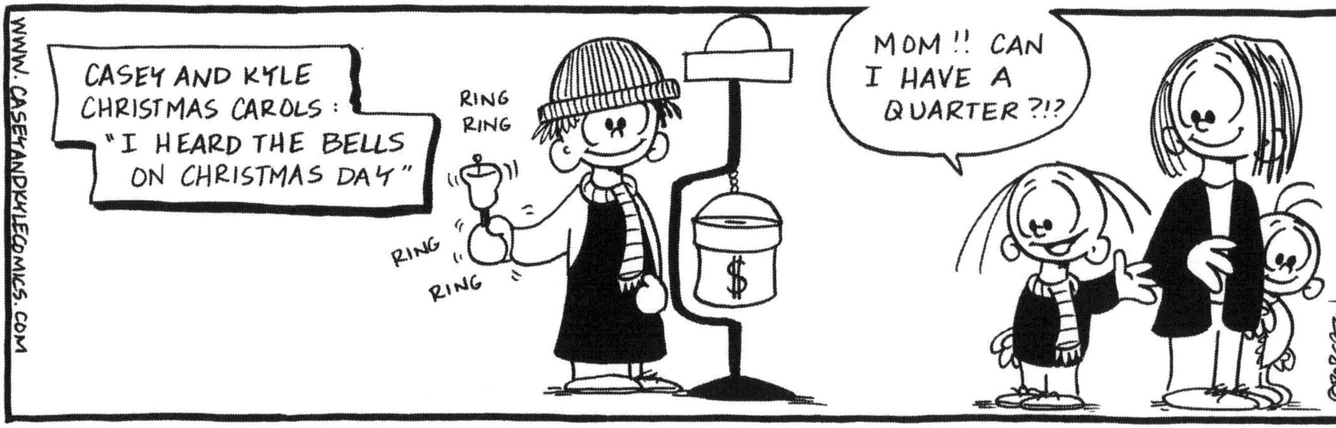
WWW.CASEYANDKYLECOMICS.COM
CASEY AND KYLE CHRISTMAS CAROLS: "I HEARD THE BELLS ON CHRISTMAS DAY"
RING RING
RING RING
MOM!! CAN I HAVE A QUARTER?!?
$
©ROBERTSON

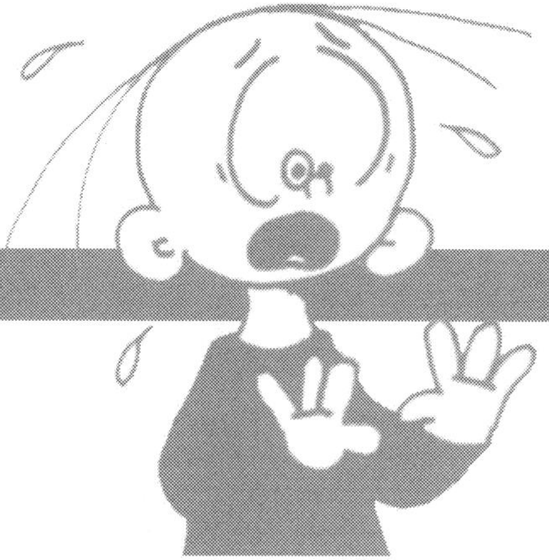

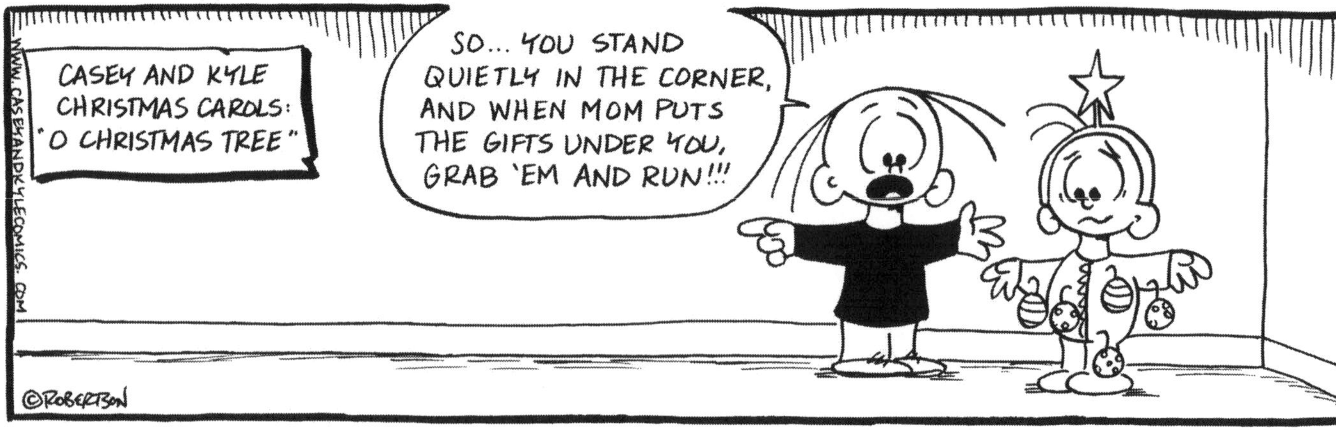
WWW.CASEYANDKYLECOMICS.COM
CASEY AND KYLE CHRISTMAS CAROLS: "O CHRISTMAS TREE"
SO... YOU STAND QUIETLY IN THE CORNER, AND WHEN MOM PUTS THE GIFTS UNDER YOU, GRAB 'EM AND RUN!!!
©ROBERTSON

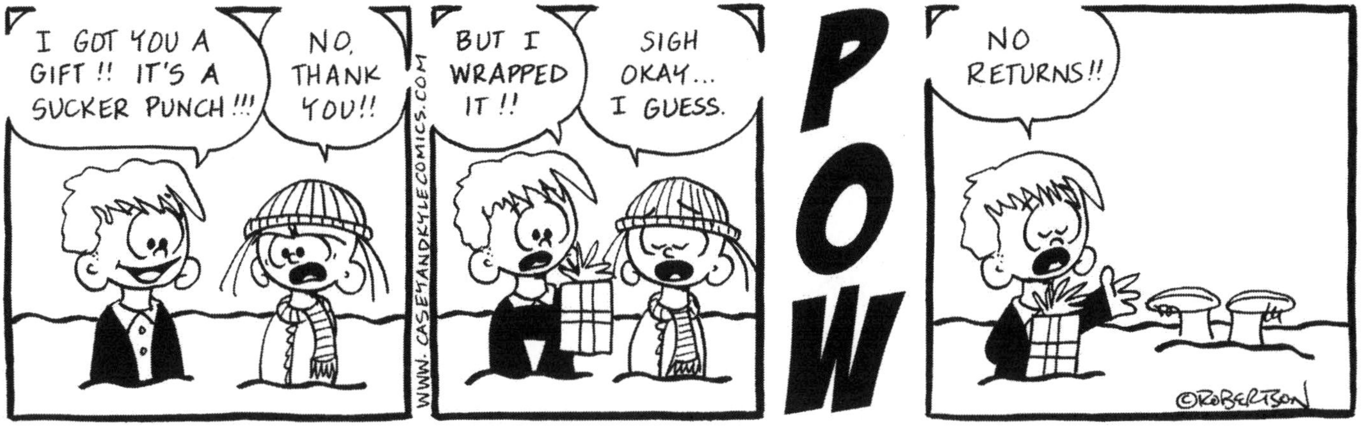
I GOT YOU A GIFT !! IT'S A SUCKER PUNCH !!!
NO, THANK YOU!!
WWW.CASEYANDKYLECOMICS.COM
BUT I WRAPPED IT !!
SIGH OKAY... I GUESS.
POW
NO RETURNS!!
©ROBERTSON

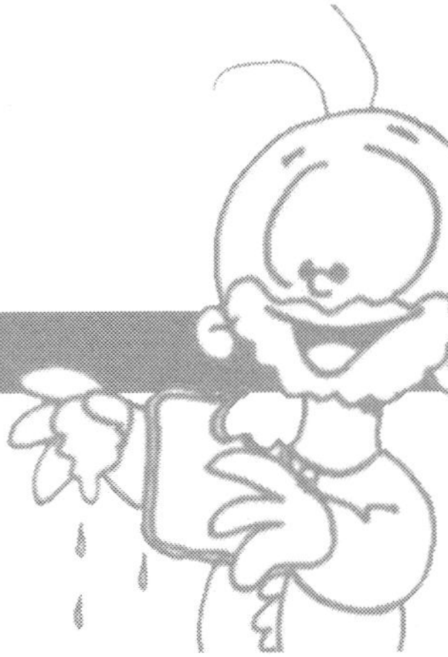

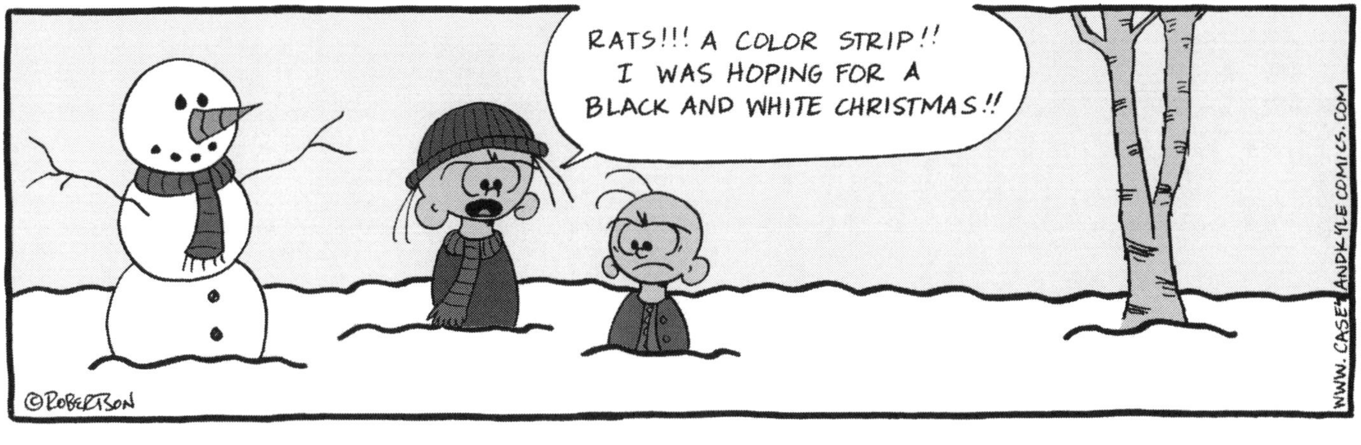
RATS!!! A COLOR STRIP!! I WAS HOPING FOR A BLACK AND WHITE CHRISTMAS!!
WWW.CASEYANDKYLECOMICS.COM
©ROBERTSON

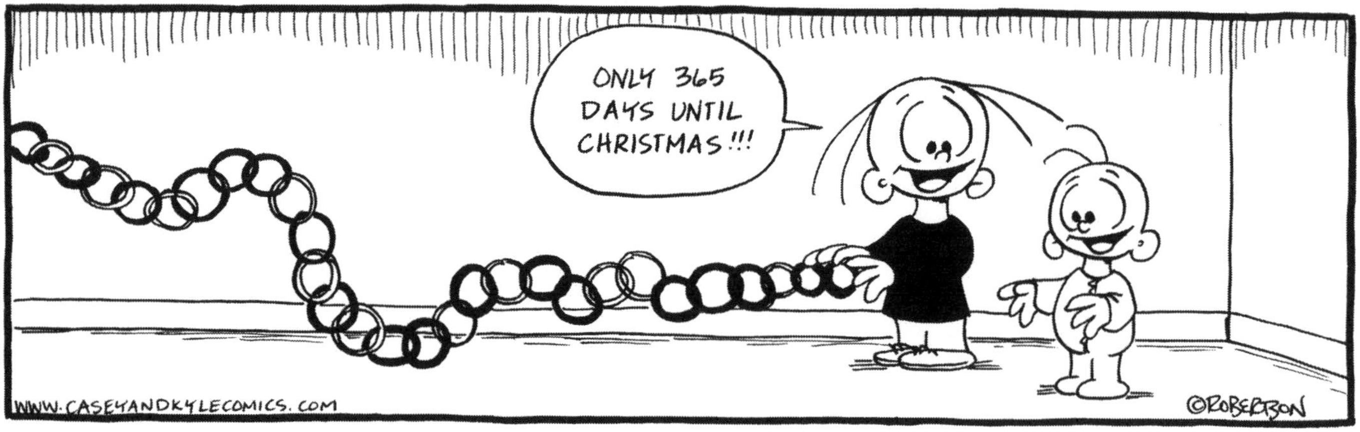
ONLY 365 DAYS UNTIL CHRISTMAS!!!
WWW.CASEYANDKYLECOMICS.COM
©ROBERTSON

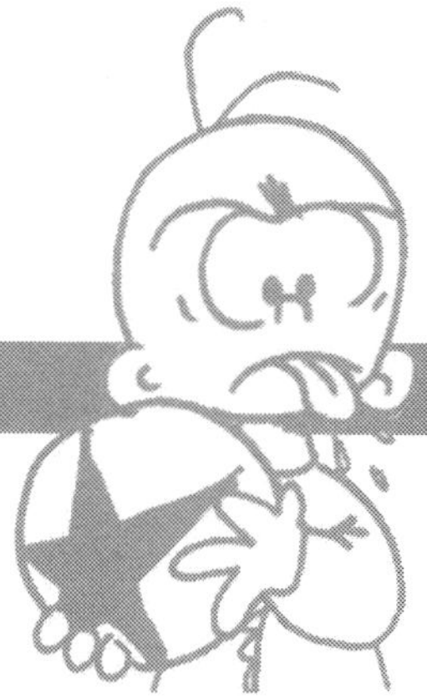

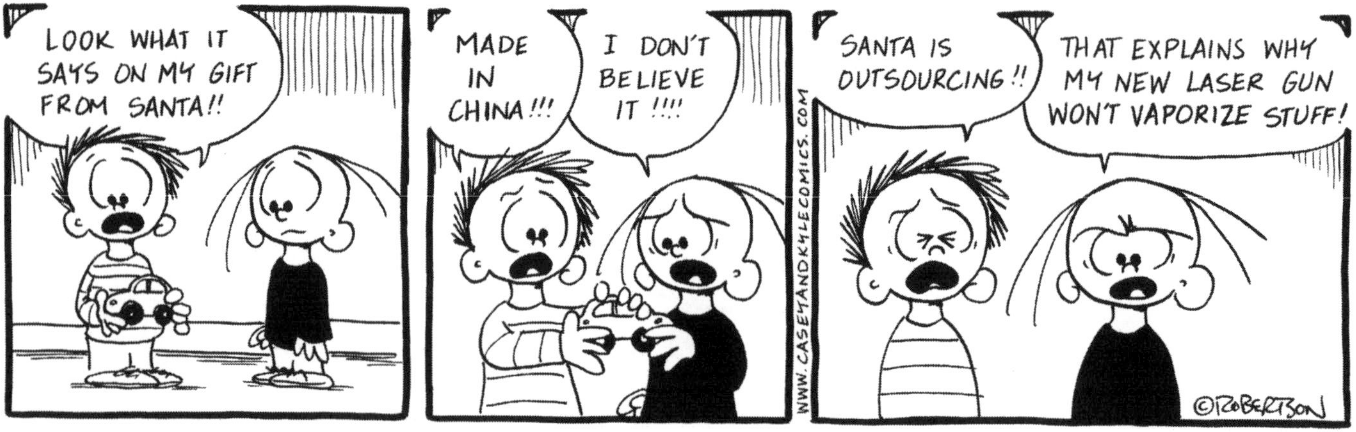
LOOK WHAT IT SAYS ON MY GIFT FROM SANTA!!
MADE IN CHINA!!!
I DON'T BELIEVE IT !!!!
WWW.CASEYANDKYLECOMICS.COM
SANTA IS OUTSOURCING!!
THAT EXPLAINS WHY MY NEW LASER GUN WON'T VAPORIZE STUFF!
©ROBERTSON

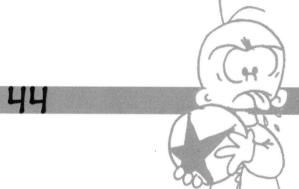

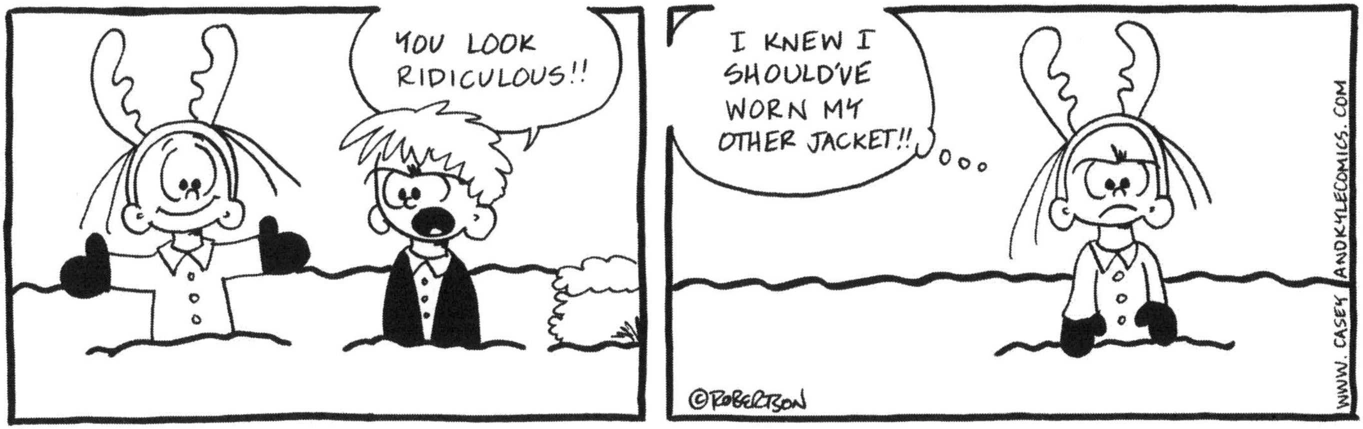
YOU LOOK RIDICULOUS!!
I KNEW I SHOULD'VE WORN MY OTHER JACKET!!
©ROBERTSON
WWW.CASEYANDKYLECOMICS.COM

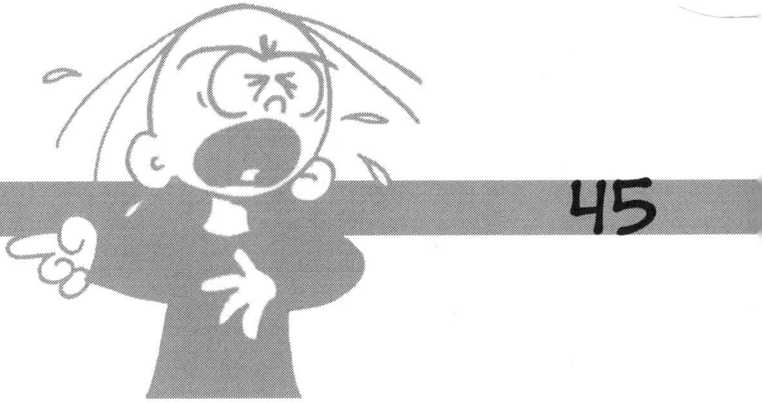

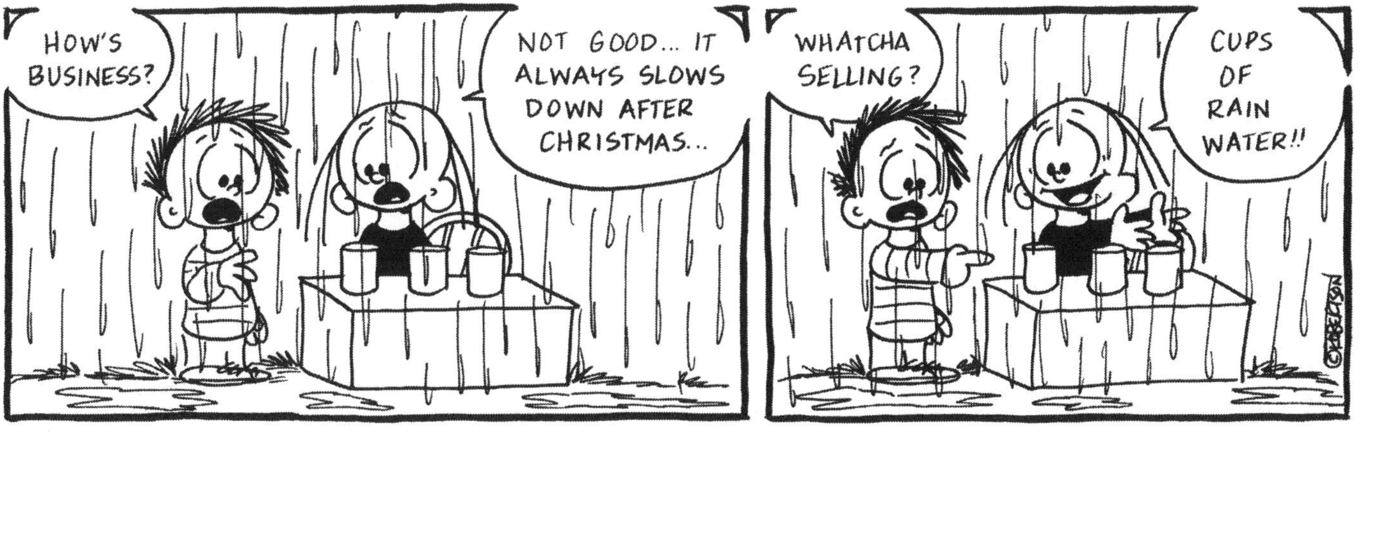
HOW'S BUSINESS?
NOT GOOD... IT ALWAYS SLOWS DOWN AFTER CHRISTMAS...
WHATCHA SELLING?
CUPS OF RAIN WATER!!
©ROBERTSON

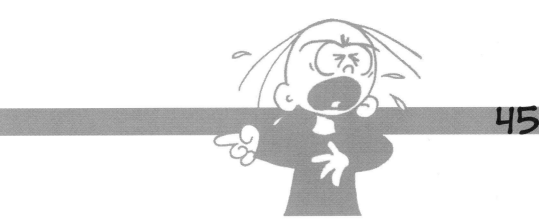

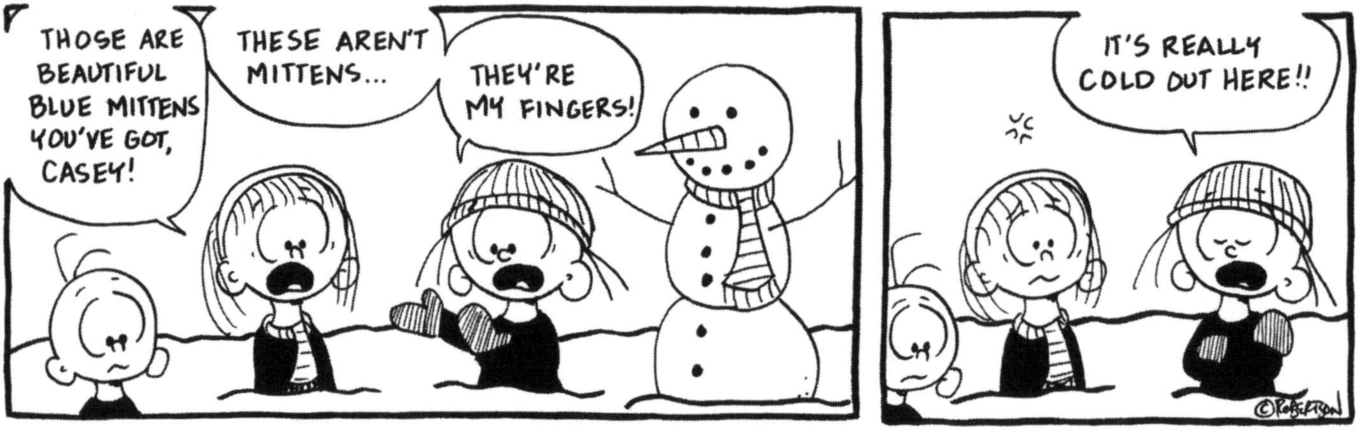
THOSE ARE BEAUTIFUL BLUE MITTENS YOU'VE GOT, CASEY!
THESE AREN'T MITTENS...
THEY'RE MY FINGERS!
IT'S REALLY COLD OUT HERE!!
©ROBERTSON

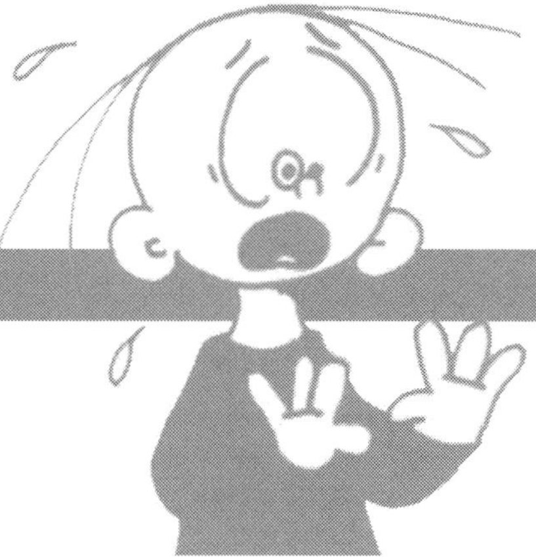

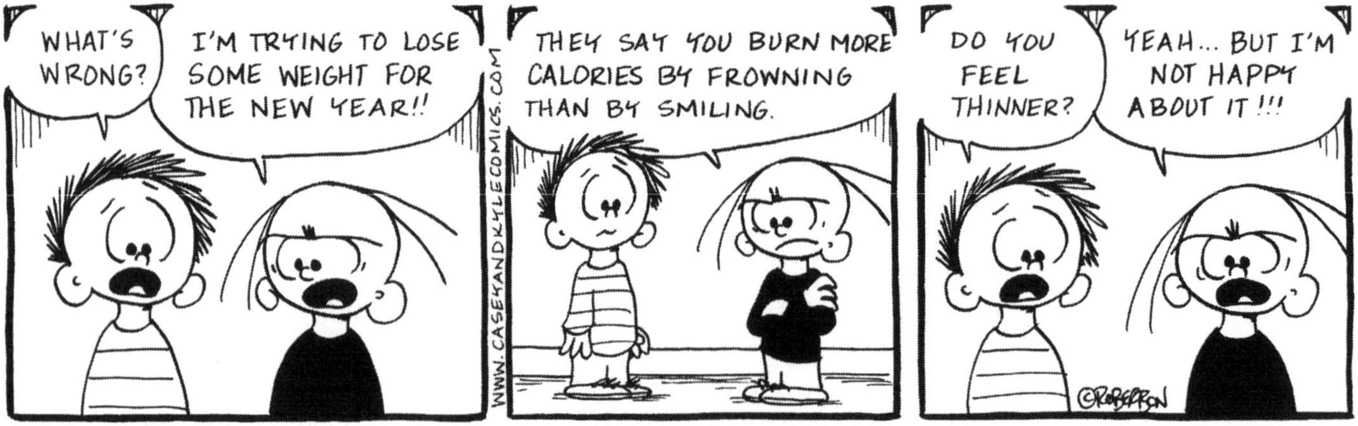
WHAT'S WRONG?
I'M TRYING TO LOSE SOME WEIGHT FOR THE NEW YEAR!!
WWW.CASEYANDKYLECOMICS.COM
THEY SAY YOU BURN MORE CALORIES BY FROWNING THAN BY SMILING.
DO YOU FEEL THINNER?
YEAH... BUT I'M NOT HAPPY ABOUT IT!!!
©ROBERTSON

THIS WINTER IS TOO RAINY!! YOU CAN'T MAKE SNOW ANGELS IN THE RAIN!!
YOU COULD MAKE A MUD PUDDLE ANGEL!!
IT'S NOT THE SAME!!!

MOM SAYS IT'S SUMMER IN AUSTRALIA RIGHT NOW!!

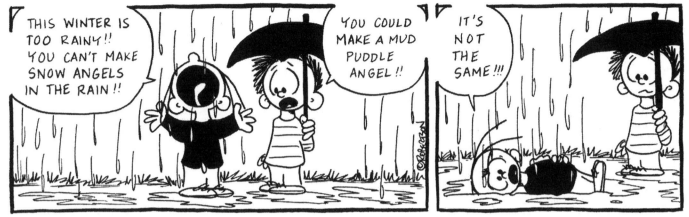

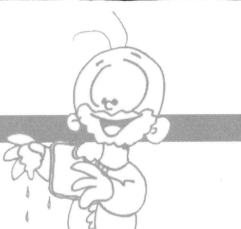

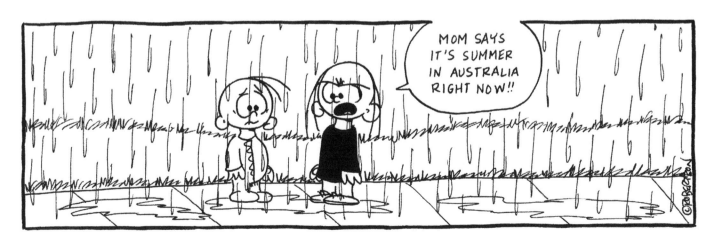

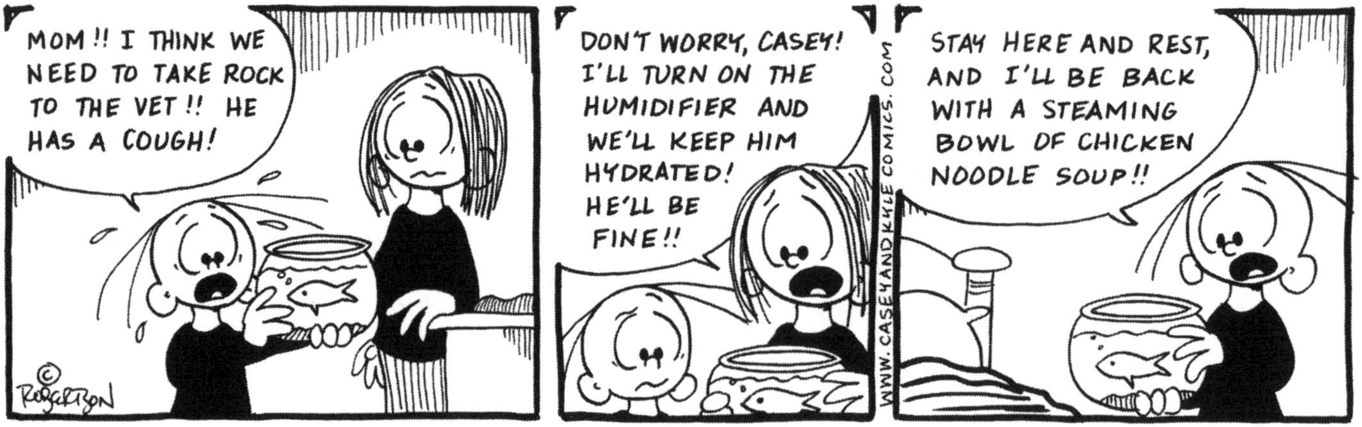
MOM!! I THINK WE NEED TO TAKE ROCK TO THE VET!! HE HAS A COUGH!
© ROBERTSON
DON'T WORRY, CASEY! I'LL TURN ON THE HUMIDIFIER AND WE'LL KEEP HIM HYDRATED! HE'LL BE FINE!!
WWW.CASEYANDKYLECOMICS.COM
STAY HERE AND REST, AND I'LL BE BACK WITH A STEAMING BOWL OF CHICKEN NOODLE SOUP!!

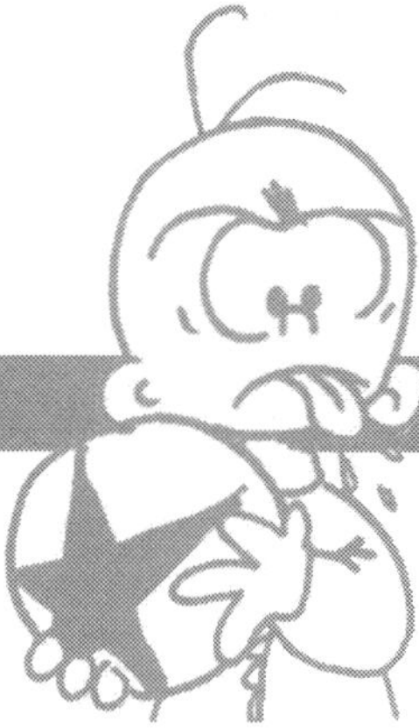

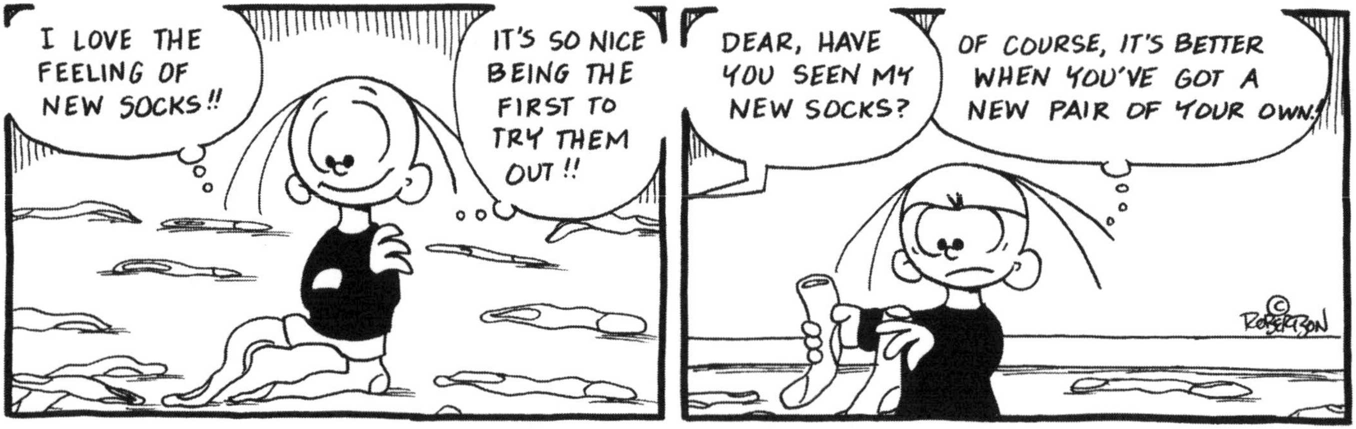
I LOVE THE FEELING OF NEW SOCKS!!
IT'S SO NICE BEING THE FIRST TO TRY THEM OUT!!
DEAR, HAVE YOU SEEN MY NEW SOCKS?
OF COURSE, IT'S BETTER WHEN YOU'VE GOT A NEW PAIR OF YOUR OWN!
© ROBERTSON

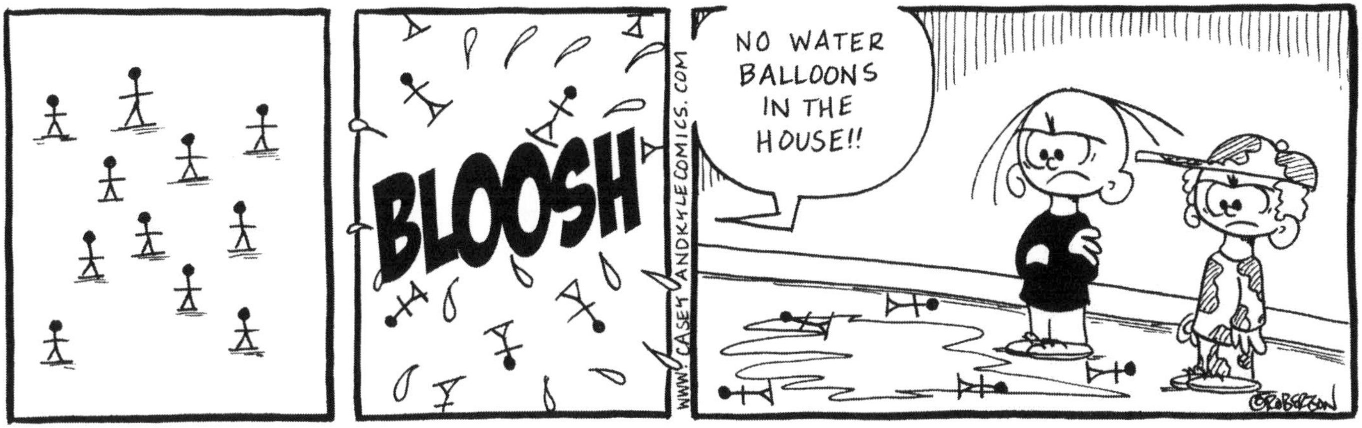
BLOOSH
WWW.CASEYANDKYLECOMICS.COM
NO WATER BALLOONS IN THE HOUSE!!

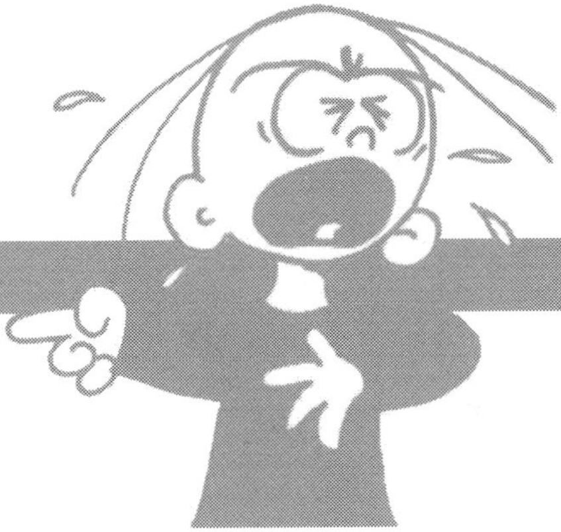

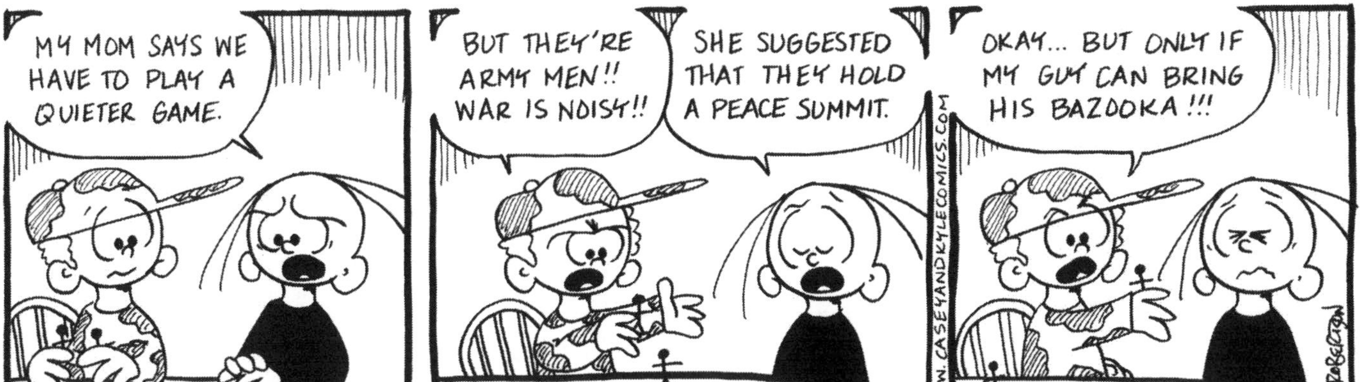
MY MOM SAYS WE HAVE TO PLAY A QUIETER GAME.
BUT THEY'RE ARMY MEN!! WAR IS NOISY!!
SHE SUGGESTED THAT THEY HOLD A PEACE SUMMIT.
WWW.CASEYANDKYLECOMICS.COM
OKAY... BUT ONLY IF MY GUY CAN BRING HIS BAZOOKA!!!

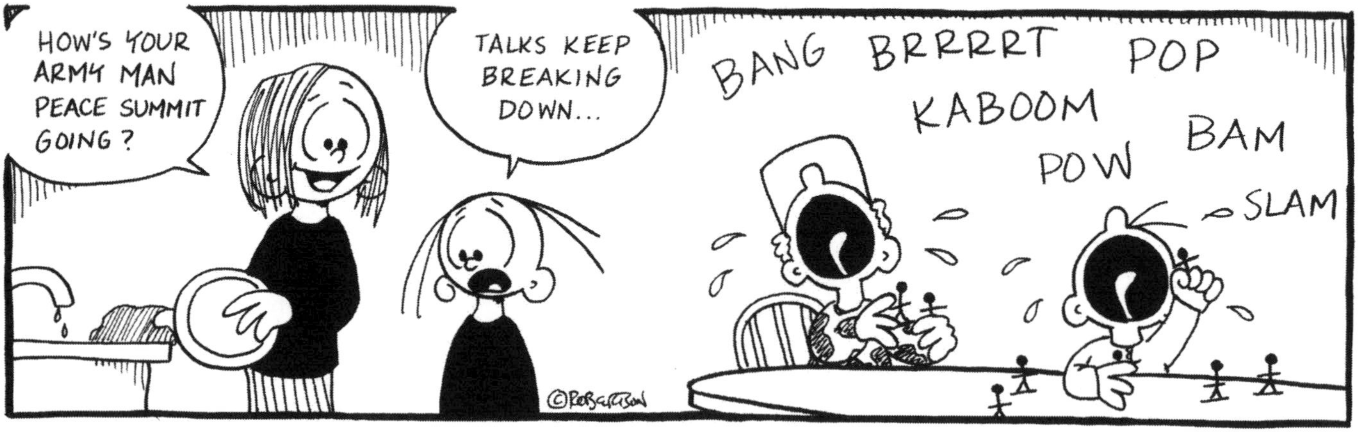
HOW'S YOUR ARMY MAN PEACE SUMMIT GOING?
TALKS KEEP BREAKING DOWN...
©ROBERTSON
BANG BRRRRT POP
KABOOM
BAM
POW
SLAM

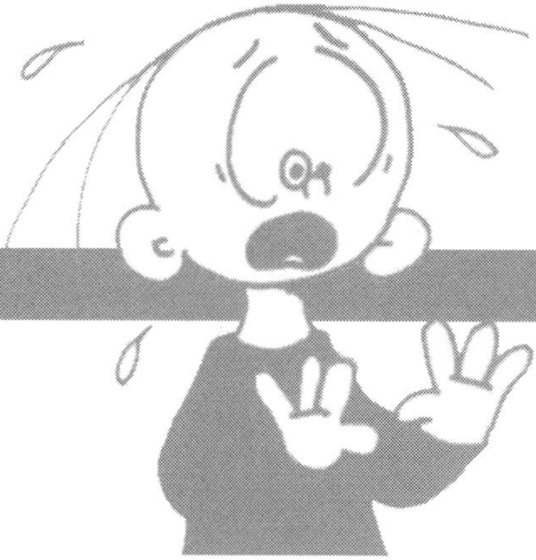

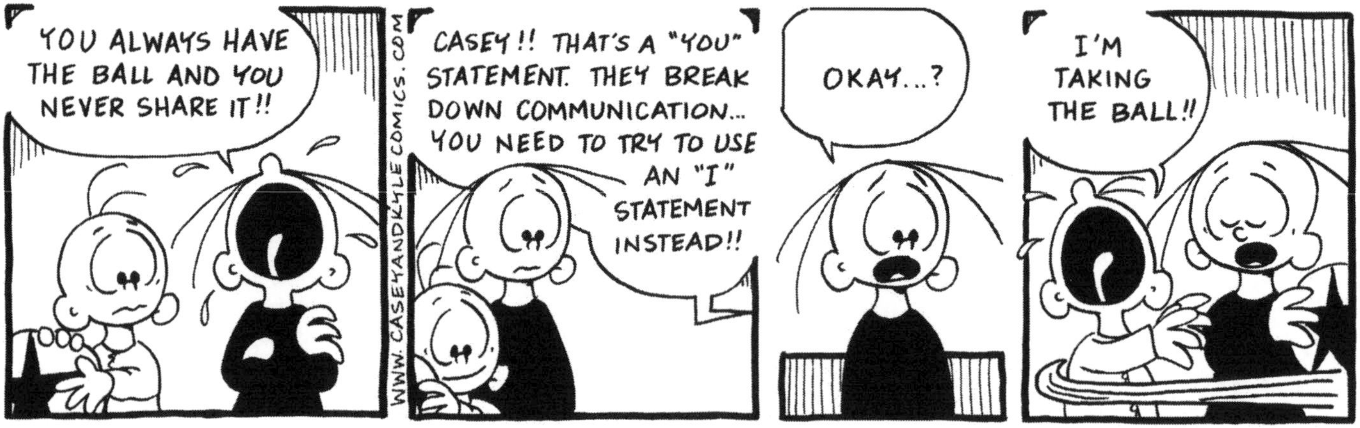
YOU ALWAYS HAVE THE BALL AND YOU NEVER SHARE IT!!
WWW.CASEYANDKYLECOMICS.COM
CASEY!! THAT'S A "YOU" STATEMENT. THEY BREAK DOWN COMMUNICATION... YOU NEED TO TRY TO USE AN "I" STATEMENT INSTEAD!!
OKAY...?
I'M TAKING THE BALL!!

BOOM
BOOM
BOOM
CASEY !!! QUIT PRETENDING TO SHOOT YOUR BROTHER WITH A MACHINE GUN!
I'M NOT, MOM !! IT'S A BAZOOKA !!
WWW.CASEYANDKYLECOMICS.COM
SOME DAYS IT'S LIKE SHE DOESN'T KNOW ANYTHING !!
© ROBERTSON

WWW.CASEYANDKYLECOMICS.COM
CASEY!!
HOW COULD I TOUCH HIM?! I'M CLEAR OVER HERE!!
©ROBERTSON

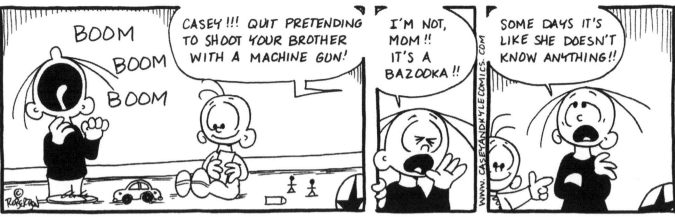

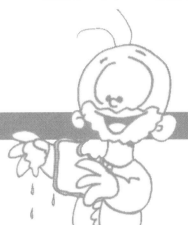

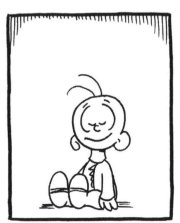

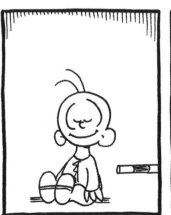

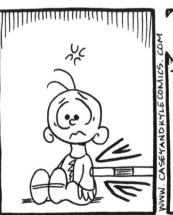

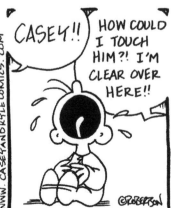

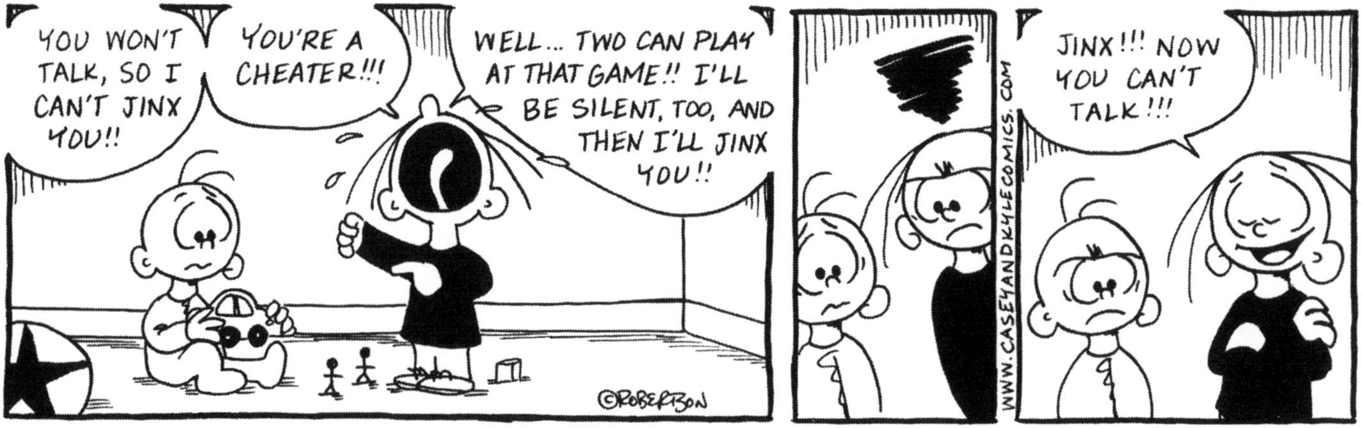
YOU WON'T TALK, SO I CAN'T JINX YOU!!
YOU'RE A CHEATER!!!
WELL... TWO CAN PLAY AT THAT GAME!! I'LL BE SILENT, TOO, AND THEN I'LL JINX YOU!!
©ROBERTSON
WWW.CASEYANDKYLECOMICS.COM
JINX!!! NOW YOU CAN'T TALK!!!

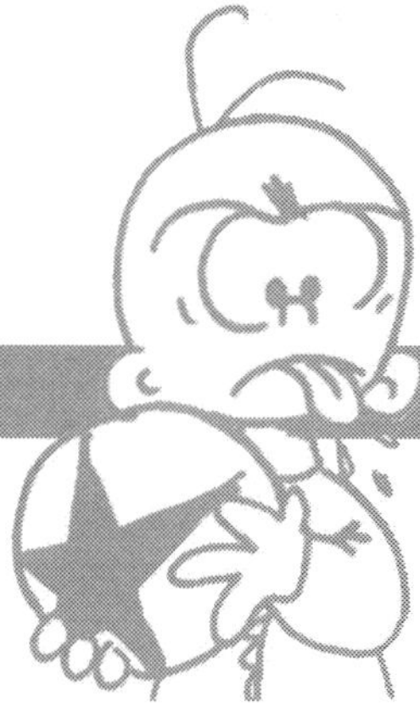

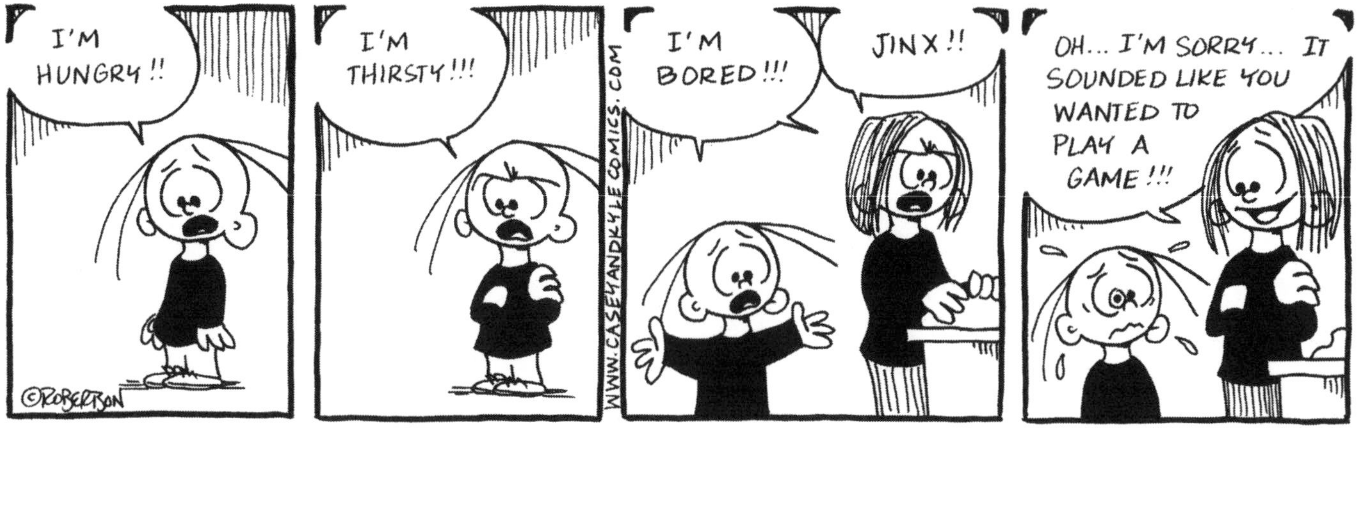
I'M HUNGRY!!
©ROBERTSON
I'M THIRSTY!!!
WWW.CASEYANDKYLECOMICS.COM
I'M BORED!!!
JINX!!
OH... I'M SORRY... IT SOUNDED LIKE YOU WANTED TO PLAY A GAME!!!

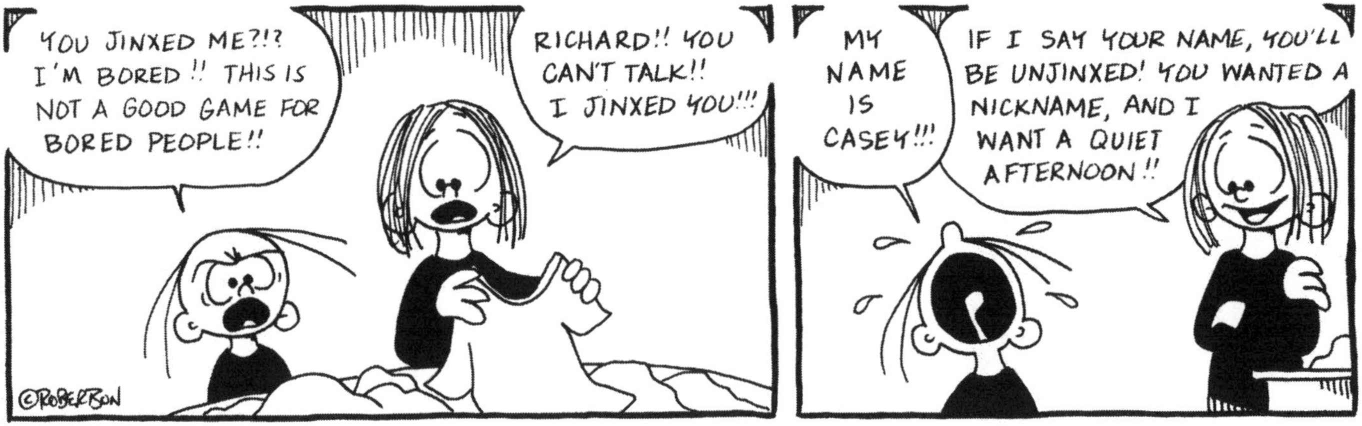
YOU JINXED ME?!? I'M BORED!! THIS IS NOT A GOOD GAME FOR BORED PEOPLE!!
RICHARD!! YOU CAN'T TALK!! I JINXED YOU!!!
MY NAME IS CASEY!!!
IF I SAY YOUR NAME, YOU'LL BE UNJINXED! YOU WANTED A NICKNAME, AND I WANT A QUIET AFTERNOON!!
©ROBERTSON

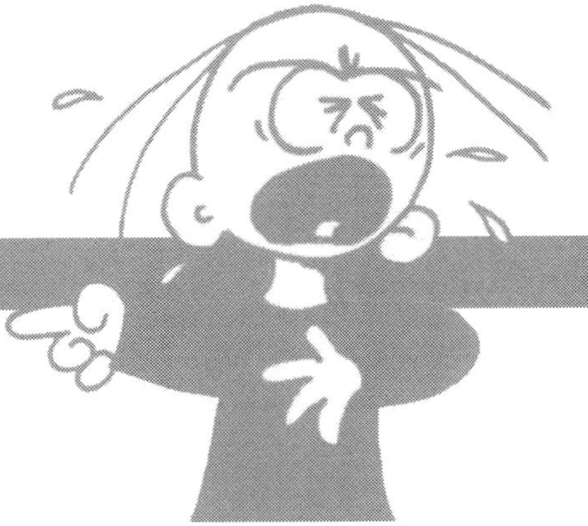

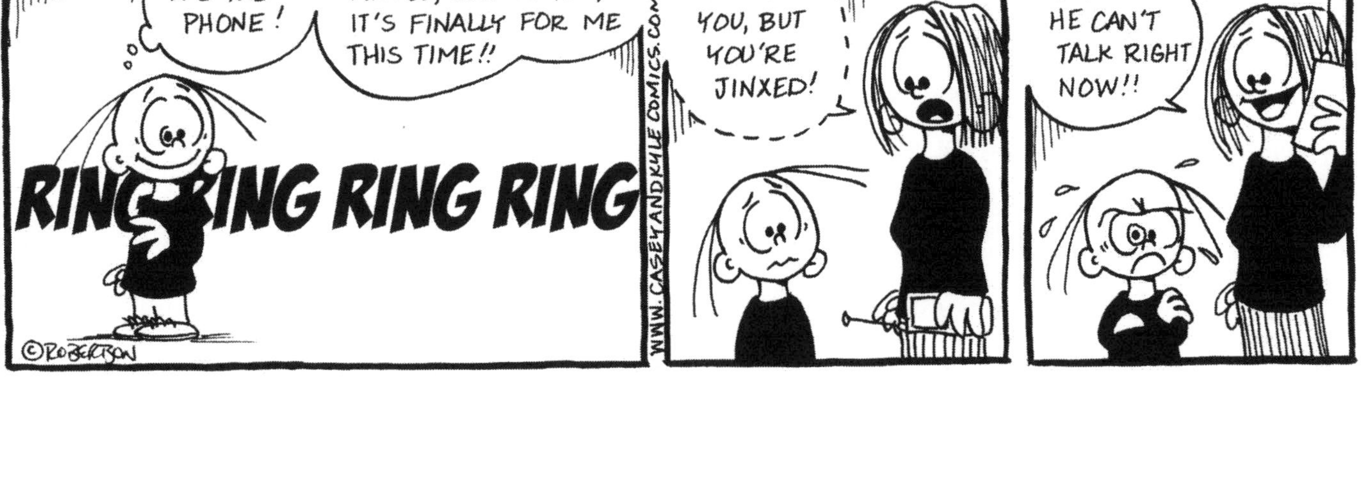
IT'S THE PHONE!
MAYBE, JUST MAYBE, IT'S FINALLY FOR ME THIS TIME!!
RING RING RING RING
©ROBERTSON
WWW.CASEYANDKYLECOMICS.COM
IT'S FOR YOU, BUT YOU'RE JINXED!
SORRY... HE CAN'T TALK RIGHT NOW!!

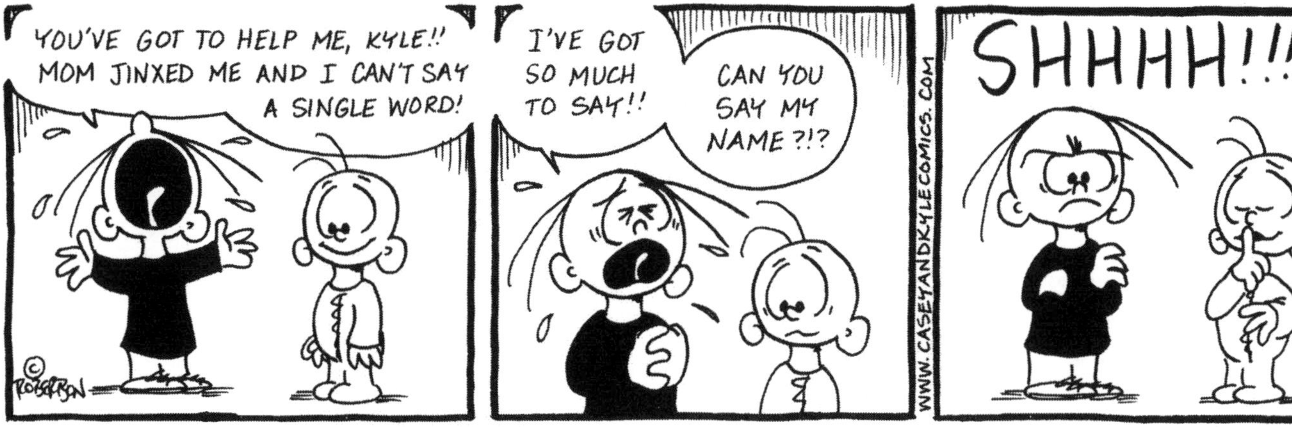
YOU'VE GOT TO HELP ME, KYLE!! MOM JINXED ME AND I CAN'T SAY A SINGLE WORD!
I'VE GOT SO MUCH TO SAY!!
CAN YOU SAY MY NAME?!?
SHHHH!!!!
© ROBERTSON
WWW.CASEYANDKYLECOMICS.COM

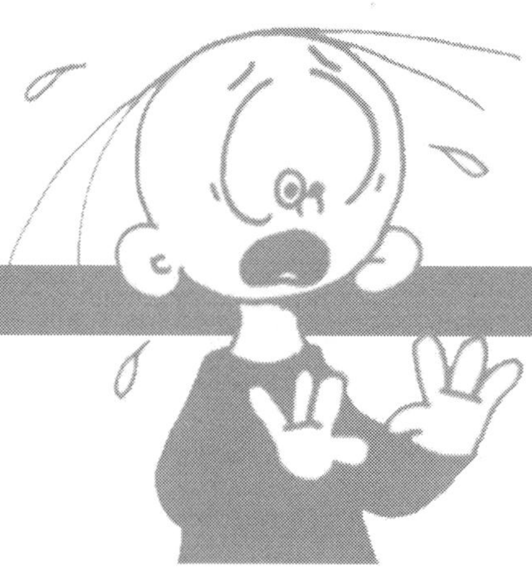

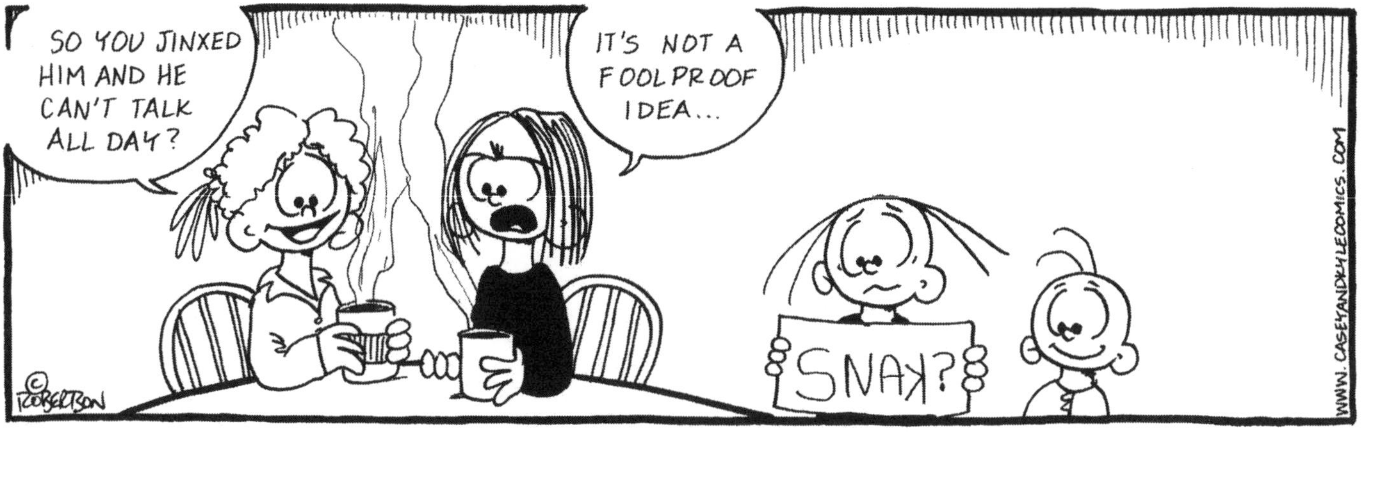
SO YOU JINXED HIM AND HE CAN'T TALK ALL DAY?
IT'S NOT A FOOLPROOF IDEA...
SNAK?
© ROBERTSON
WWW.CASEYANDKYLECOMICS.COM

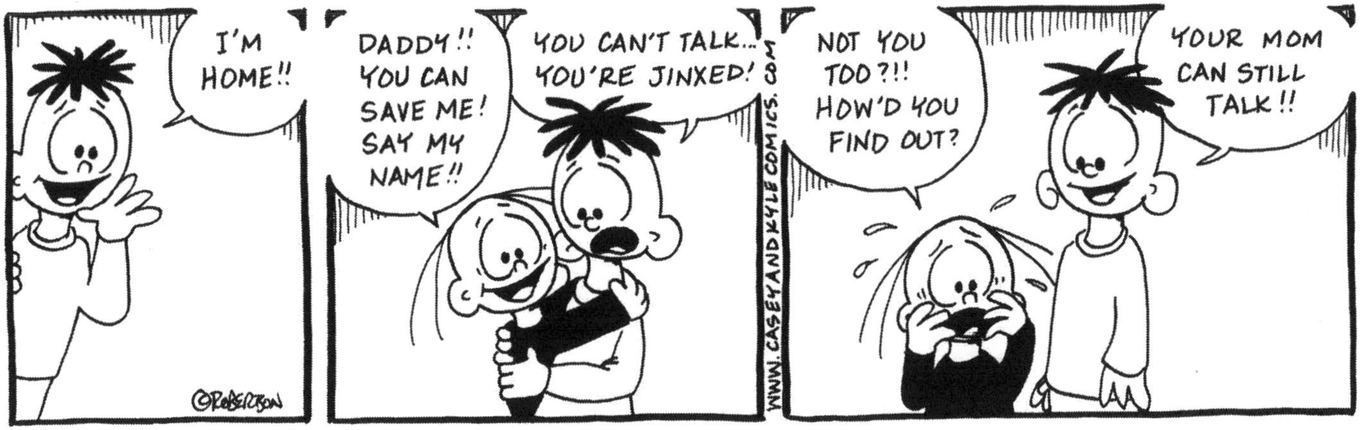
I'M HOME!!
DADDY!! YOU CAN SAVE ME! SAY MY NAME!!
YOU CAN'T TALK... YOU'RE JINXED!
NOT YOU TOO?!! HOW'D YOU FIND OUT?
YOUR MOM CAN STILL TALK!!
©ROBERSON
WWW.CASEYANDKYLECOMICS.COM

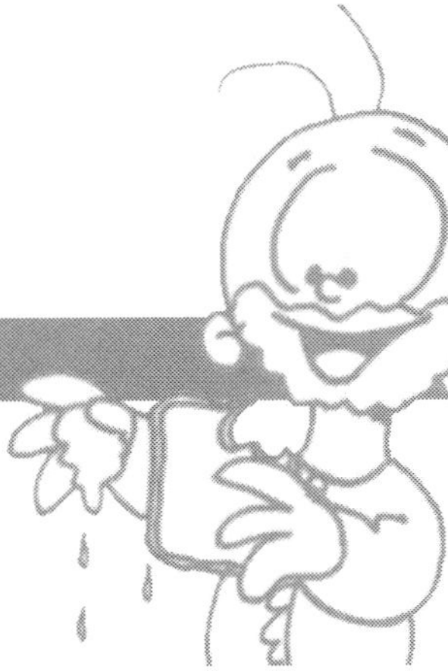

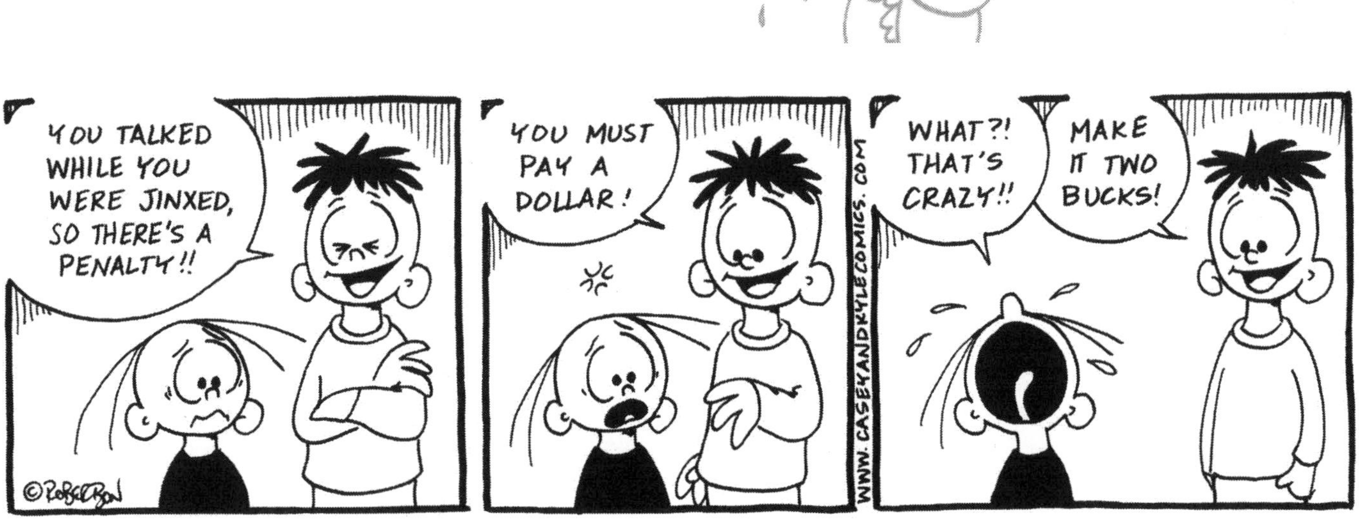
YOU TALKED WHILE YOU WERE JINXED, SO THERE'S A PENALTY!!
YOU MUST PAY A DOLLAR!
WHAT?! THAT'S CRAZY!!
MAKE IT TWO BUCKS!
©ROBERSON
WWW.CASEYANDKYLECOMICS.COM

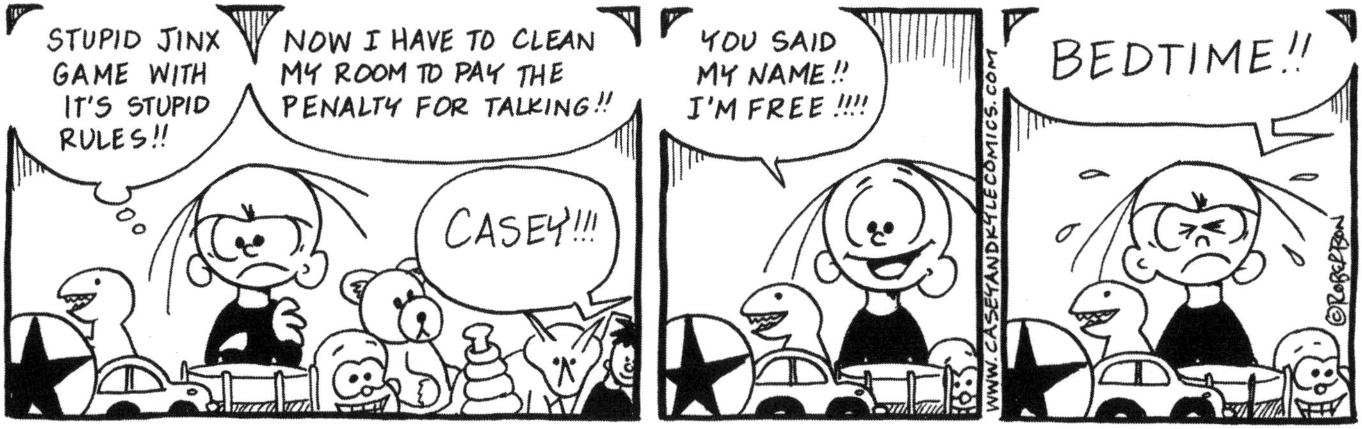
STUPID JINX GAME WITH IT'S STUPID RULES!!
NOW I HAVE TO CLEAN MY ROOM TO PAY THE PENALTY FOR TALKING!!
CASEY!!!
YOU SAID MY NAME!! I'M FREE!!!!
WWW.CASEYANDKYLECOMICS.COM
BEDTIME!!
©ROBERTSON

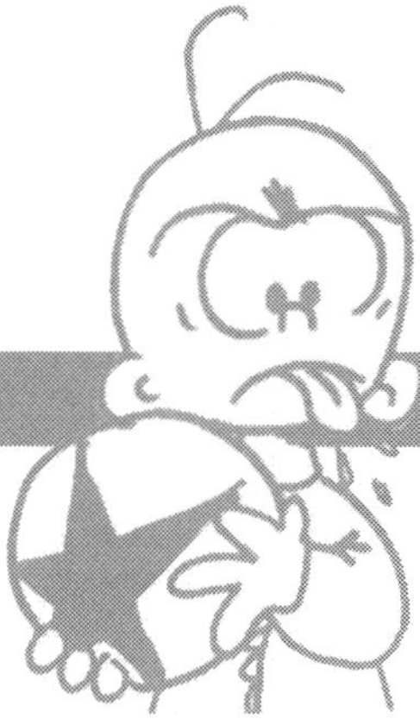

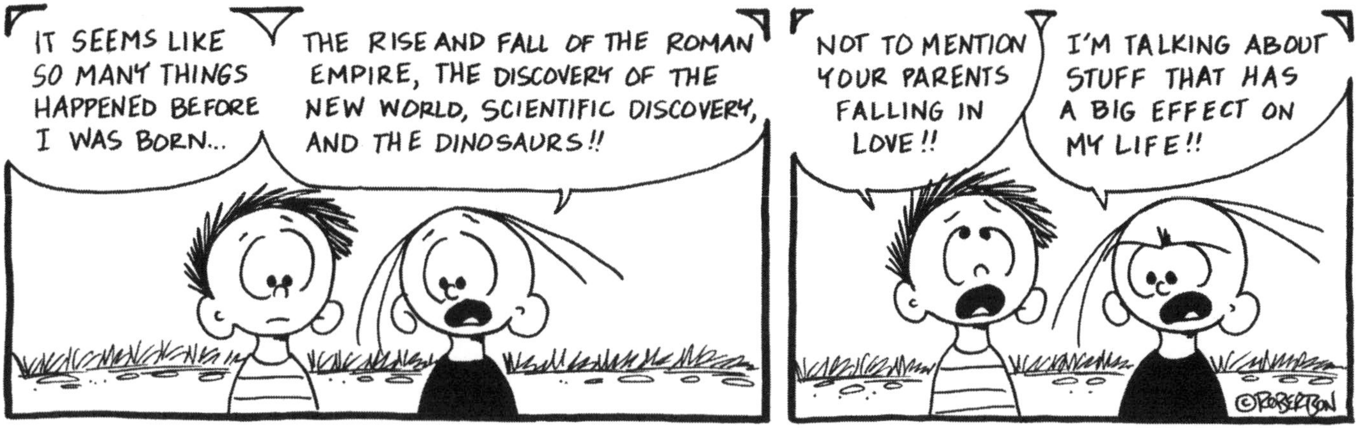
IT SEEMS LIKE SO MANY THINGS HAPPENED BEFORE I WAS BORN...
THE RISE AND FALL OF THE ROMAN EMPIRE, THE DISCOVERY OF THE NEW WORLD, SCIENTIFIC DISCOVERY, AND THE DINOSAURS!!
NOT TO MENTION YOUR PARENTS FALLING IN LOVE!!
I'M TALKING ABOUT STUFF THAT HAS A BIG EFFECT ON MY LIFE!!
©ROBERTSON

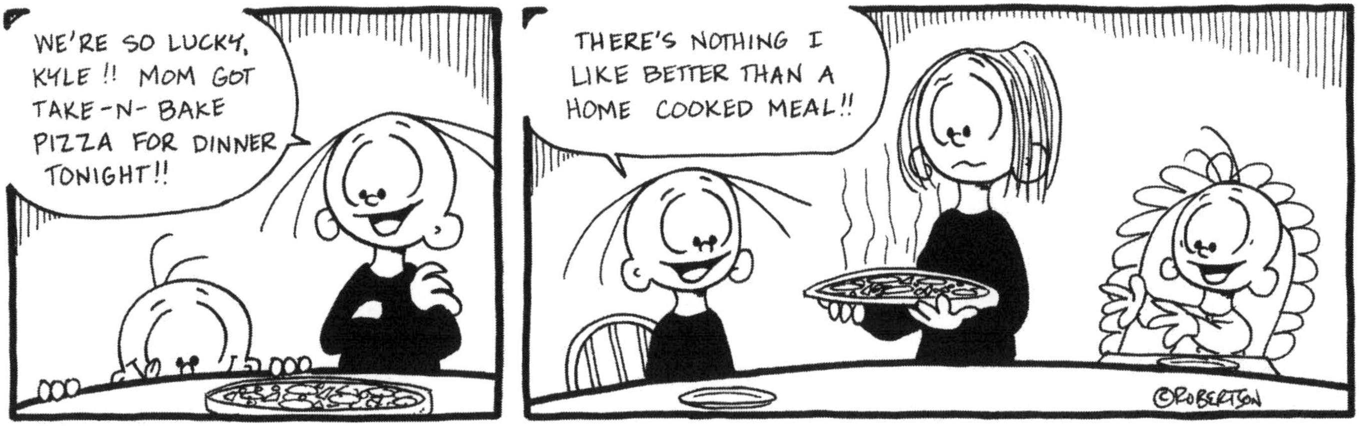
WE'RE SO LUCKY, KYLE !! MOM GOT TAKE-N-BAKE PIZZA FOR DINNER TONIGHT!!
THERE'S NOTHING I LIKE BETTER THAN A HOME COOKED MEAL!!
©ROBERTSON

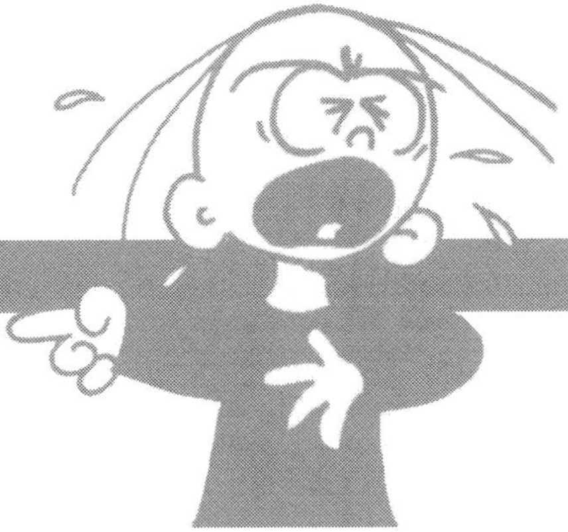

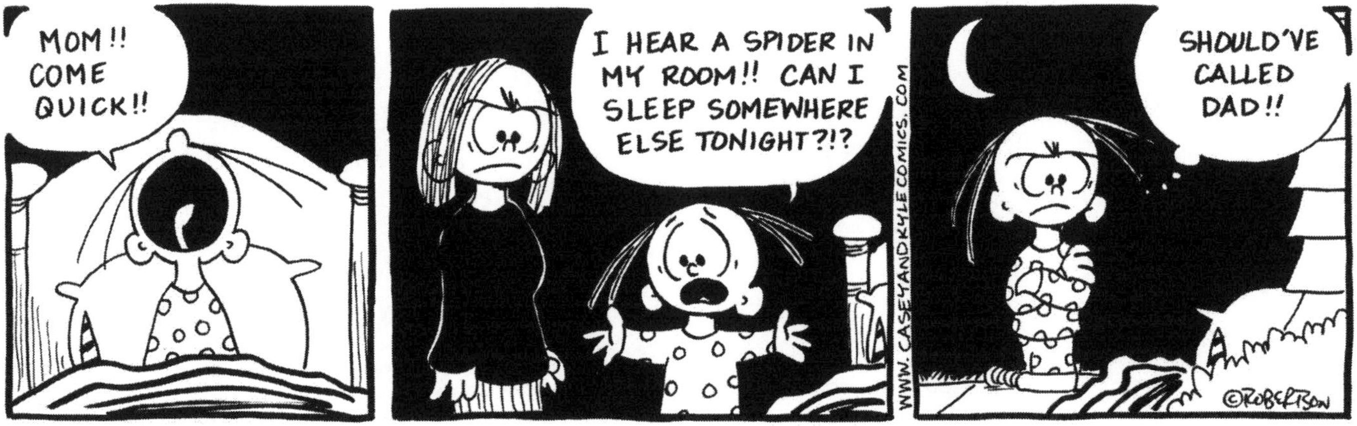
MOM!! COME QUICK!!
I HEAR A SPIDER IN MY ROOM!! CAN I SLEEP SOMEWHERE ELSE TONIGHT?!?
WWW.CASEYANDKYLECOMICS.COM
SHOULD'VE CALLED DAD!!
©ROBERTSON

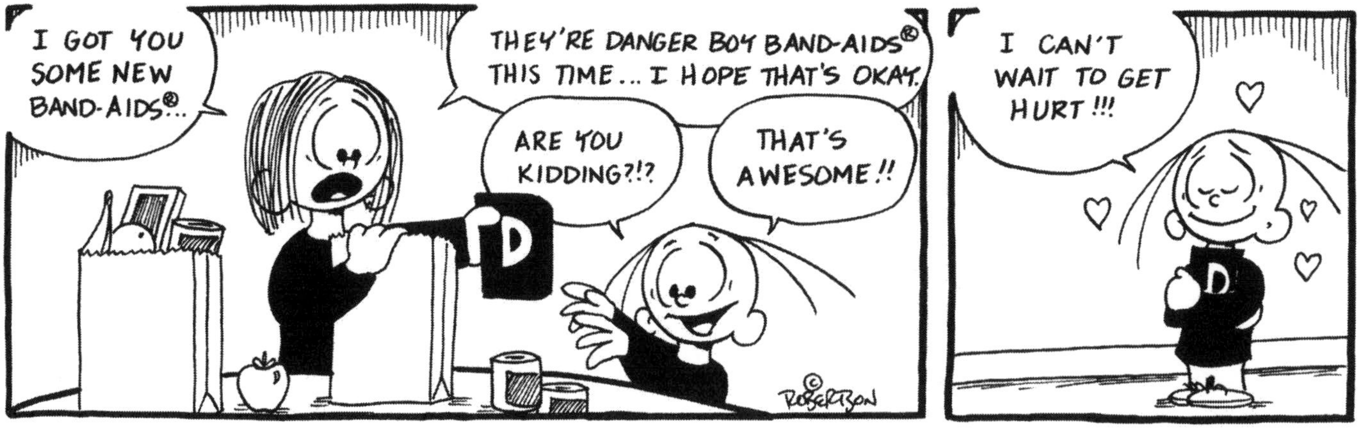
I GOT YOU SOME NEW BAND-AIDS®...
THEY'RE DANGER BOY BAND-AIDS® THIS TIME... I HOPE THAT'S OKAY.
ARE YOU KIDDING?!?
THAT'S AWESOME!!
I CAN'T WAIT TO GET HURT!!!

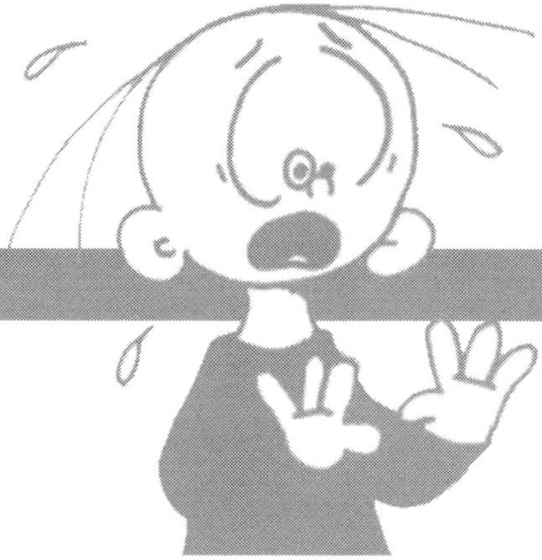

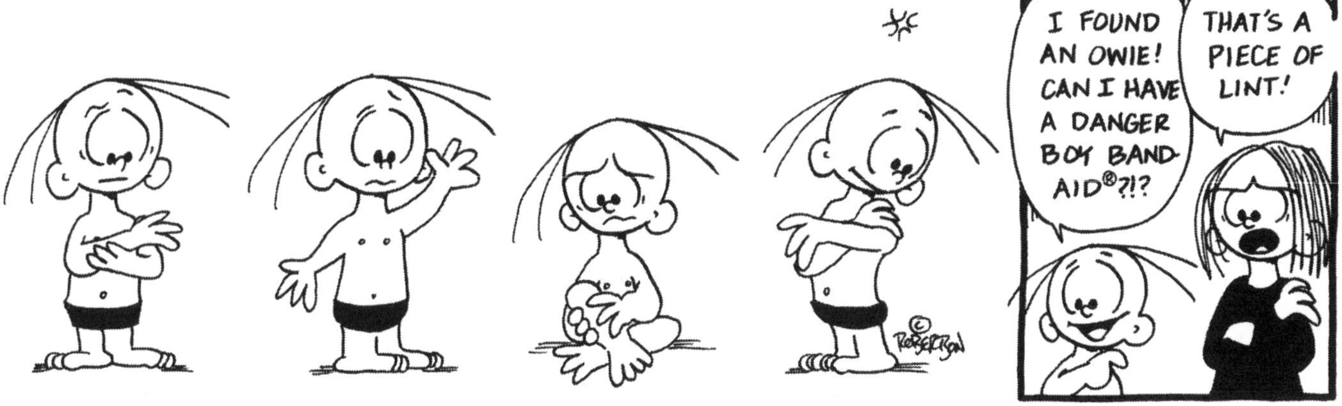
I FOUND AN OWIE! CAN I HAVE A DANGER BOY BAND-AID®?!?
THAT'S A PIECE OF LINT!

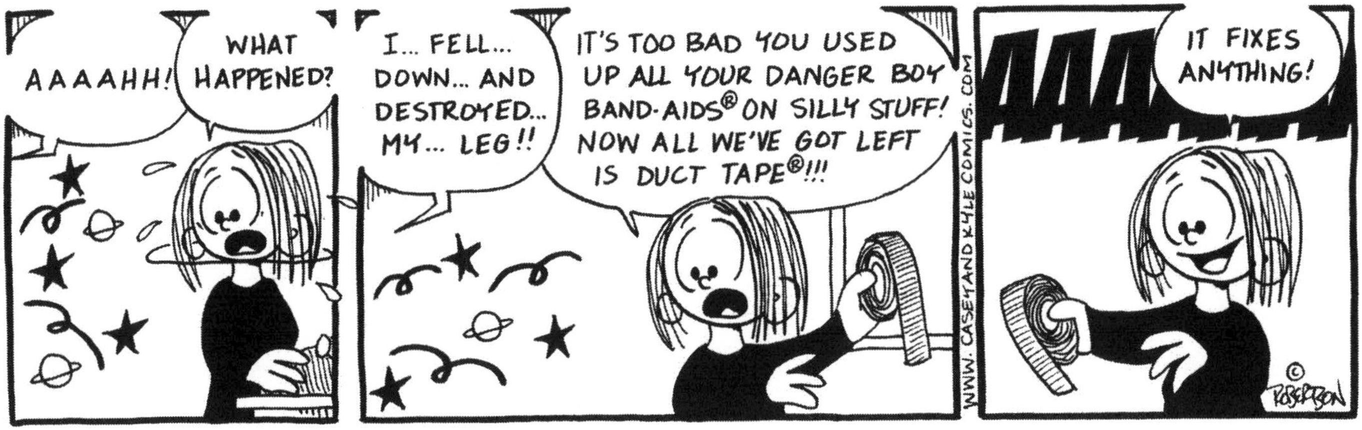
AAAAHH!
WHAT HAPPENED?
I... FELL... DOWN... AND DESTROYED... MY... LEG!!
IT'S TOO BAD YOU USED UP ALL YOUR DANGER BOY BAND-AIDS® ON SILLY STUFF! NOW ALL WE'VE GOT LEFT IS DUCT TAPE®!!!
WWW.CASEYANDKYLECOMICS.COM
AAAA
IT FIXES ANYTHING!
© ROBERTSON

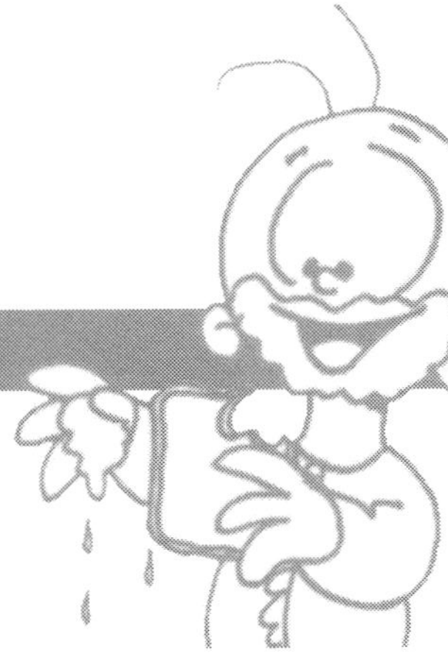

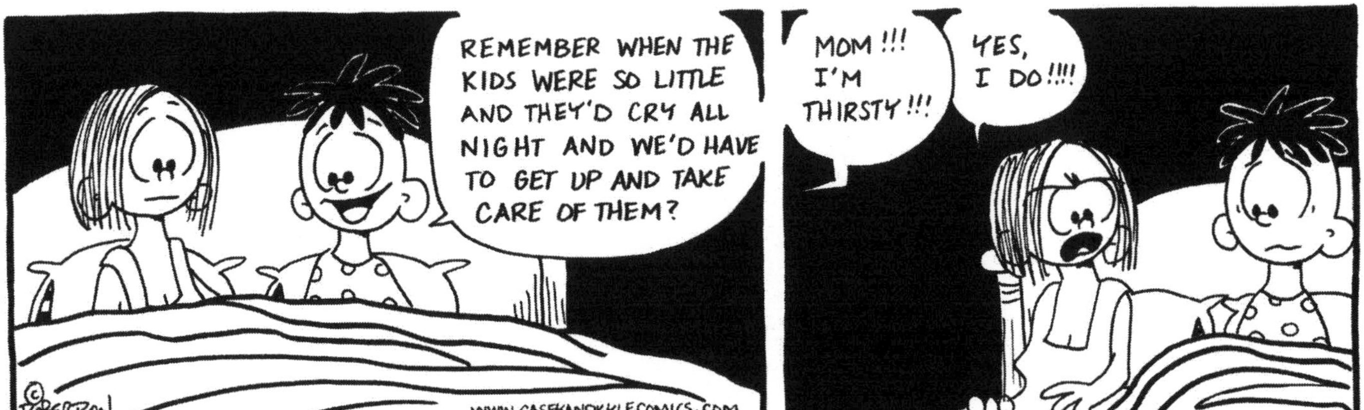
REMEMBER WHEN THE KIDS WERE SO LITTLE AND THEY'D CRY ALL NIGHT AND WE'D HAVE TO GET UP AND TAKE CARE OF THEM?
© ROBERTSON
WWW.CASEYANDKYLECOMICS.COM
MOM!!! I'M THIRSTY!!!
YES, I DO!!!!

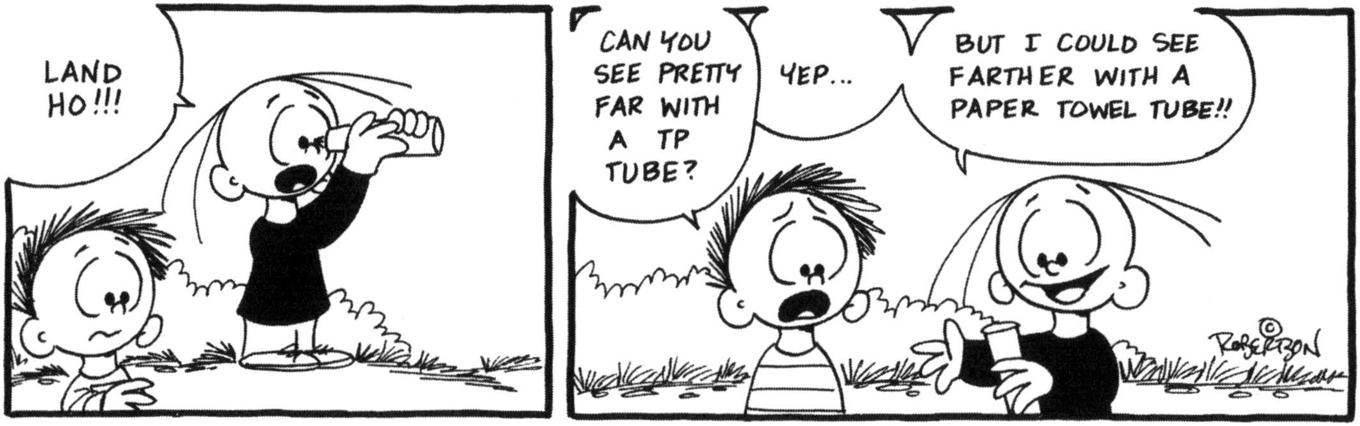
LAND HO!!!
CAN YOU SEE PRETTY FAR WITH A TP TUBE?
YEP...
BUT I COULD SEE FARTHER WITH A PAPER TOWEL TUBE!!
©ROBERTSON

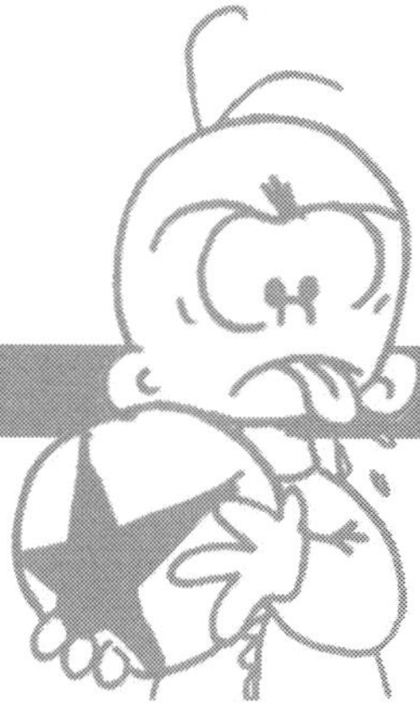

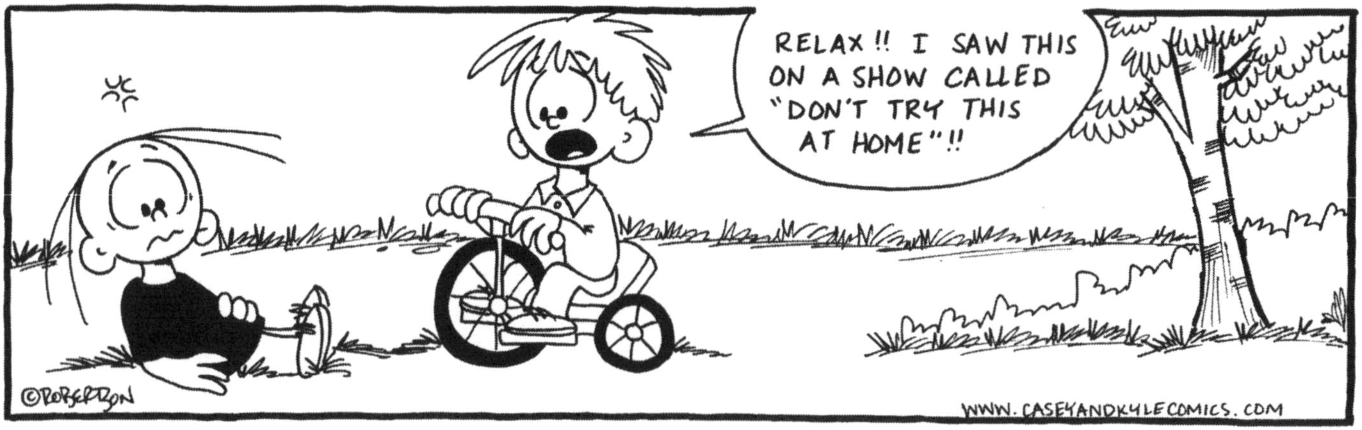
RELAX!! I SAW THIS ON A SHOW CALLED "DON'T TRY THIS AT HOME"!!
©ROBERTSON
WWW.CASEYANDKYLECOMICS.COM

I COULDN'T FIND A BOW AND ARROW, SO THIS WILL HAVE TO DO.
WWW.CASEYANDKYLECOMIKS.COM
NOW YOU RUN AROUND THE NEIGHBORHOOD AND SHOOT PRETTY GIRLS!!
THIS IS KIND OF A WEIRD HOLIDAY!!
CASEY JAMES!!
© ROBERTSON

CASEY, HAVE YOU SEEN YOUR BROTHER?
I FOUND HIS CLOTHES IN A PILE IN THE HALL.
WWW.CASEYANDKYLECOMICS.COM
THAT'S WEIRD! I TOLD HIM TO LEAVE THEM IN OUR ROOM.
YOU REALLY SHOULD TEACH HIM TO LISTEN BETTER!!
WHERE IS YOUR BROTHER!
©ROBERTSON

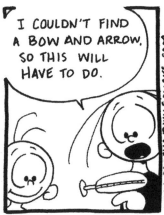

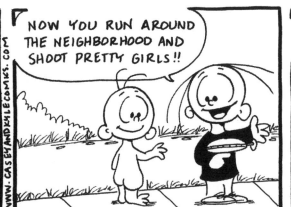

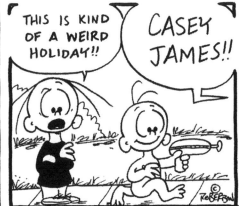

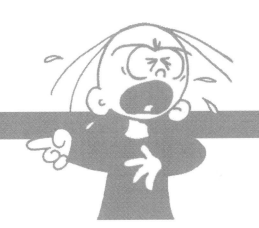

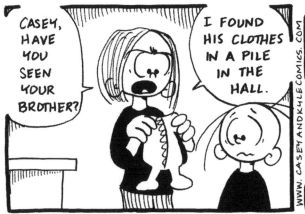

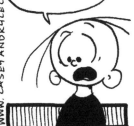

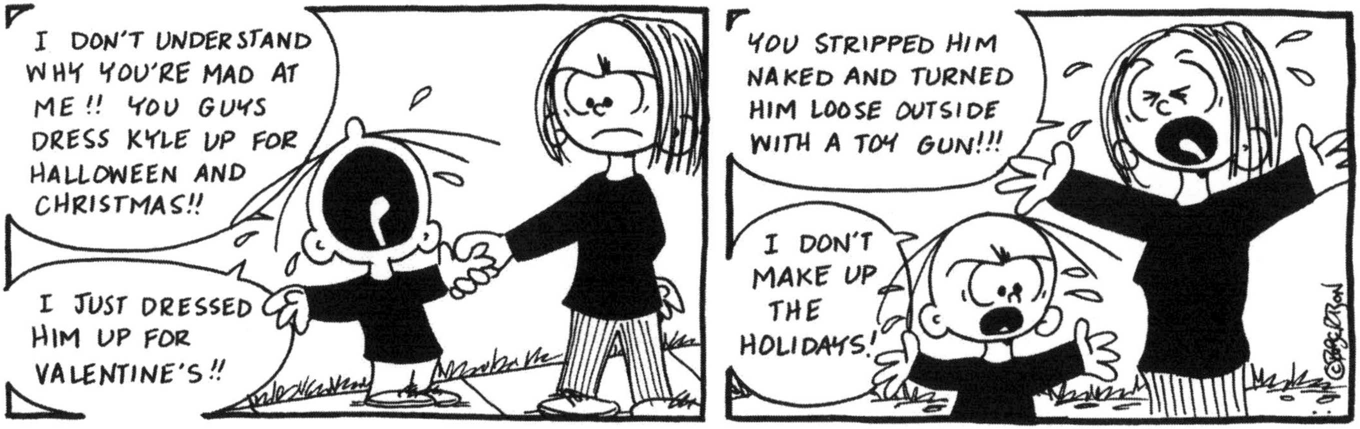
I DON'T UNDERSTAND WHY YOU'RE MAD AT ME!! YOU GUYS DRESS KYLE UP FOR HALLOWEEN AND CHRISTMAS!!
I JUST DRESSED HIM UP FOR VALENTINE'S!!
YOU STRIPPED HIM NAKED AND TURNED HIM LOOSE OUTSIDE WITH A TOY GUN!!!
I DON'T MAKE UP THE HOLIDAYS!

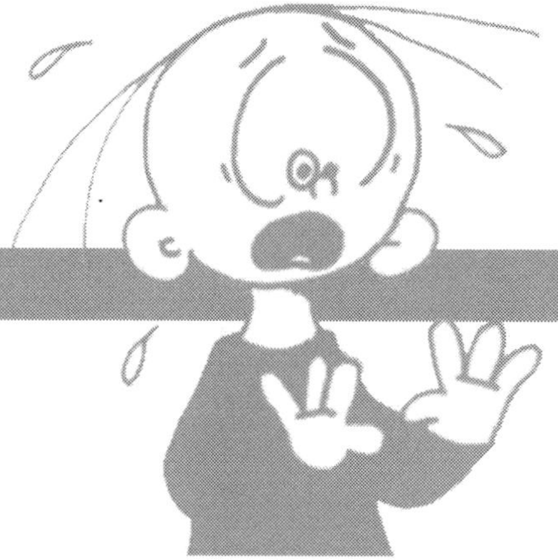

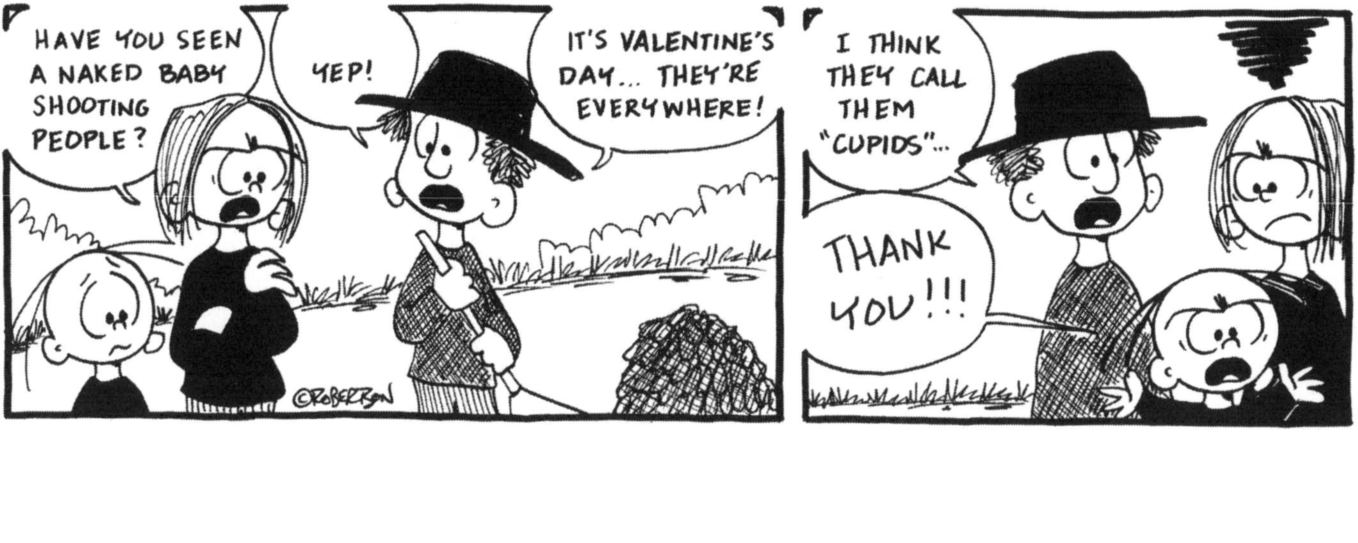
HAVE YOU SEEN A NAKED BABY SHOOTING PEOPLE?
YEP!
IT'S VALENTINE'S DAY... THEY'RE EVERYWHERE!
I THINK THEY CALL THEM "CUPIDS"...
THANK YOU!!!

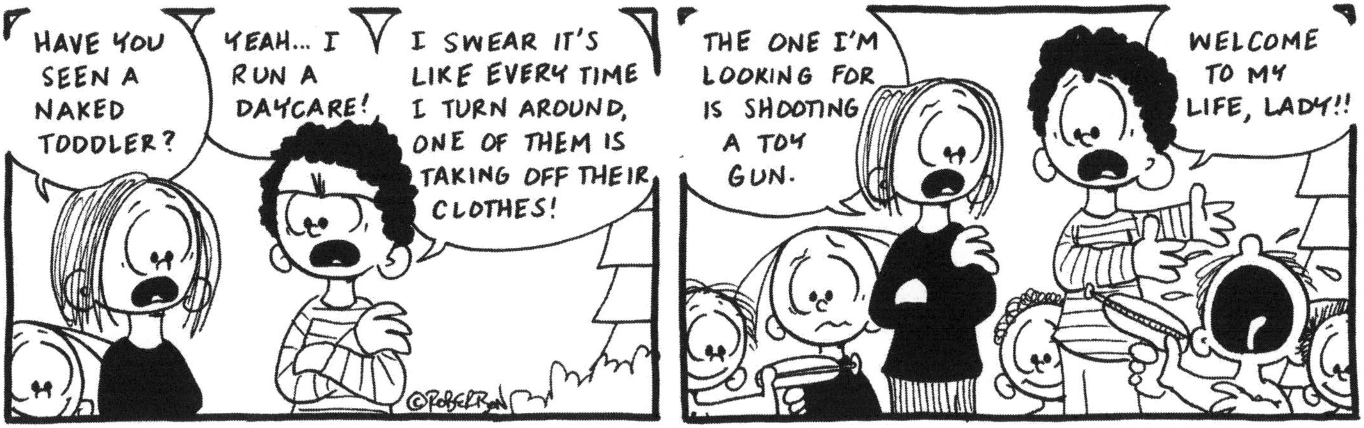
HAVE YOU SEEN A NAKED TODDLER?
YEAH... I RUN A DAYCARE!
I SWEAR IT'S LIKE EVERY TIME I TURN AROUND, ONE OF THEM IS TAKING OFF THEIR CLOTHES!
©ROBERTSON
THE ONE I'M LOOKING FOR IS SHOOTING A TOY GUN.
WELCOME TO MY LIFE, LADY!!

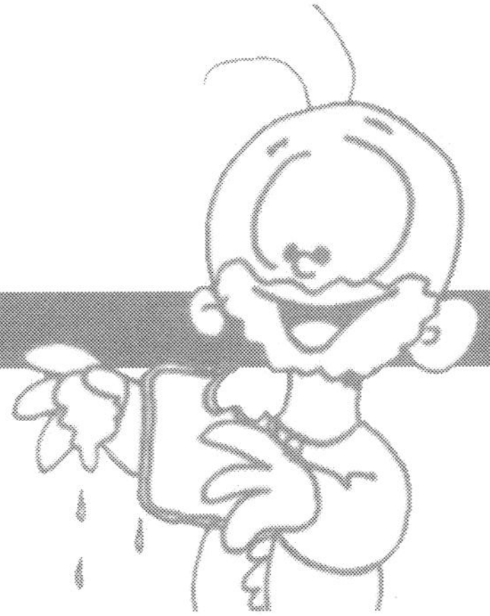

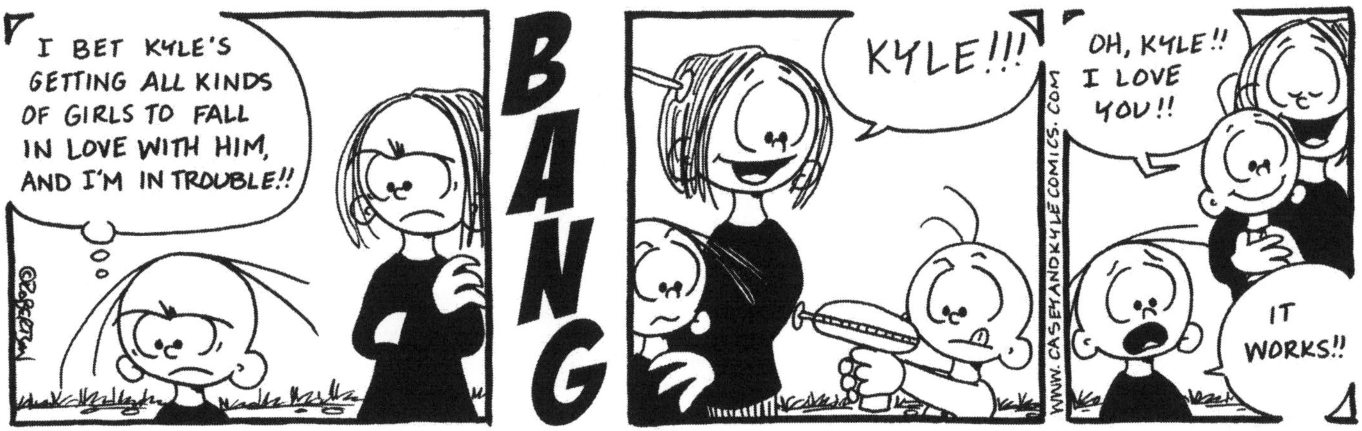
I BET KYLE'S GETTING ALL KINDS OF GIRLS TO FALL IN LOVE WITH HIM, AND I'M IN TROUBLE!!
©ROBERTSON
BANG
KYLE!!!
WWW.CASEYANDKYLECOMICS.COM
OH, KYLE!! I LOVE YOU!!
IT WORKS!!

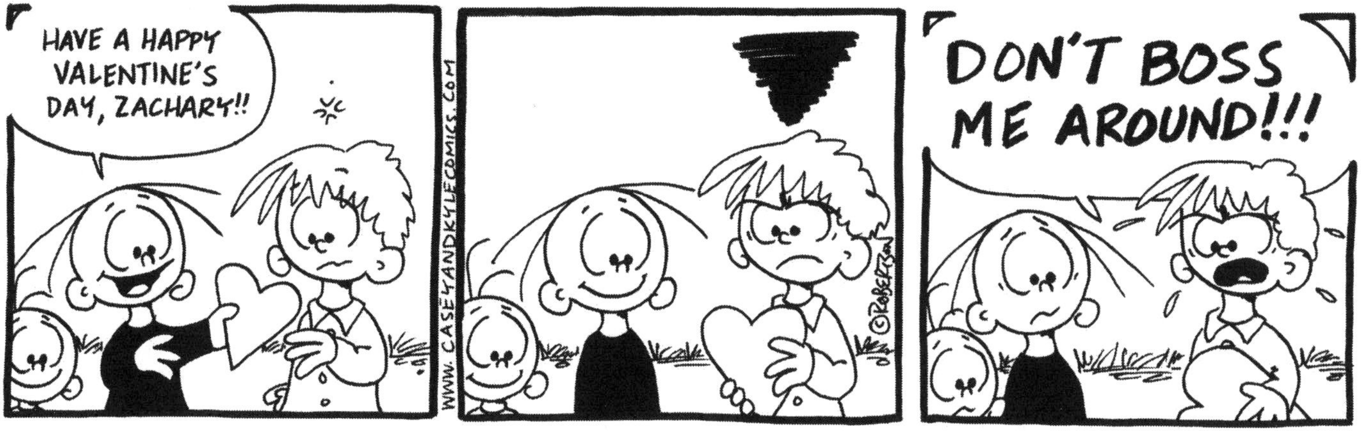
HAVE A HAPPY VALENTINE'S DAY, ZACHARY!!
WWW.CASEYANDKYLECOMICS.COM
©ROBERTSON
DON'T BOSS ME AROUND!!!

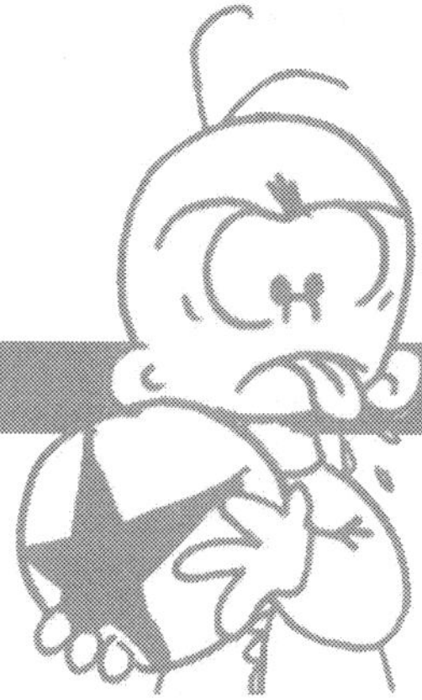

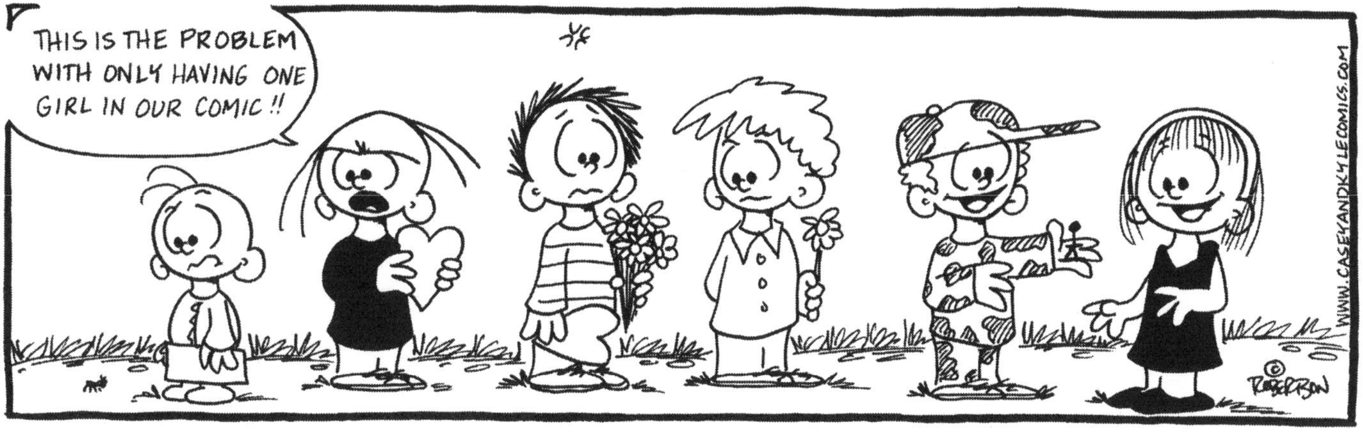
THIS IS THE PROBLEM WITH ONLY HAVING ONE GIRL IN OUR COMIC!!
WWW.CASEYANDKYLECOMICS.COM
© ROBERTSON

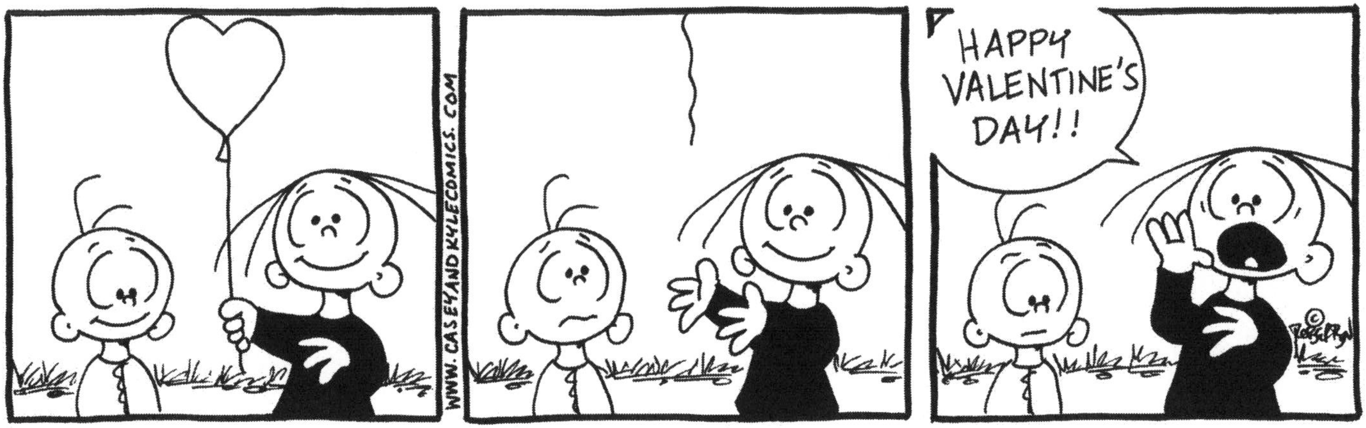
WWW.CASEYANDKYLECOMICS.COM
HAPPY VALENTINE'S DAY!!

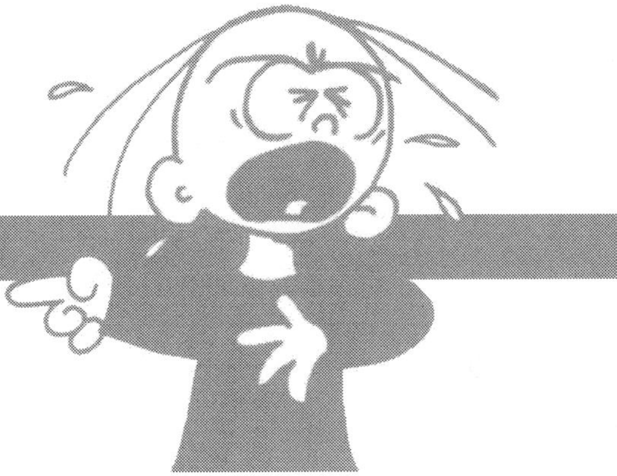

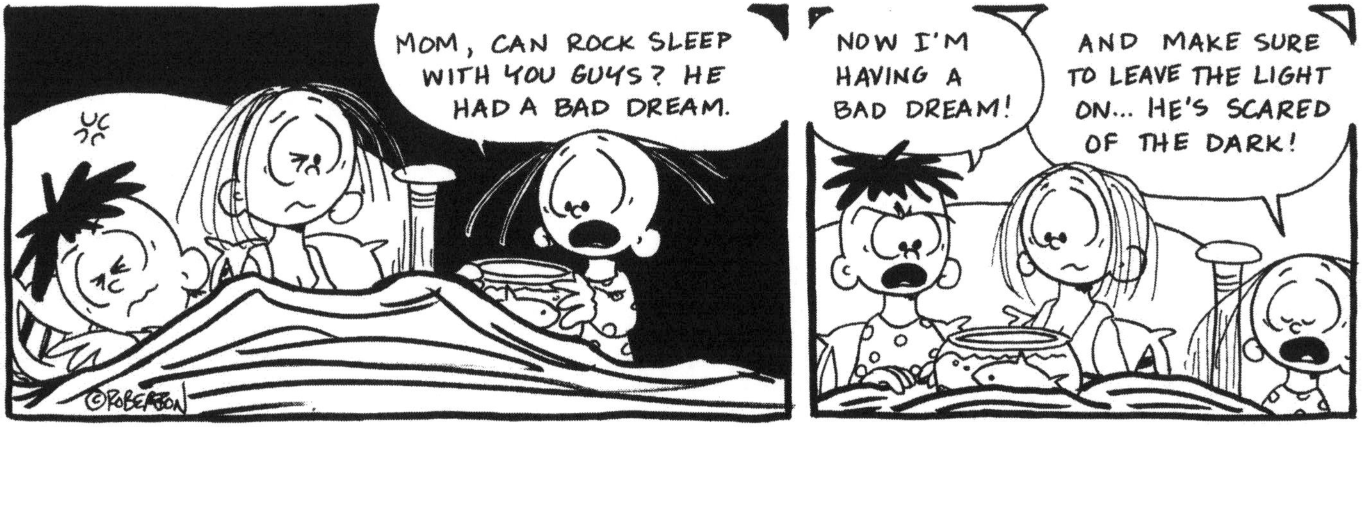
MOM, CAN ROCK SLEEP WITH YOU GUYS? HE HAD A BAD DREAM.
©ROBERTSON
NOW I'M HAVING A BAD DREAM!
AND MAKE SURE TO LEAVE THE LIGHT ON... HE'S SCARED OF THE DARK!

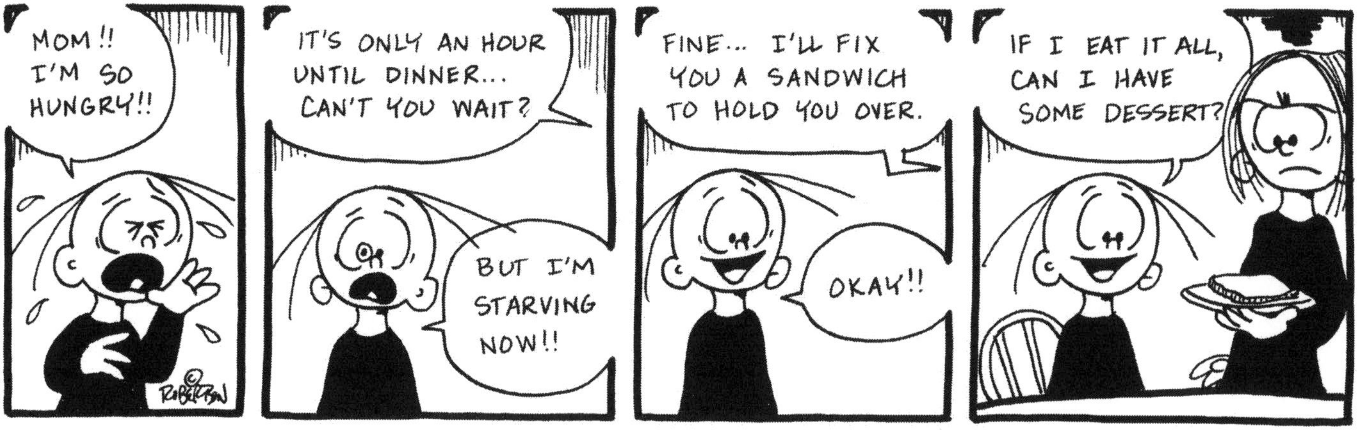
MOM!! I'M SO HUNGRY!!
IT'S ONLY AN HOUR UNTIL DINNER... CAN'T YOU WAIT?
BUT I'M STARVING NOW!!
FINE... I'LL FIX YOU A SANDWICH TO HOLD YOU OVER.
OKAY!!
IF I EAT IT ALL, CAN I HAVE SOME DESSERT?

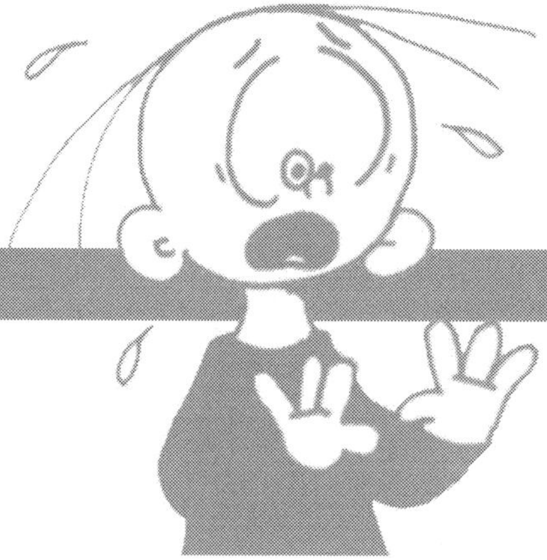

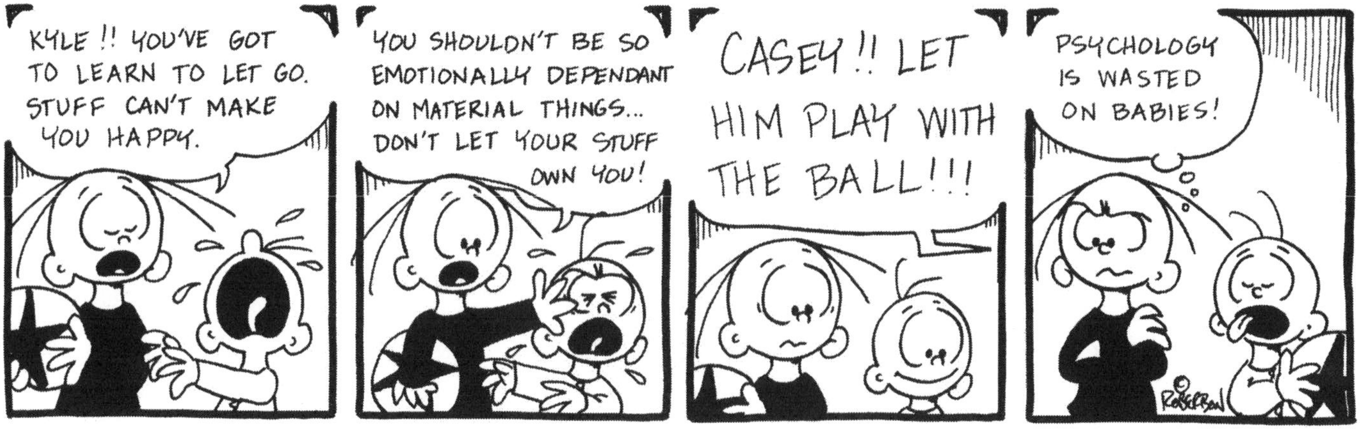
KYLE!! YOU'VE GOT TO LEARN TO LET GO. STUFF CAN'T MAKE YOU HAPPY.
YOU SHOULDN'T BE SO EMOTIONALLY DEPENDANT ON MATERIAL THINGS... DON'T LET YOUR STUFF OWN YOU!
CASEY!! LET HIM PLAY WITH THE BALL!!!
PSYCHOLOGY IS WASTED ON BABIES!

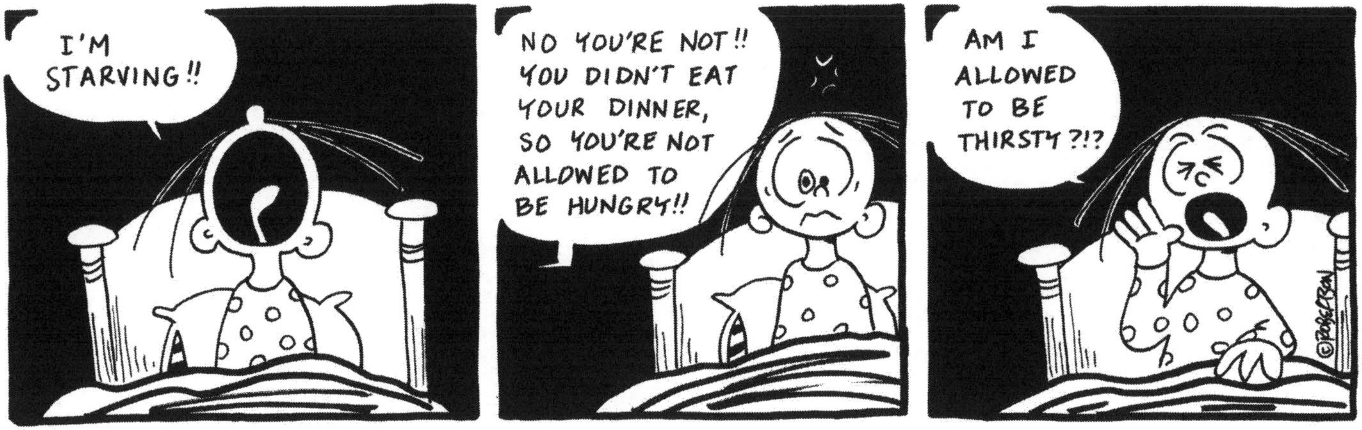
I'M STARVING!!
NO YOU'RE NOT!! YOU DIDN'T EAT YOUR DINNER, SO YOU'RE NOT ALLOWED TO BE HUNGRY!!
AM I ALLOWED TO BE THIRSTY?!?
©ROBERTSON

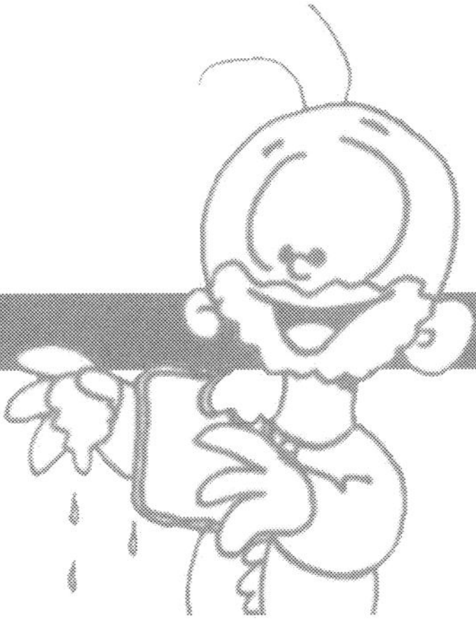

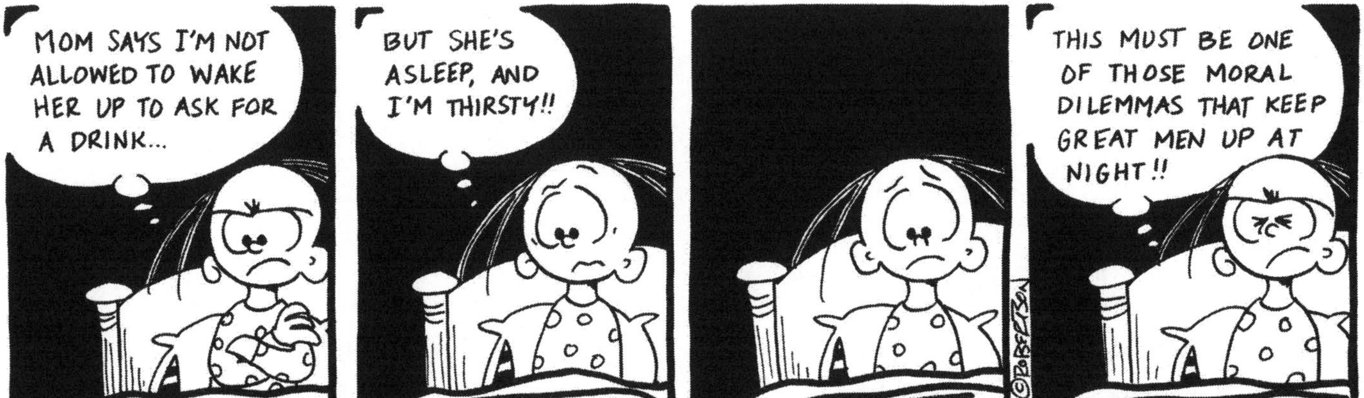
MOM SAYS I'M NOT ALLOWED TO WAKE HER UP TO ASK FOR A DRINK...
BUT SHE'S ASLEEP, AND I'M THIRSTY!!
THIS MUST BE ONE OF THOSE MORAL DILEMMAS THAT KEEP GREAT MEN UP AT NIGHT!!
©ROBERTSON

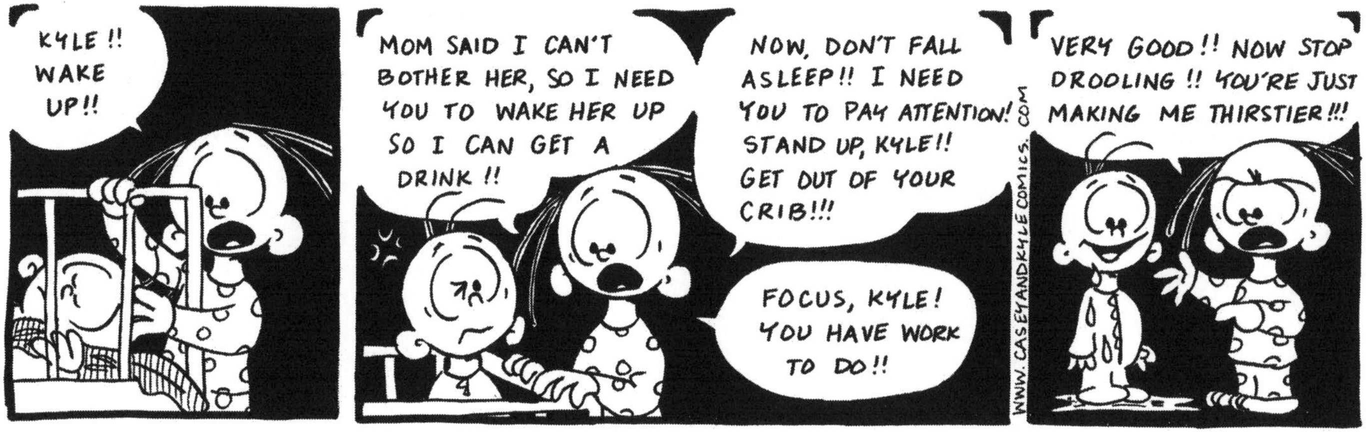
KYLE !! WAKE UP!!
MOM SAID I CAN'T BOTHER HER, SO I NEED YOU TO WAKE HER UP SO I CAN GET A DRINK !!
NOW, DON'T FALL ASLEEP!! I NEED YOU TO PAY ATTENTION! STAND UP, KYLE!! GET OUT OF YOUR CRIB!!!
FOCUS, KYLE! YOU HAVE WORK TO DO!!
WWW.CASEYANDKYLECOMICS.COM
VERY GOOD!! NOW STOP DROOLING !! YOU'RE JUST MAKING ME THIRSTIER!!!

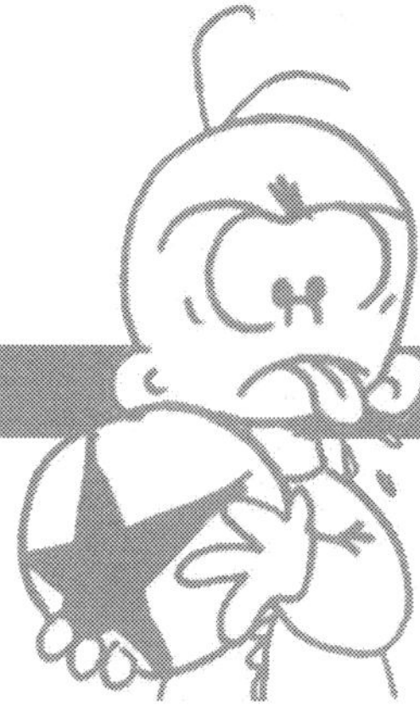

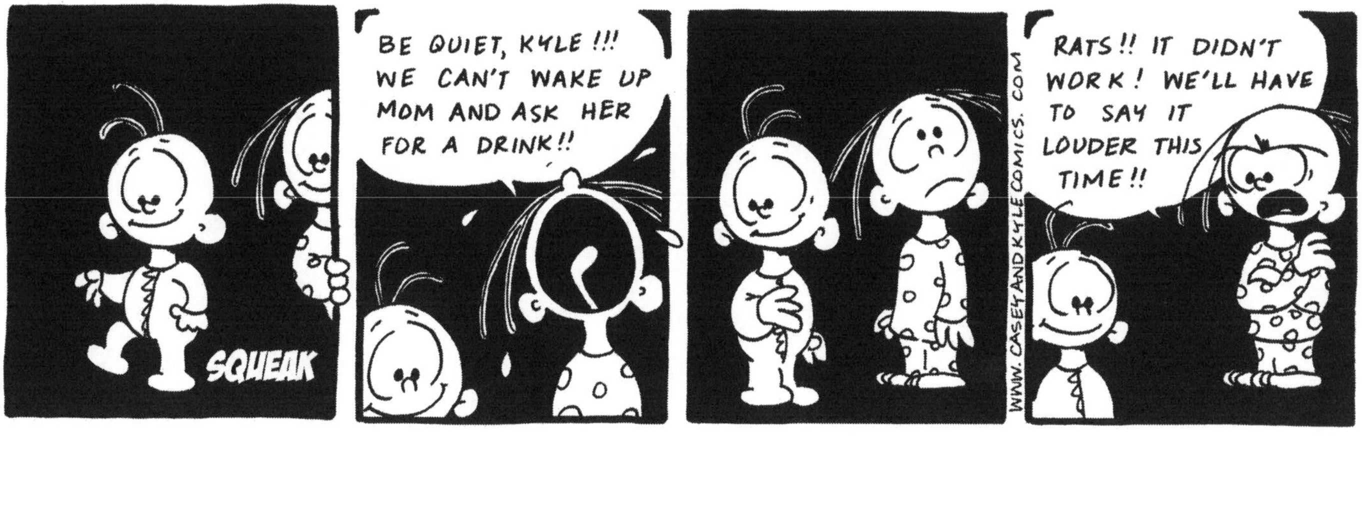
SQUEAK
BE QUIET, KYLE !!! WE CAN'T WAKE UP MOM AND ASK HER FOR A DRINK!!
WWW.CASEYANDKYLECOMICS.COM
RATS!! IT DIDN'T WORK! WE'LL HAVE TO SAY IT LOUDER THIS TIME!!

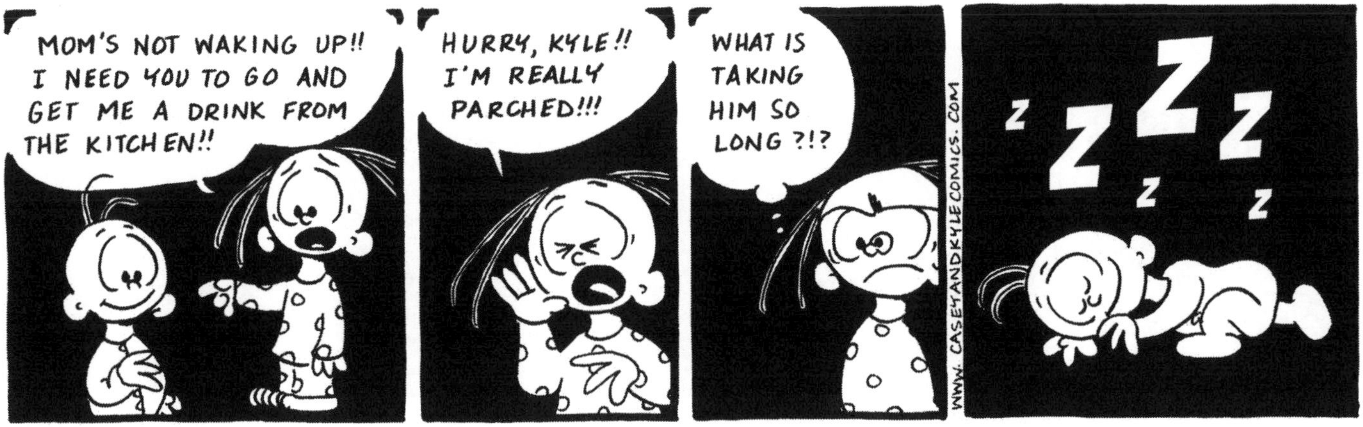
MOM'S NOT WAKING UP!! I NEED YOU TO GO AND GET ME A DRINK FROM THE KITCHEN!!
HURRY, KYLE!! I'M REALLY PARCHED!!!
WHAT IS TAKING HIM SO LONG ?!?
WWW.CASEYANDKYLECOMICS.COM
Z Z Z Z Z Z

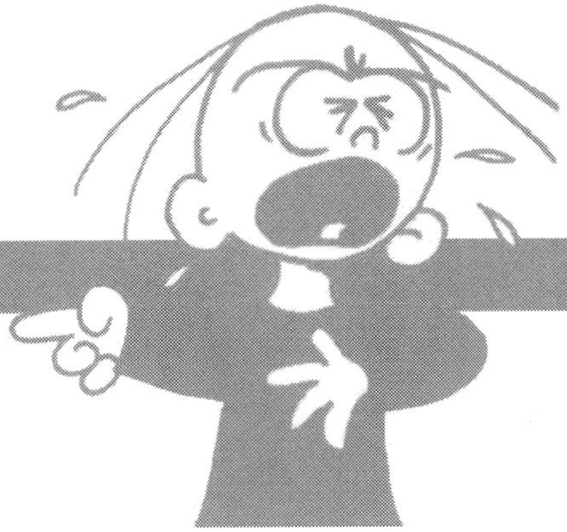

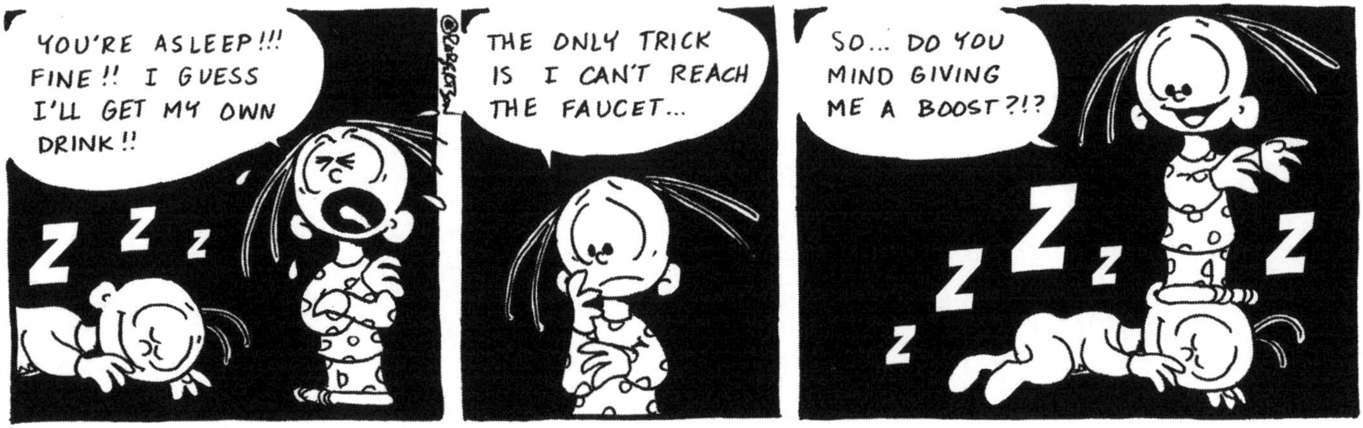
YOU'RE ASLEEP!!! FINE!! I GUESS I'LL GET MY OWN DRINK!!
Z Z Z
THE ONLY TRICK IS I CAN'T REACH THE FAUCET...
SO... DO YOU MIND GIVING ME A BOOST?!?
Z Z Z Z Z Z

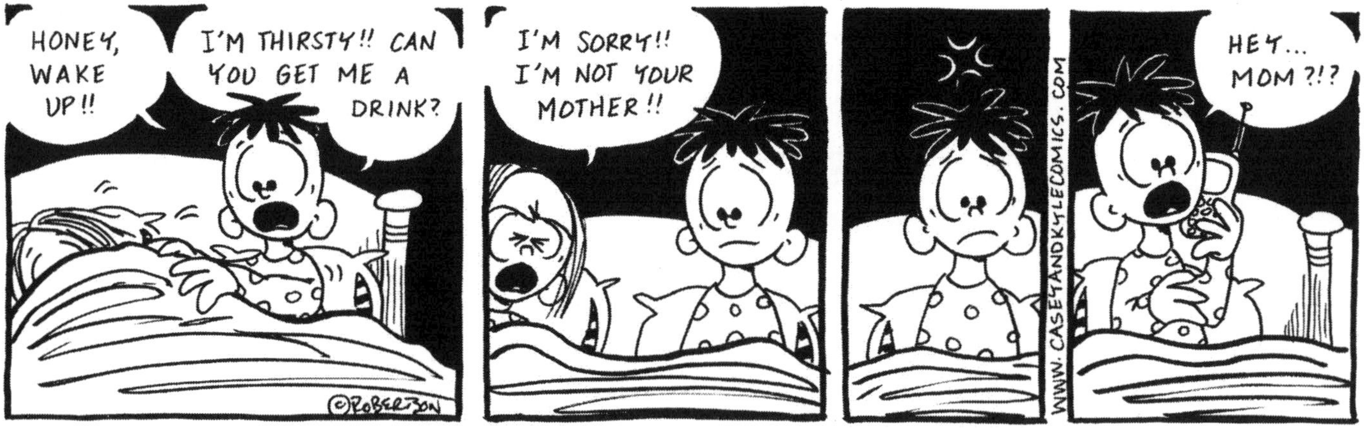
HONEY, WAKE UP!!
I'M THIRSTY!! CAN YOU GET ME A DRINK?
©ROBERTSON
I'M SORRY!! I'M NOT YOUR MOTHER!!
WWW.CASEYANDKYLECOMICS.COM
HEY... MOM?!?

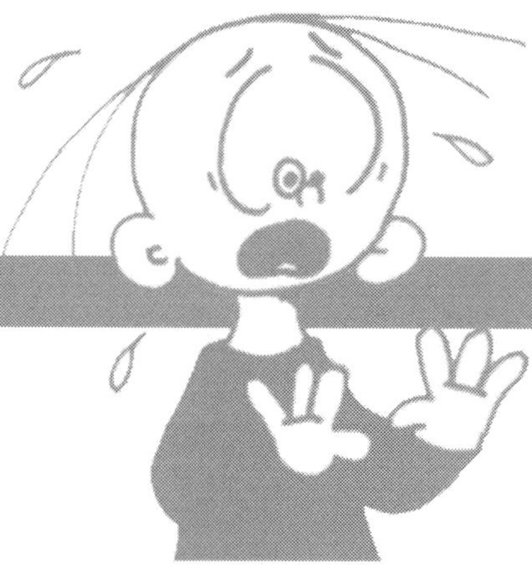

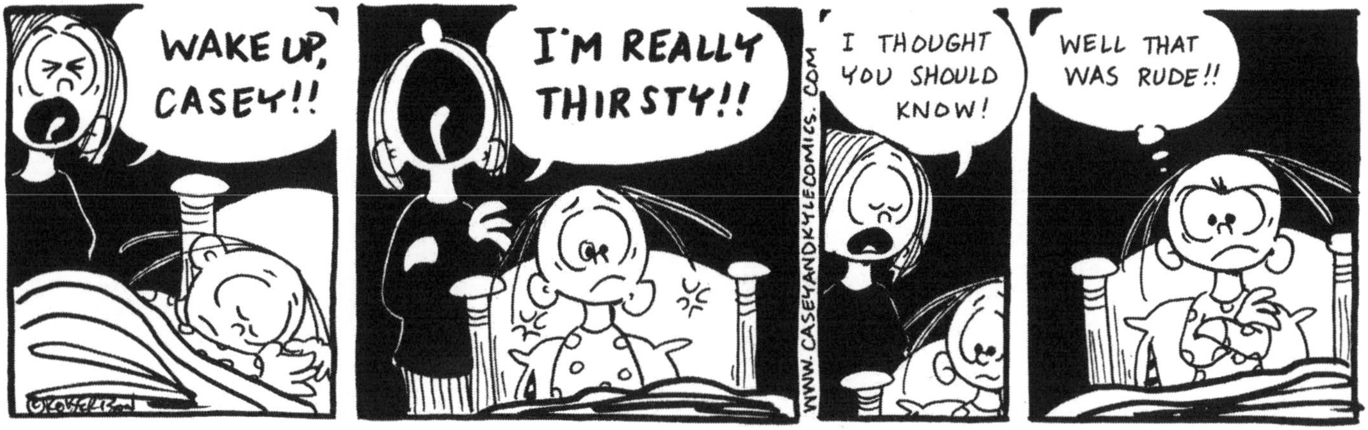
WAKE UP, CASEY!!
©ROBERTSON
I'M REALLY THIRSTY!!
WWW.CASEYANDKYLECOMICS.COM
I THOUGHT YOU SHOULD KNOW!
WELL THAT WAS RUDE!!

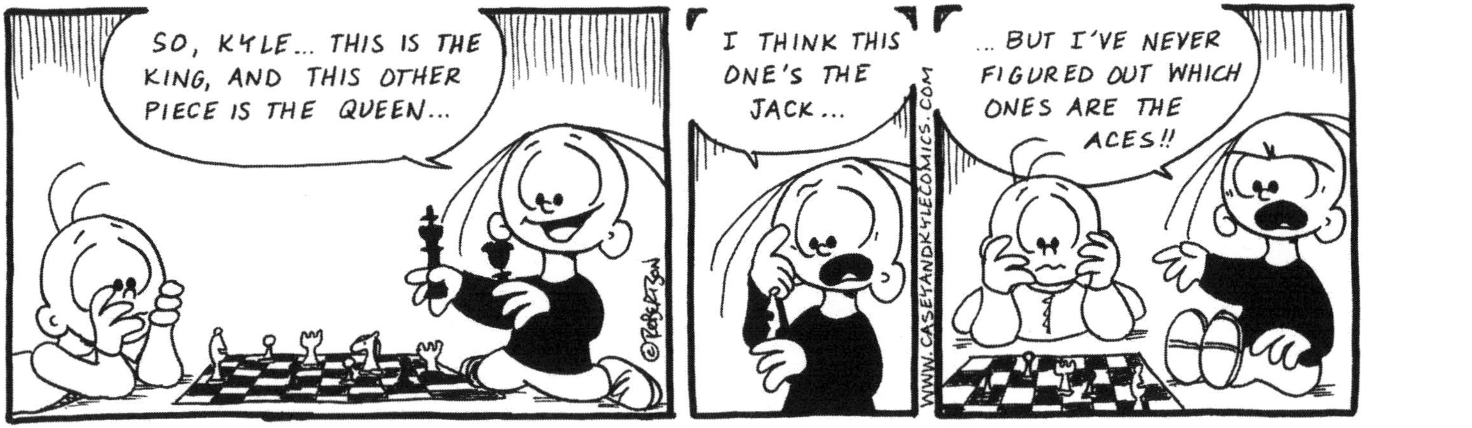
SO, KYLE... THIS IS THE KING, AND THIS OTHER PIECE IS THE QUEEN...
©ROBERTSON
I THINK THIS ONE'S THE JACK...
WWW.CASEYANDKYLECOMICS.COM
... BUT I'VE NEVER FIGURED OUT WHICH ONES ARE THE ACES!!

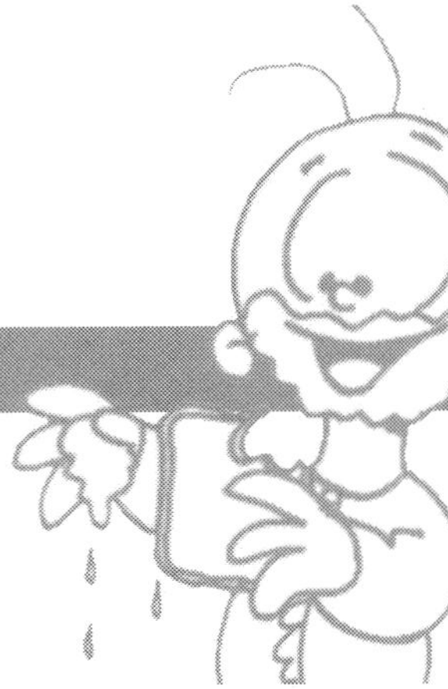

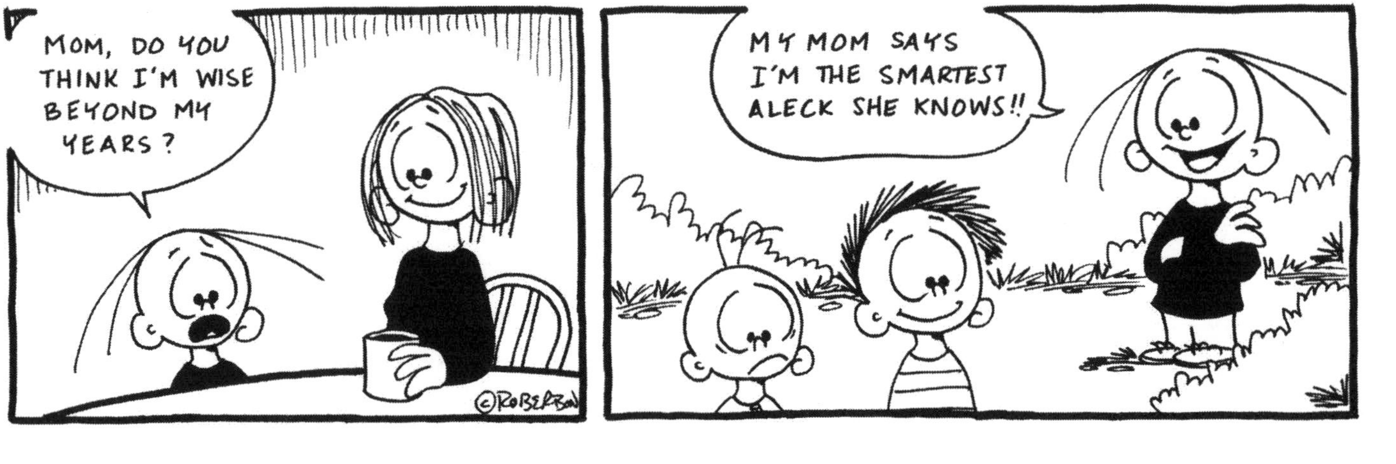
MOM, DO YOU THINK I'M WISE BEYOND MY YEARS?
©ROBERTSON
MY MOM SAYS I'M THE SMARTEST ALECK SHE KNOWS!!

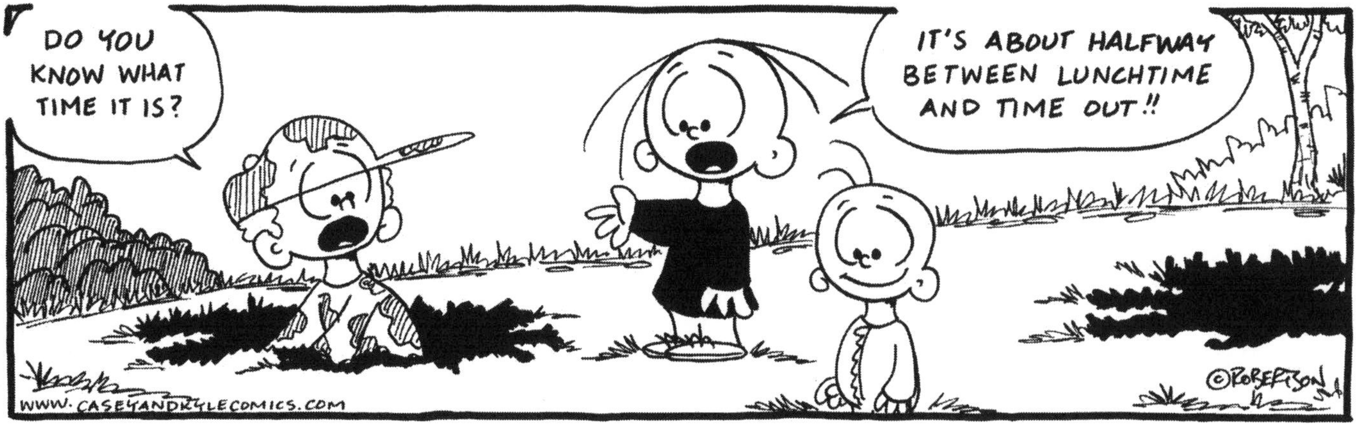
DO YOU KNOW WHAT TIME IT IS?
IT'S ABOUT HALFWAY BETWEEN LUNCHTIME AND TIME OUT!!
©ROBERTSON
WWW.CASEYANDKYLECOMICS.COM

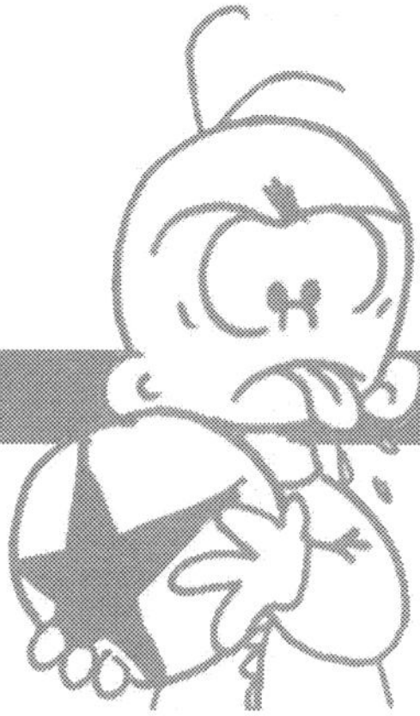

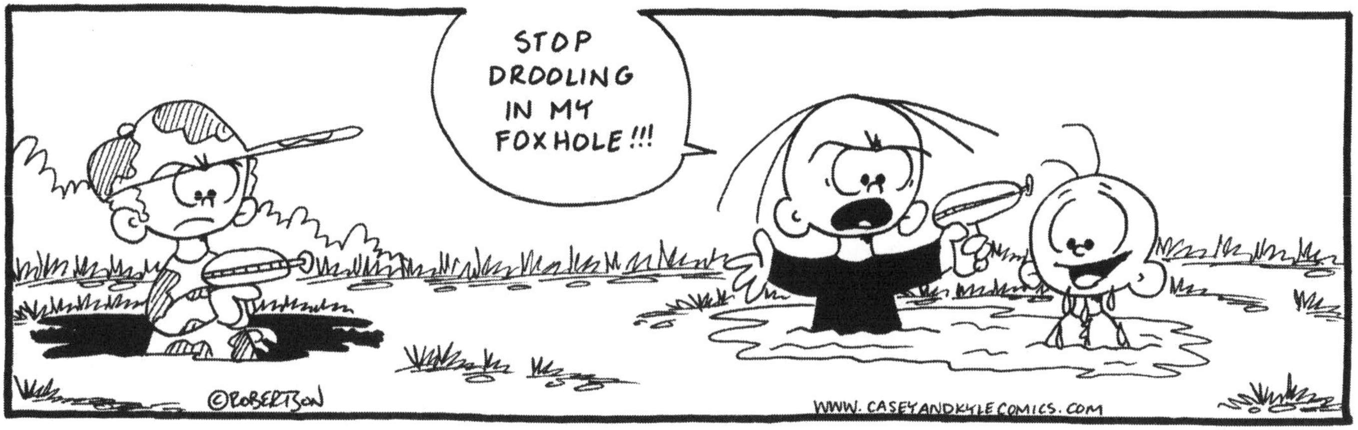
STOP DROOLING IN MY FOXHOLE!!!
©ROBERTSON
WWW.CASEYANDKYLECOMICS.COM

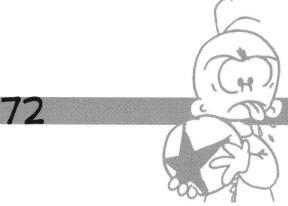

CAN I TAKE YOUR ORDER?
YEP!!
WWW.CASEYANDKYLECOMICS.COM
DROP AND GIVE ME TWENTY!!!
©ROBERTSON

IN THE SECOND WORLD WAR, THE MEN WOULD SOMETIMES RUN LOW ON COFFEE, AND THEY'D GRIND UP ACORNS TO MAKE A SUBSTITUTE.
WWW.CASEYANDKYLECOMICS.COM
CAN YOU DO SOMETHING LIKE THAT?!?
I CAN DO "WHIP" OR "NO WHIP"!!
©ROBERTSON

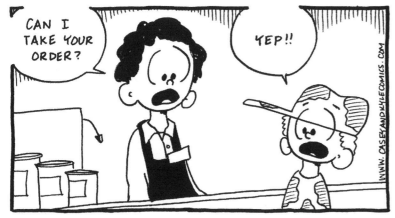

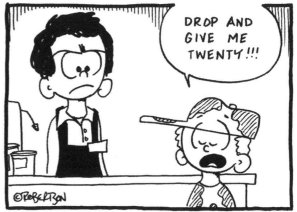

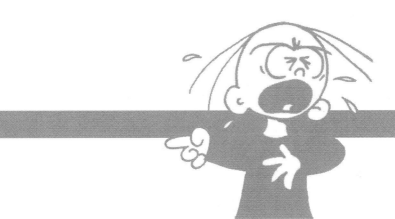

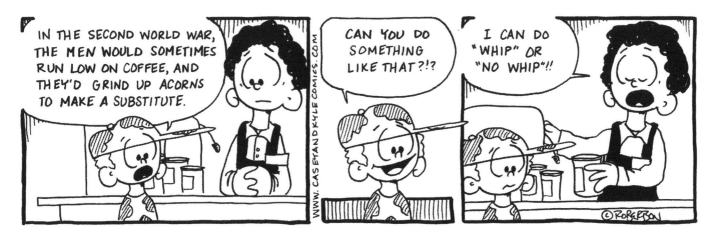

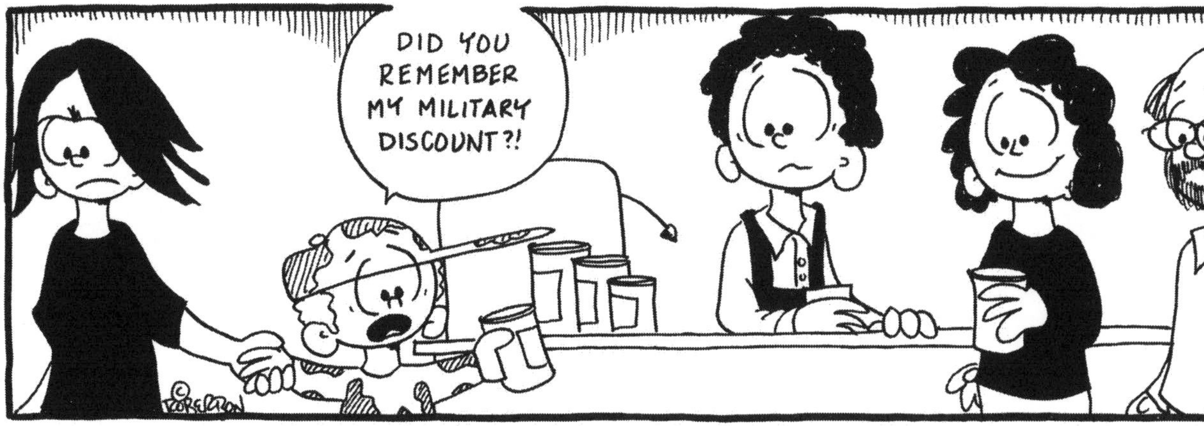
DID YOU REMEMBER MY MILITARY DISCOUNT?!
©ROBERTSON

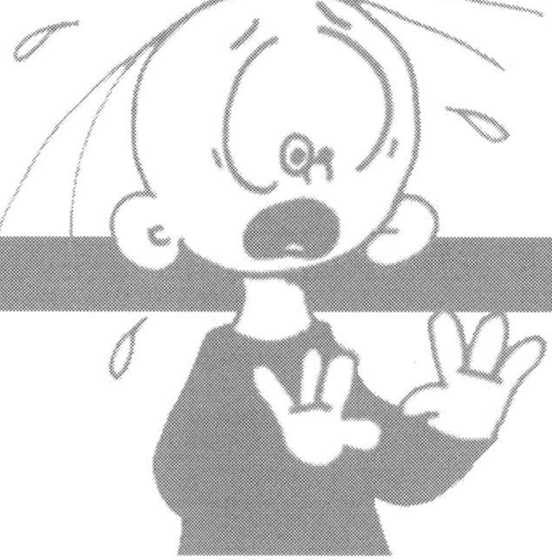

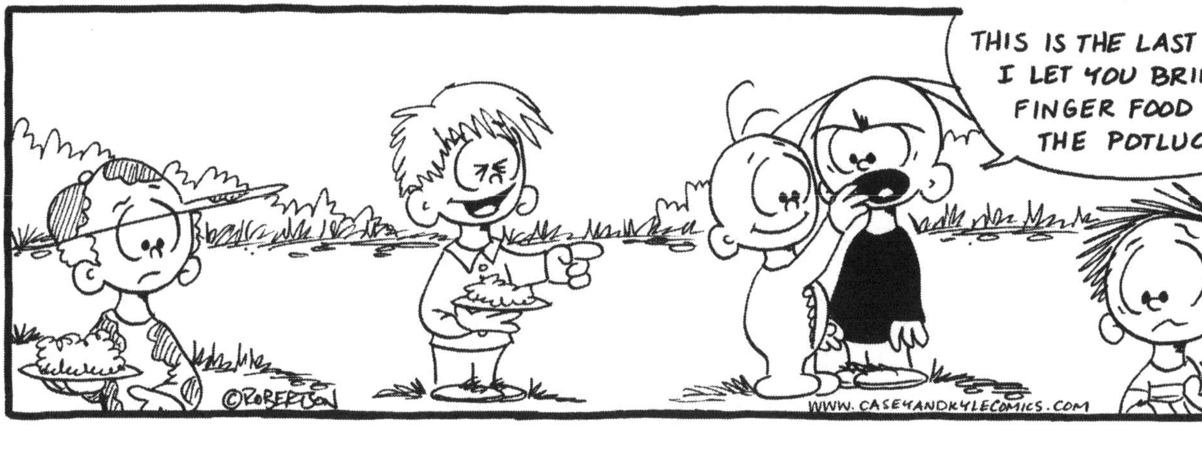
THIS IS THE LAST TIME I LET YOU BRING THE FINGER FOOD FOR THE POTLUCK!!
©ROBERTSON
WWW.CASEYANDKYLECOMICS.COM

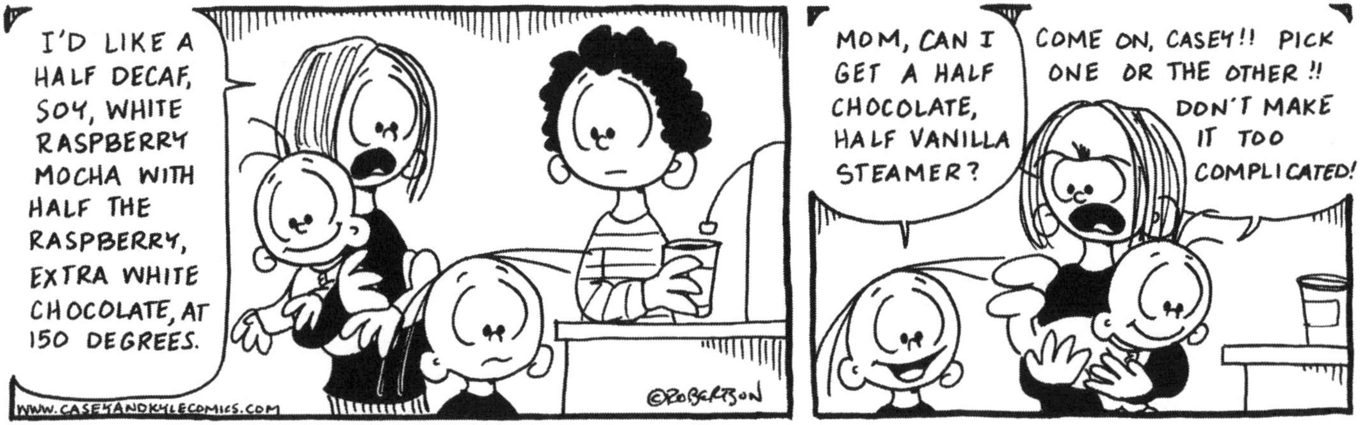
I'D LIKE A HALF DECAF, SOY, WHITE RASPBERRY MOCHA WITH HALF THE RASPBERRY, EXTRA WHITE CHOCOLATE, AT 150 DEGREES.
WWW.CASEYANDKYLECOMICS.COM
©ROBERTSON
MOM, CAN I GET A HALF CHOCOLATE, HALF VANILLA STEAMER?
COME ON, CASEY!! PICK ONE OR THE OTHER!!
DON'T MAKE IT TOO COMPLICATED!

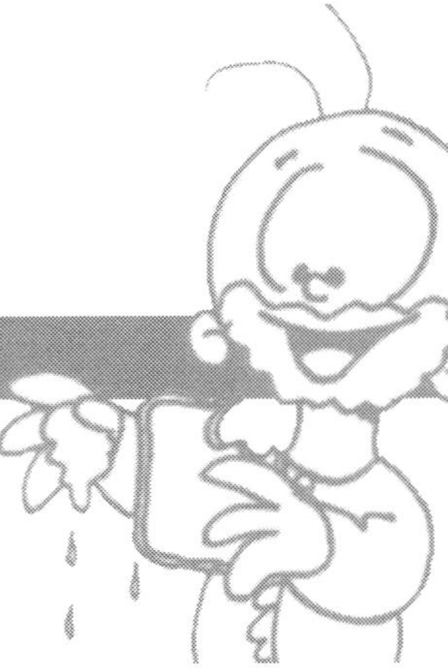

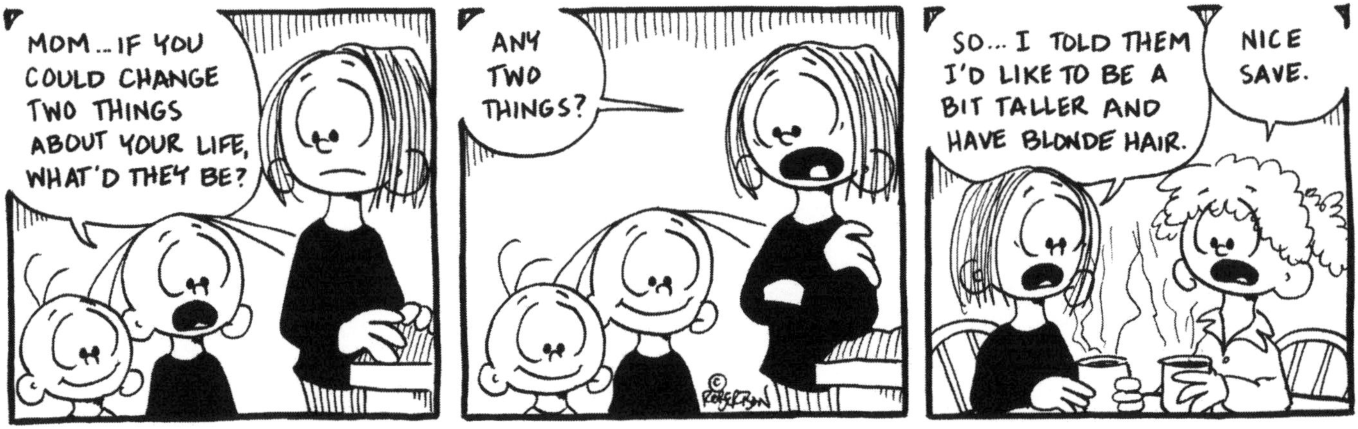
MOM... IF YOU COULD CHANGE TWO THINGS ABOUT YOUR LIFE, WHAT'D THEY BE?
ANY TWO THINGS?
© ROBERTSON
SO... I TOLD THEM I'D LIKE TO BE A BIT TALLER AND HAVE BLONDE HAIR.
NICE SAVE.

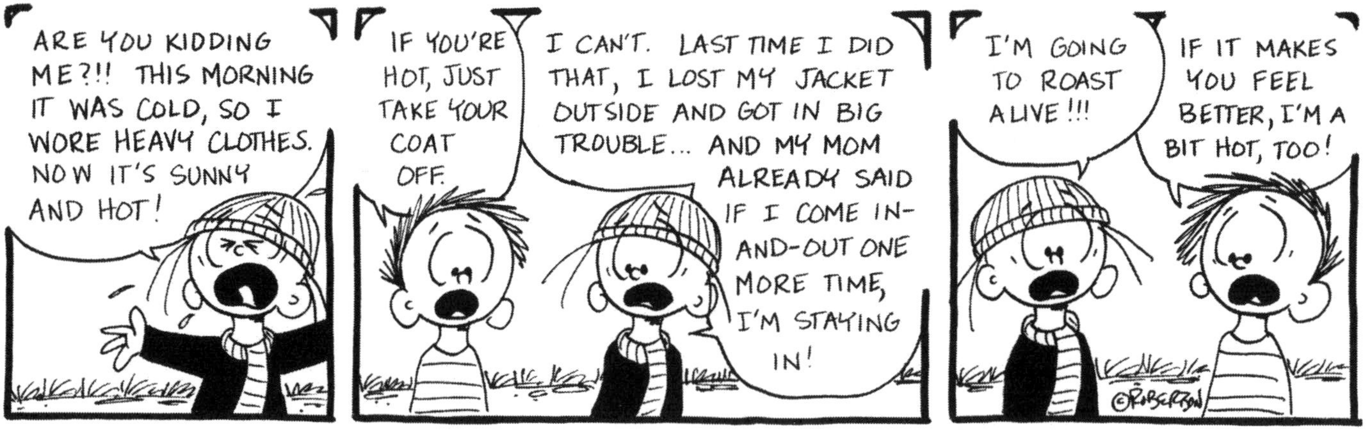
ARE YOU KIDDING ME?!! THIS MORNING IT WAS COLD, SO I WORE HEAVY CLOTHES. NOW IT'S SUNNY AND HOT!
IF YOU'RE HOT, JUST TAKE YOUR COAT OFF.
I CAN'T. LAST TIME I DID THAT, I LOST MY JACKET OUTSIDE AND GOT IN BIG TROUBLE... AND MY MOM ALREADY SAID IF I COME IN-AND-OUT ONE MORE TIME, I'M STAYING IN!
I'M GOING TO ROAST ALIVE!!!
IF IT MAKES YOU FEEL BETTER, I'M A BIT HOT, TOO!
©ROBERTSON

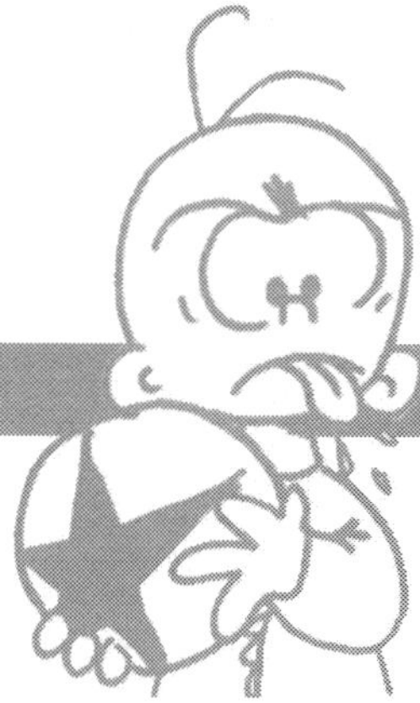

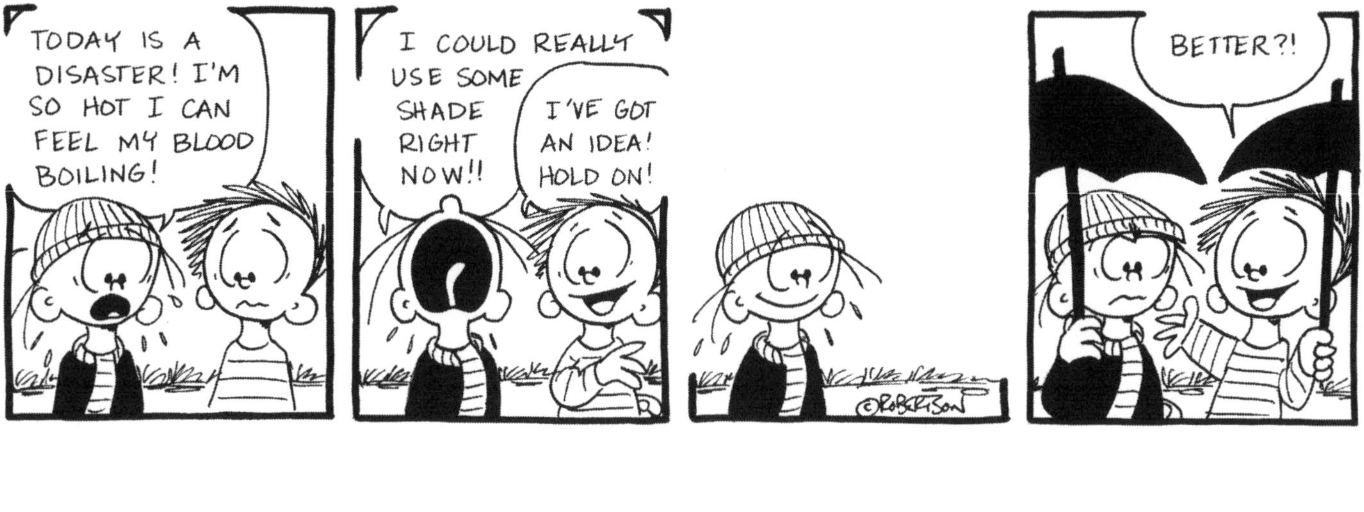
TODAY IS A DISASTER! I'M SO HOT I CAN FEEL MY BLOOD BOILING!
I COULD REALLY USE SOME SHADE RIGHT NOW!!
I'VE GOT AN IDEA! HOLD ON!
©ROBERTSON
BETTER?!

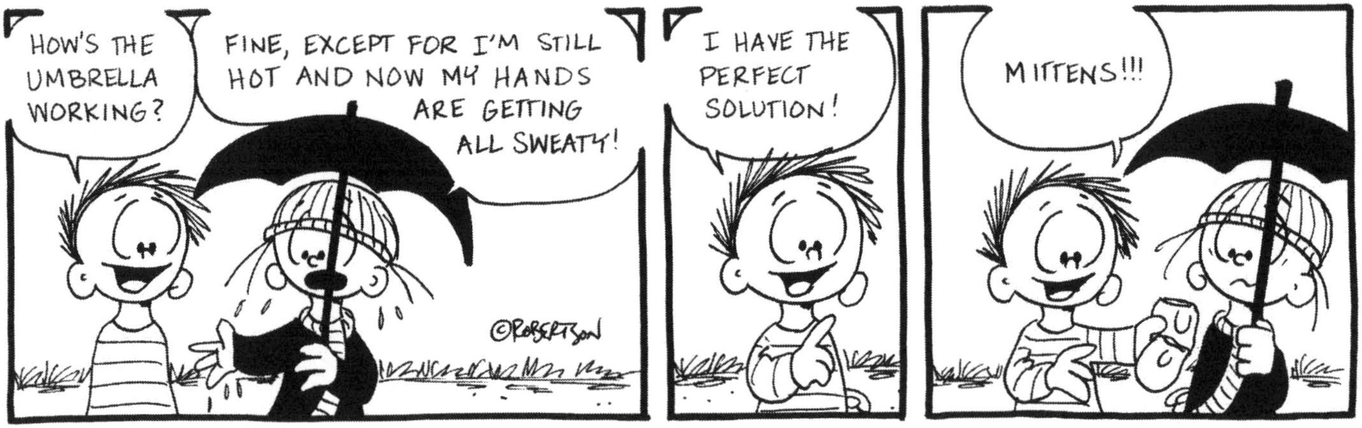
HOW'S THE UMBRELLA WORKING?
FINE, EXCEPT FOR I'M STILL HOT AND NOW MY HANDS ARE GETTING ALL SWEATY!
©ROBERTSON
I HAVE THE PERFECT SOLUTION!
MITTENS!!!

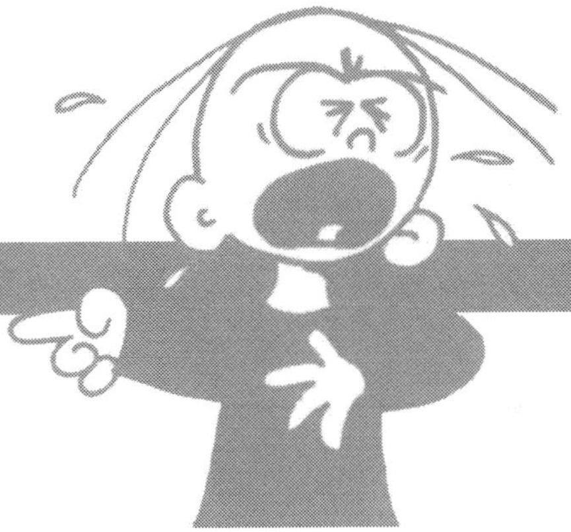

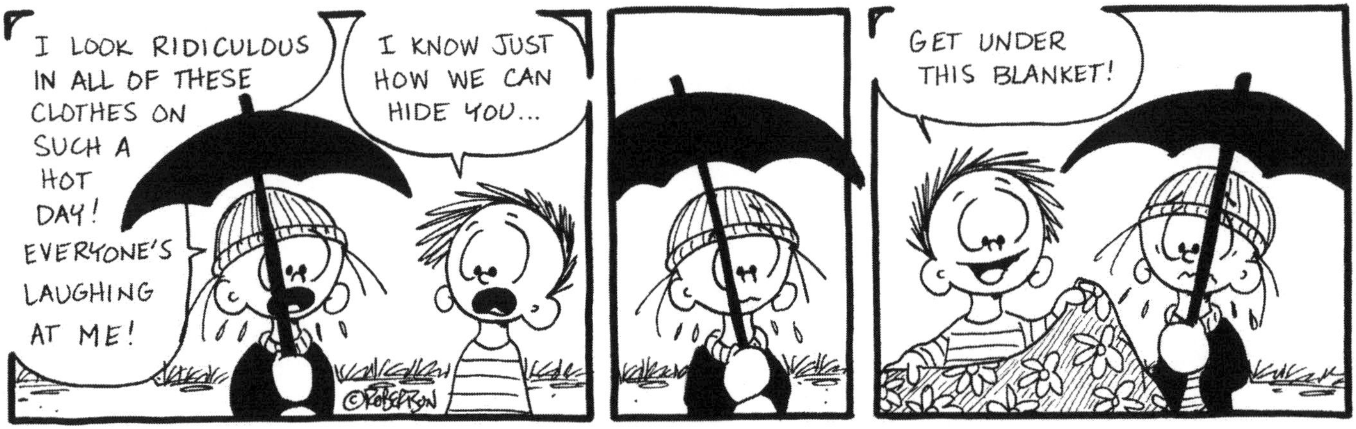
I LOOK RIDICULOUS IN ALL OF THESE CLOTHES ON SUCH A HOT DAY! EVERYONE'S LAUGHING AT ME!
I KNOW JUST HOW WE CAN HIDE YOU...
©ROBERTSON
GET UNDER THIS BLANKET!

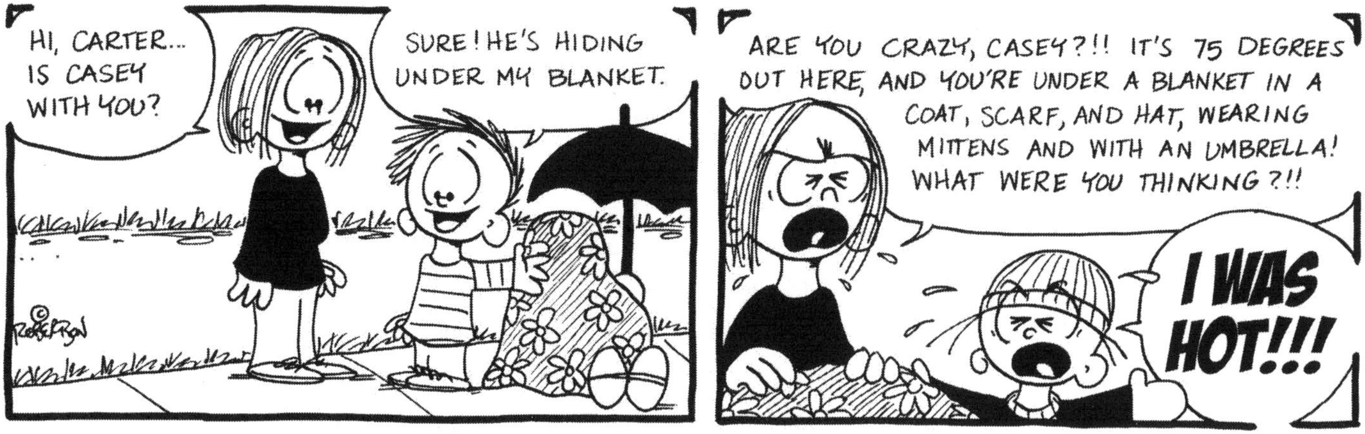
HI, CARTER... IS CASEY WITH YOU?
SURE! HE'S HIDING UNDER MY BLANKET.
© ROBERTSON
ARE YOU CRAZY, CASEY?!! IT'S 75 DEGREES OUT HERE, AND YOU'RE UNDER A BLANKET IN A COAT, SCARF, AND HAT, WEARING MITTENS AND WITH AN UMBRELLA! WHAT WERE YOU THINKING?!!
I WAS HOT!!!

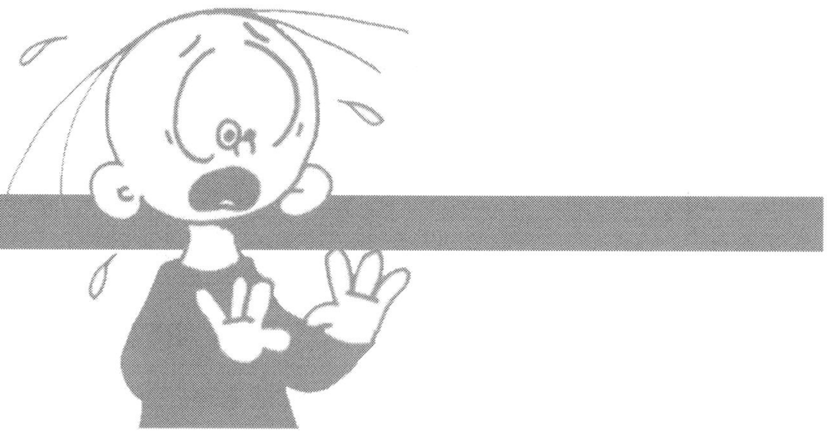

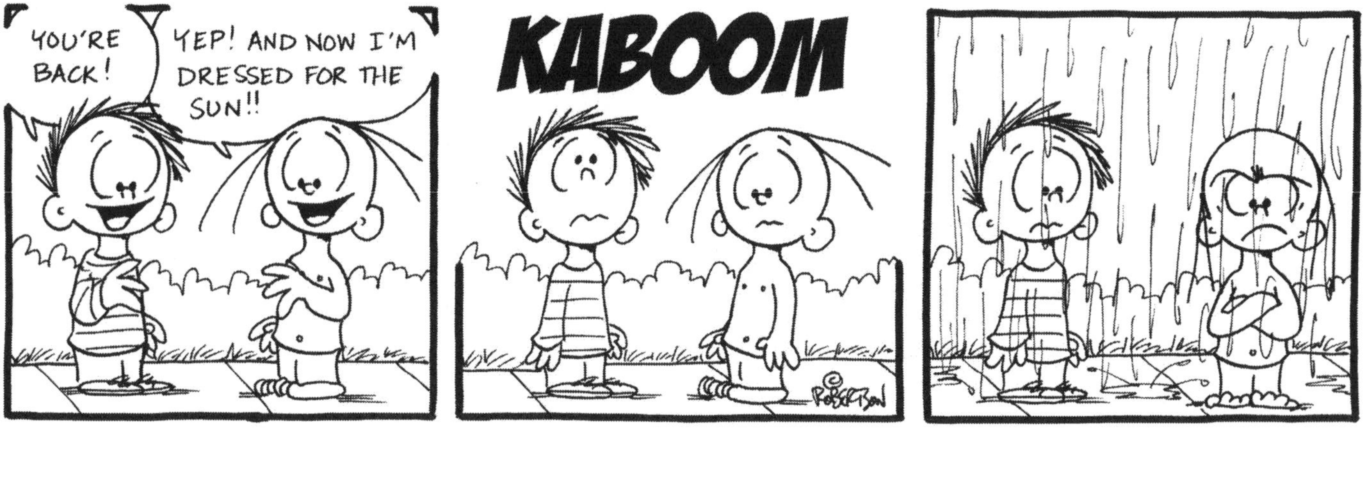
YOU'RE BACK!
YEP! AND NOW I'M DRESSED FOR THE SUN!!
KABOOM
© ROBERTSON

MY MOM TOOK US TO A TRACK MEET YESTERDAY.

WAS IT FUN?

I GUESS... BUT THIS ONE GUY WAS THROWING A STONE FRISBEE, AND HE WAS SWEATING SO MUCH IT GROSSED US OUT!! IT WAS ALL WE COULD TALK ABOUT.

YOU WERE DISCUSSING DISGUSTING DISCUS-ING?!?

AND DON'T GET ME STARTED ABOUT THE TINY HEAVY BASEBALL!

IF YOU LOOK THAT WAY, IT'S ALL BLACK RAIN CLOUDS...

BUT IF YOU LOOK THIS WAY, THERE'S A BEAUTIFUL PATCH OF BLUE SKY!!

I LIKE TO LOOK THIS WAY AND PRETEND IT'S SUMMER!!

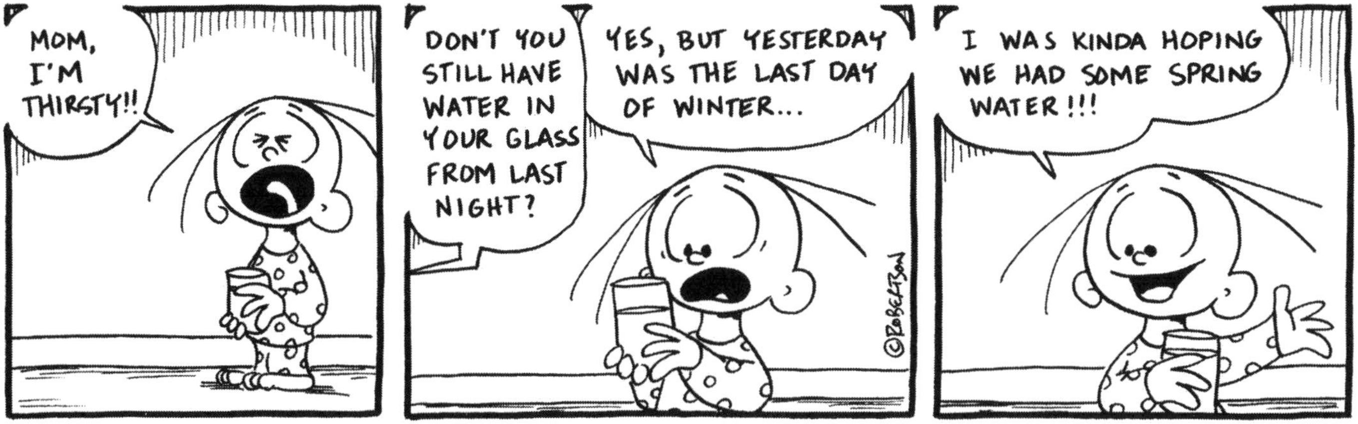
MOM, I'M THIRSTY!!
DON'T YOU STILL HAVE WATER IN YOUR GLASS FROM LAST NIGHT?
YES, BUT YESTERDAY WAS THE LAST DAY OF WINTER...
I WAS KINDA HOPING WE HAD SOME SPRING WATER!!!

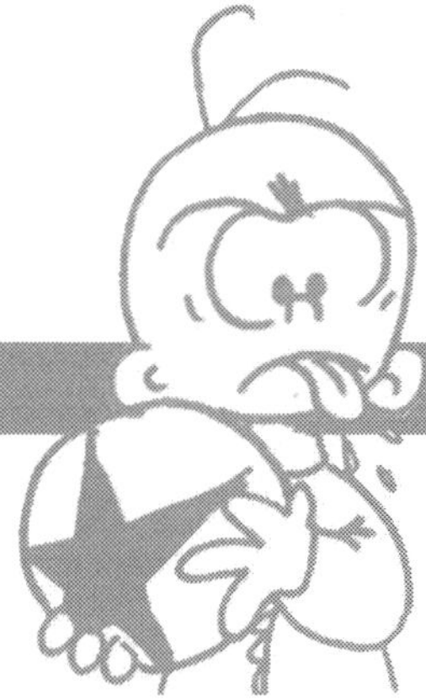

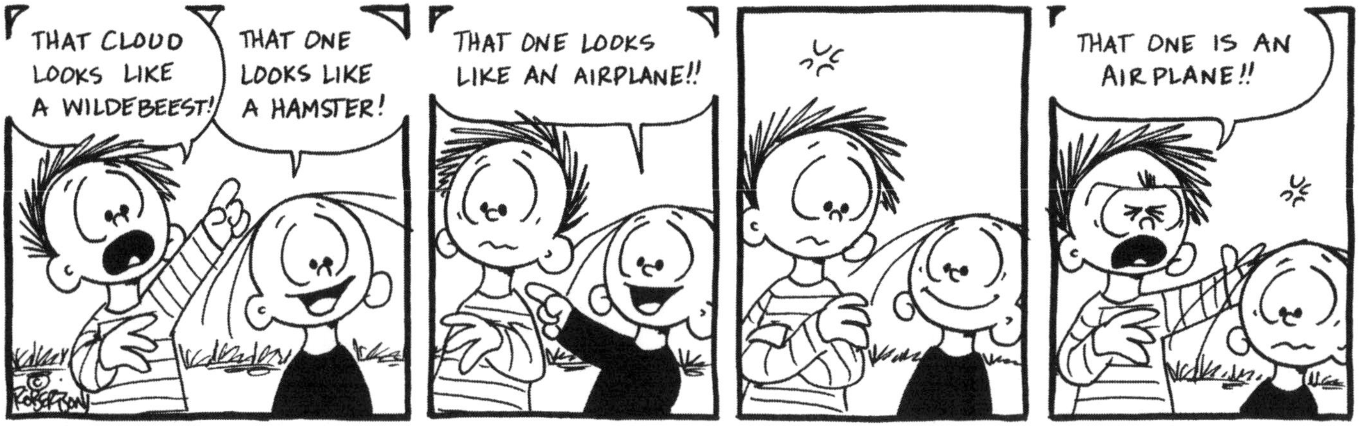
THAT CLOUD LOOKS LIKE A WILDEBEEST!
THAT ONE LOOKS LIKE A HAMSTER!
THAT ONE LOOKS LIKE AN AIRPLANE!!
THAT ONE IS AN AIRPLANE!!

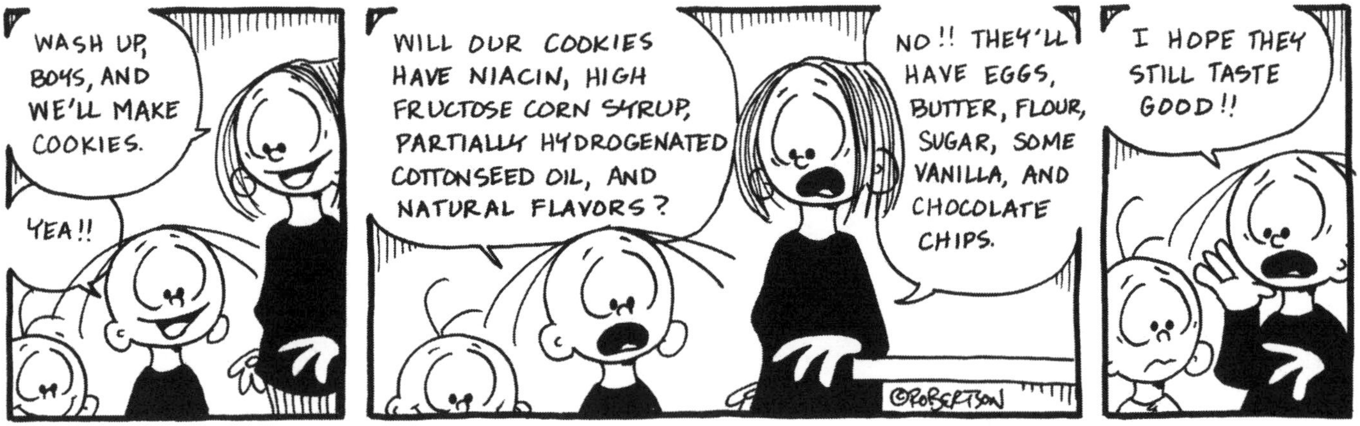
WASH UP, BOYS, AND WE'LL MAKE COOKIES.
YEA!!
WILL OUR COOKIES HAVE NIACIN, HIGH FRUCTOSE CORN SYRUP, PARTIALLY HYDROGENATED COTTONSEED OIL, AND NATURAL FLAVORS?
NO!! THEY'LL HAVE EGGS, BUTTER, FLOUR, SUGAR, SOME VANILLA, AND CHOCOLATE CHIPS.
©ROBERTSON
I HOPE THEY STILL TASTE GOOD!!

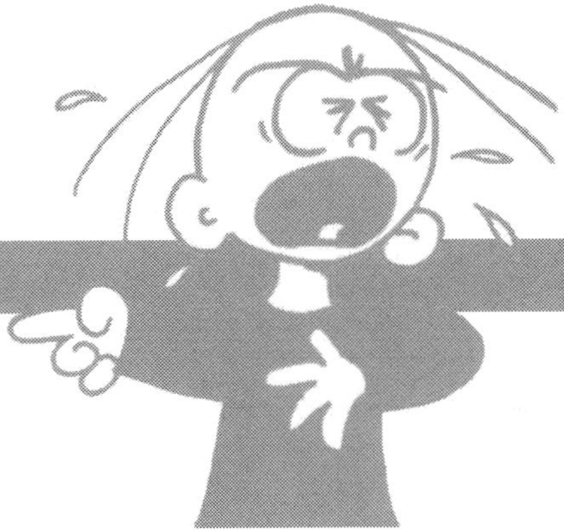

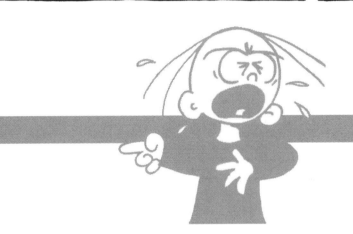

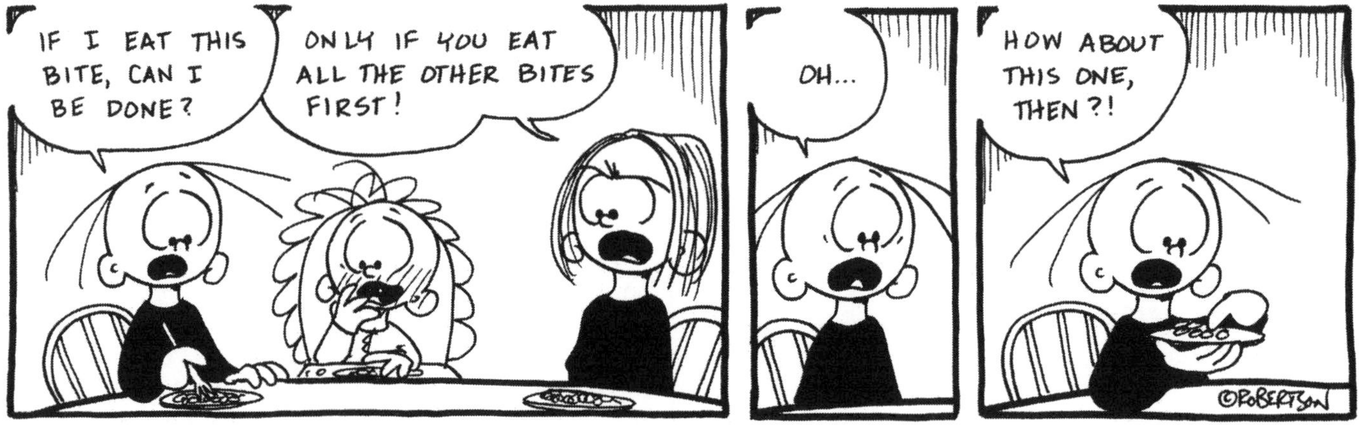
IF I EAT THIS BITE, CAN I BE DONE?
ONLY IF YOU EAT ALL THE OTHER BITES FIRST!
OH...
HOW ABOUT THIS ONE, THEN?!
©ROBERTSON

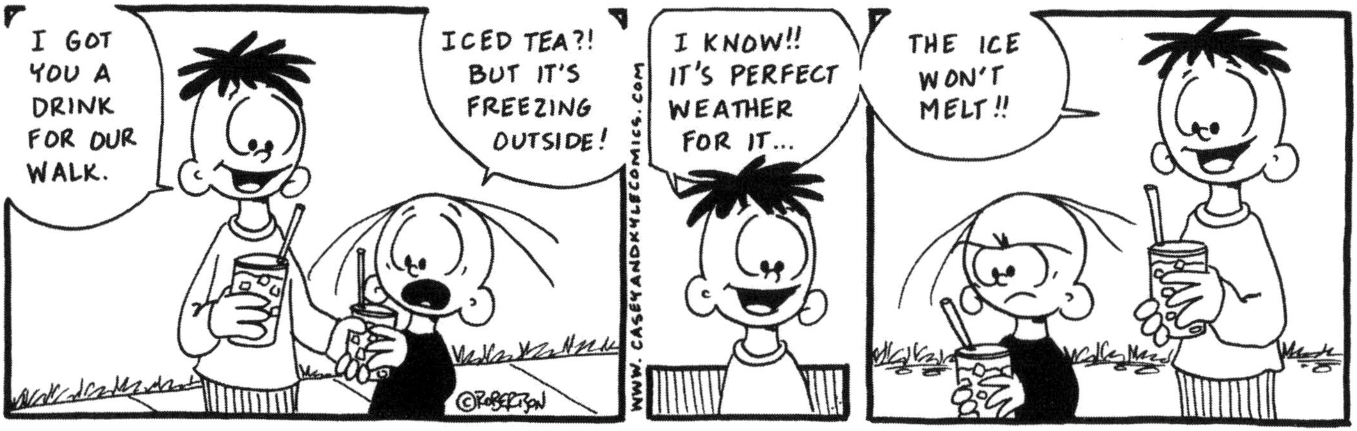
I GOT YOU A DRINK FOR OUR WALK.
ICED TEA?! BUT IT'S FREEZING OUTSIDE!
I KNOW!! IT'S PERFECT WEATHER FOR IT...
THE ICE WON'T MELT!!
©ROBERTSON
WWW.CASEYANDKYLECOMICS.COM

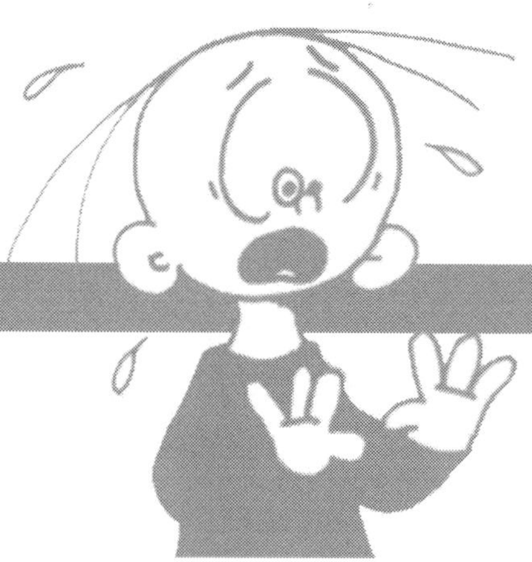

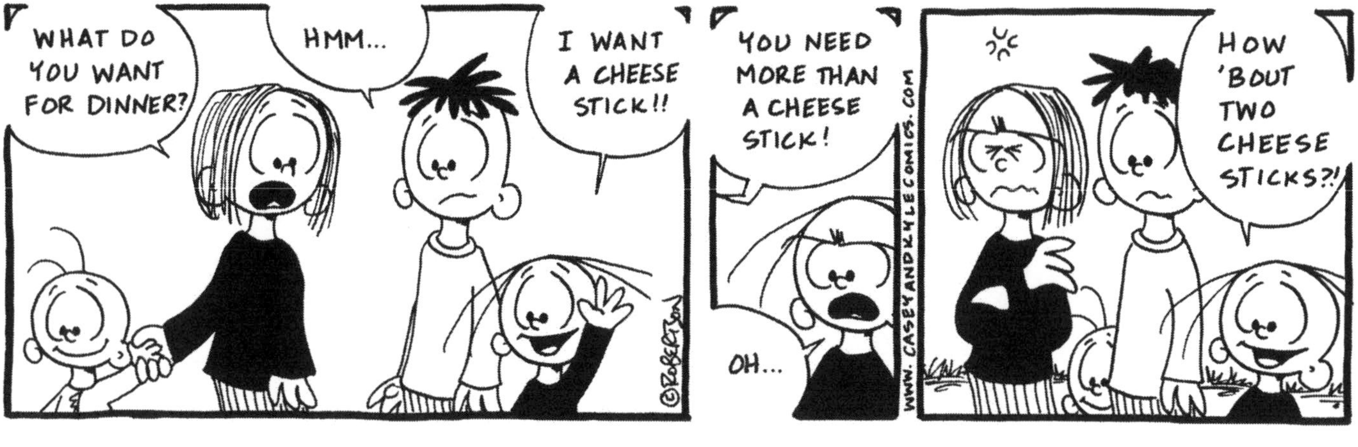
WHAT DO YOU WANT FOR DINNER?
HMM...
I WANT A CHEESE STICK!!
YOU NEED MORE THAN A CHEESE STICK!
OH...
HOW 'BOUT TWO CHEESE STICKS?!
©ROBERTSON
WWW.CASEYANDKYLECOMICS.COM

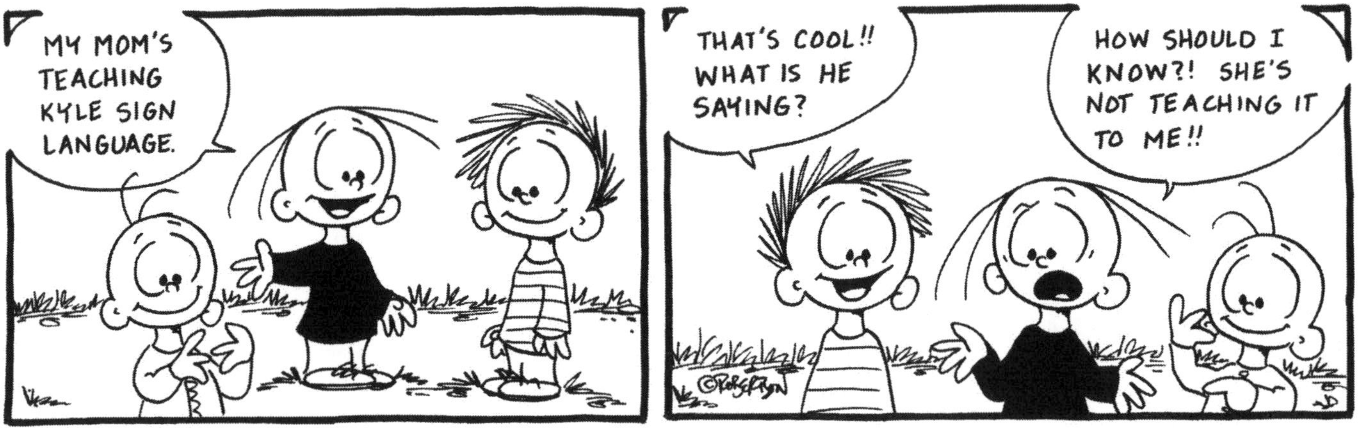
MY MOM'S TEACHING KYLE SIGN LANGUAGE.
THAT'S COOL!! WHAT IS HE SAYING?
HOW SHOULD I KNOW?! SHE'S NOT TEACHING IT TO ME!!
©ROBERTSON

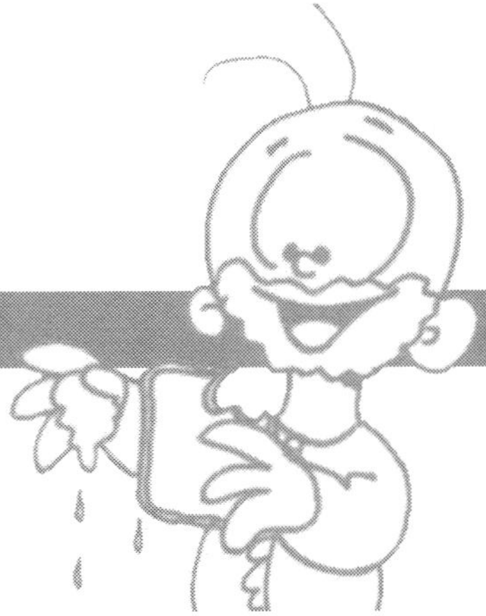

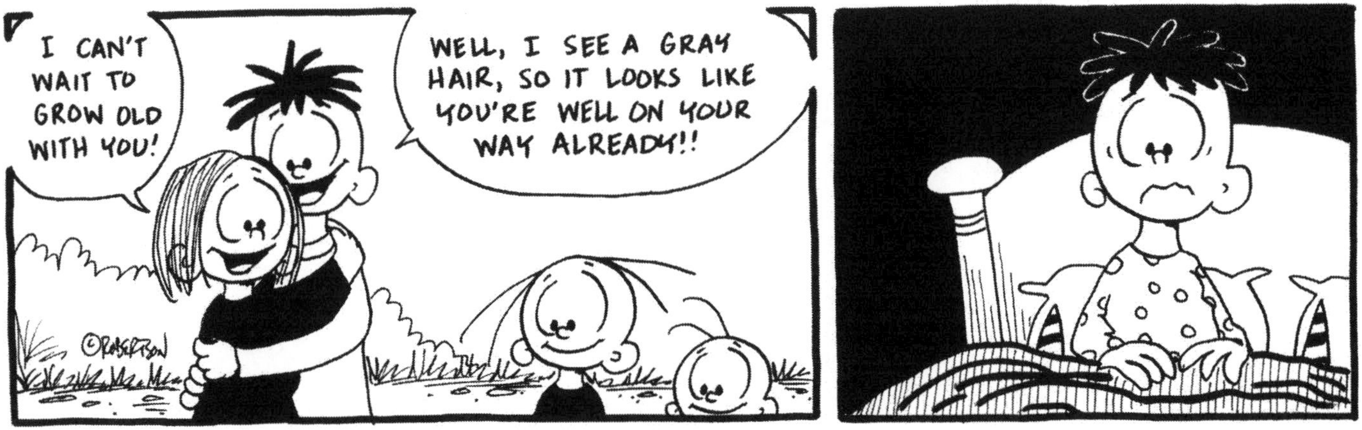
I CAN'T WAIT TO GROW OLD WITH YOU!
WELL, I SEE A GRAY HAIR, SO IT LOOKS LIKE YOU'RE WELL ON YOUR WAY ALREADY!!
©ROBERTSON

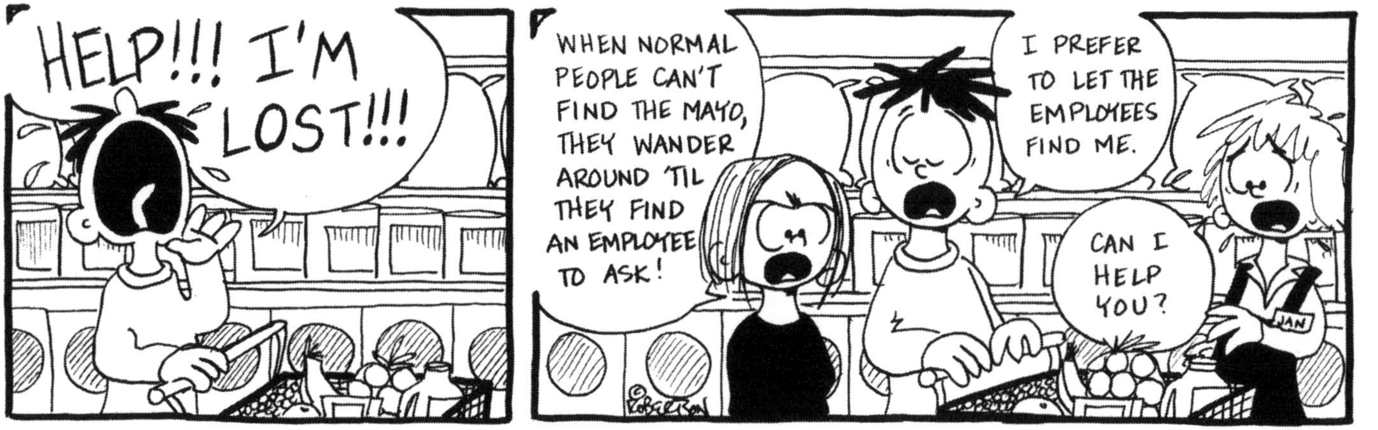
HELP!!! I'M LOST!!!
WHEN NORMAL PEOPLE CAN'T FIND THE MAYO, THEY WANDER AROUND 'TIL THEY FIND AN EMPLOYEE TO ASK!
I PREFER TO LET THE EMPLOYEES FIND ME.
CAN I HELP YOU?
JAN
©ROBERTSON

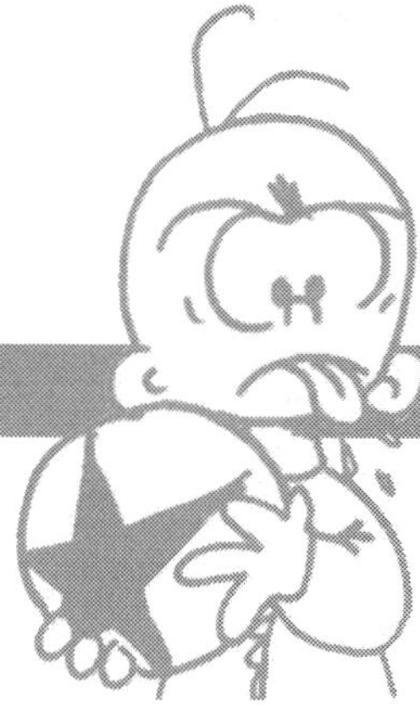

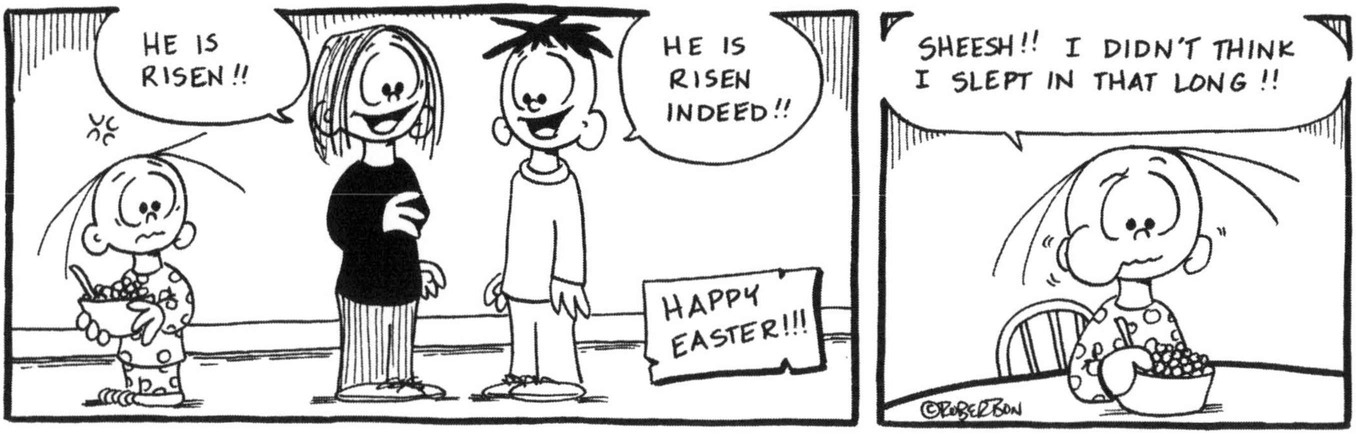
HE IS RISEN!!
HE IS RISEN INDEED!!
HAPPY EASTER!!!
SHEESH!! I DIDN'T THINK I SLEPT IN THAT LONG!!
©ROBERTSON

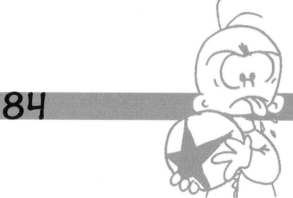

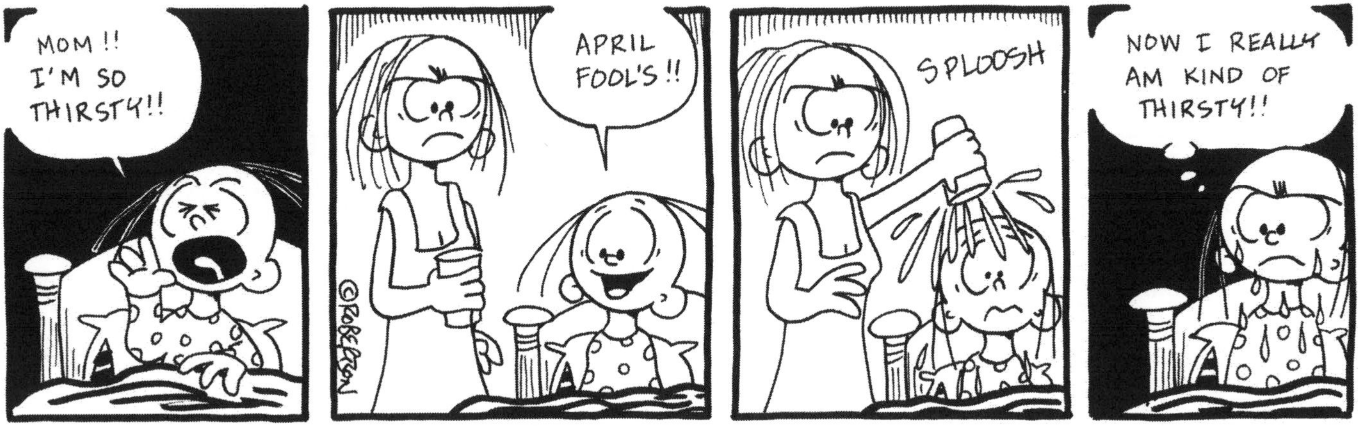
MOM !! I'M SO THIRSTY!!
APRIL FOOL'S !!
SPLOOSH
NOW I REALLY AM KIND OF THIRSTY!!
©ROBERTSON

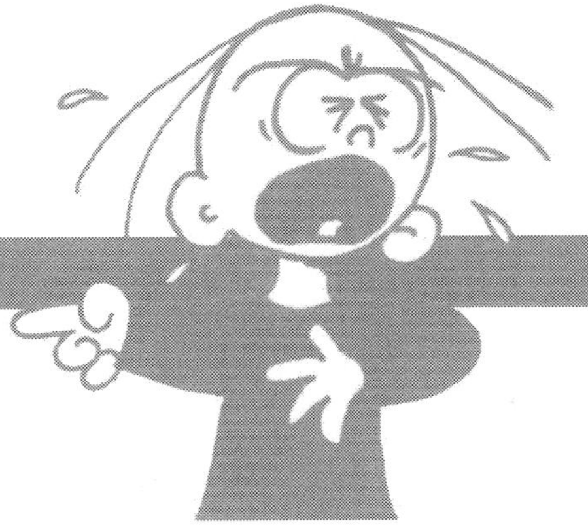

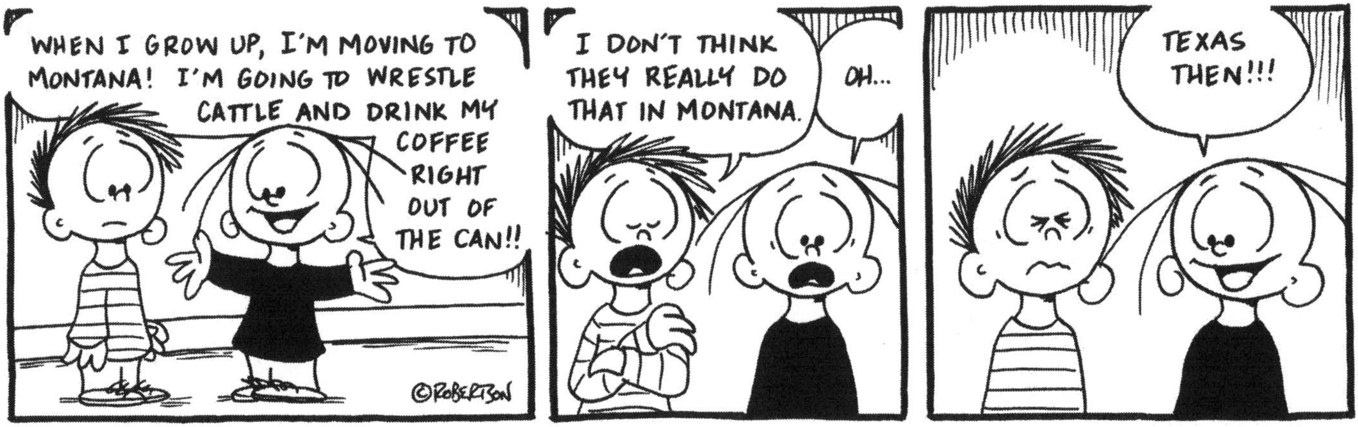
WHEN I GROW UP, I'M MOVING TO MONTANA! I'M GOING TO WRESTLE CATTLE AND DRINK MY COFFEE RIGHT OUT OF THE CAN!!
©ROBERTSON
I DON'T THINK THEY REALLY DO THAT IN MONTANA.
OH...
TEXAS THEN!!!

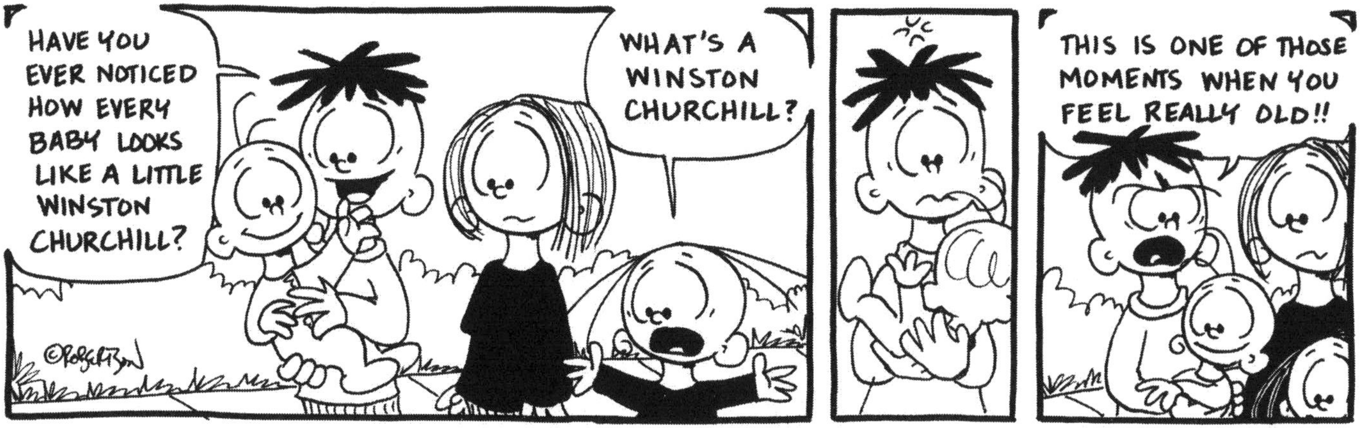
HAVE YOU EVER NOTICED HOW EVERY BABY LOOKS LIKE A LITTLE WINSTON CHURCHILL?
WHAT'S A WINSTON CHURCHILL?
THIS IS ONE OF THOSE MOMENTS WHEN YOU FEEL REALLY OLD!!
©ROBERTSON

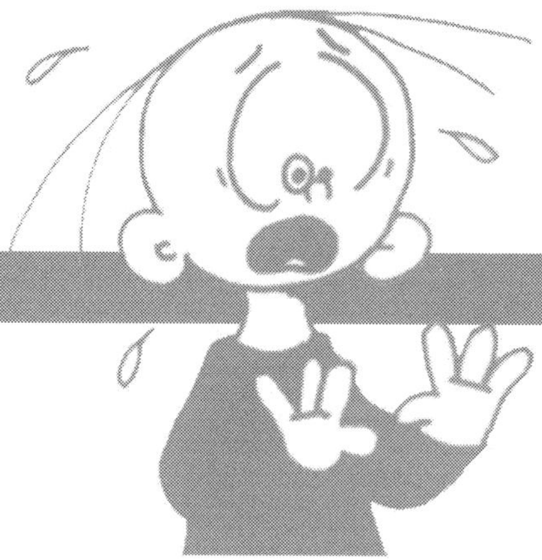

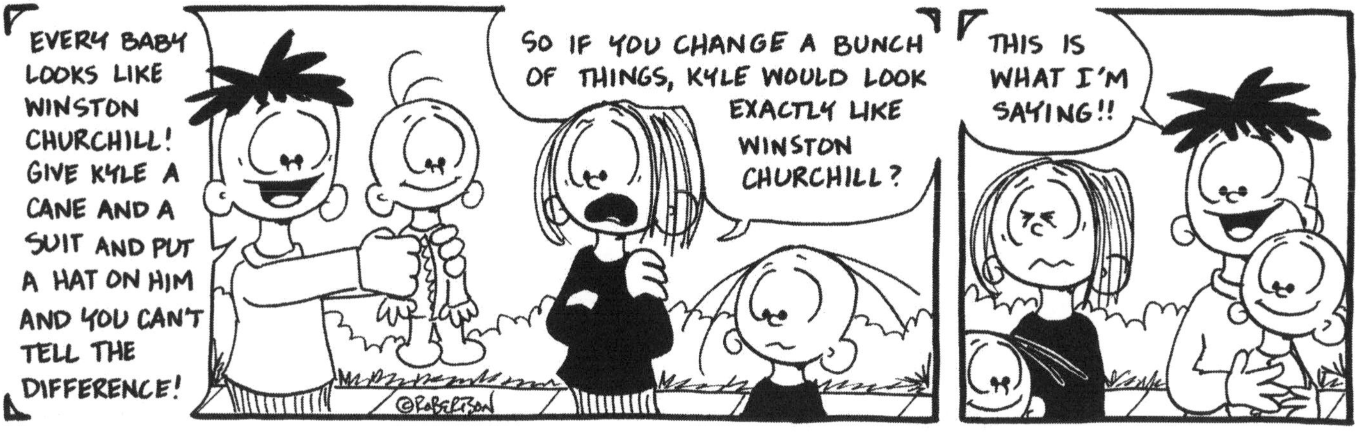
EVERY BABY LOOKS LIKE WINSTON CHURCHILL! GIVE KYLE A CANE AND A SUIT AND PUT A HAT ON HIM AND YOU CAN'T TELL THE DIFFERENCE!
SO IF YOU CHANGE A BUNCH OF THINGS, KYLE WOULD LOOK EXACTLY LIKE WINSTON CHURCHILL?
THIS IS WHAT I'M SAYING!!
©ROBERTSON

AAAAAHHH!!!!!
WHY ARE YOU BOTH NAKED IN A MUD PIT?!
©ROBERSON
YOU SAID NOT TO GET OUR CLOTHES DIRTY!!

THE GOOD NEWS IS...
WE GOT SO DIRTY...
©ROBERSON
WE CAN MAKE MUD PIES IN THE BATH!!

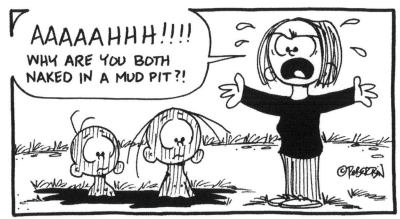

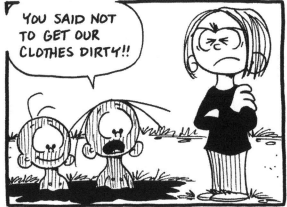

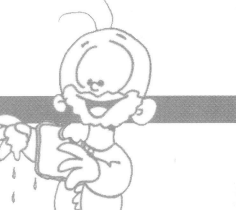

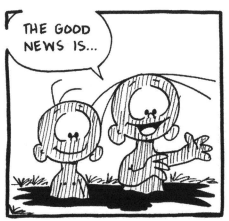

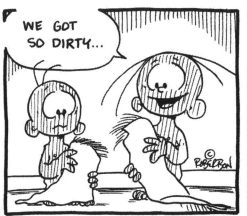

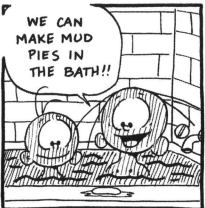

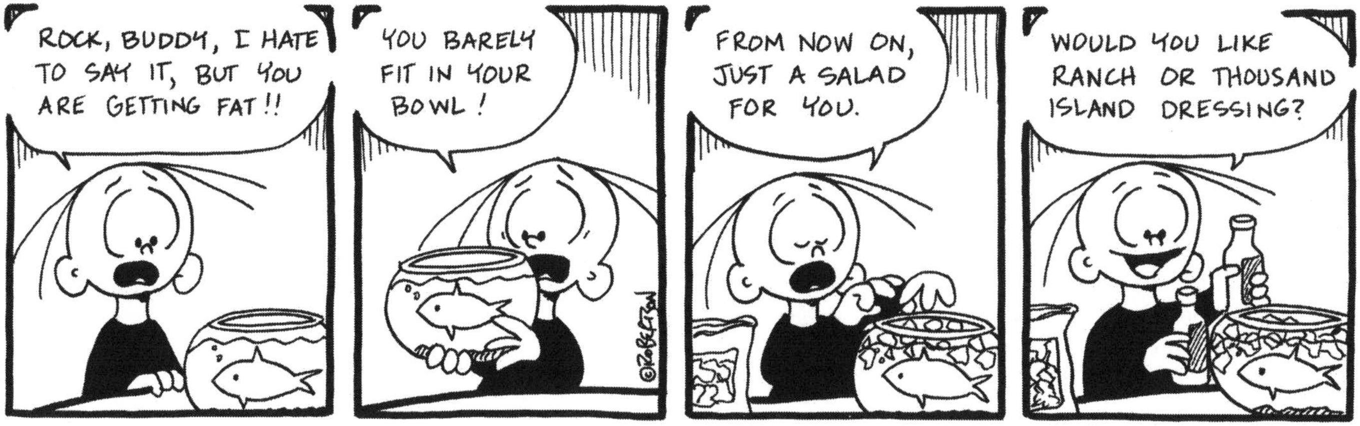
ROCK, BUDDY, I HATE TO SAY IT, BUT YOU ARE GETTING FAT!!
YOU BARELY FIT IN YOUR BOWL!
FROM NOW ON, JUST A SALAD FOR YOU.
WOULD YOU LIKE RANCH OR THOUSAND ISLAND DRESSING?

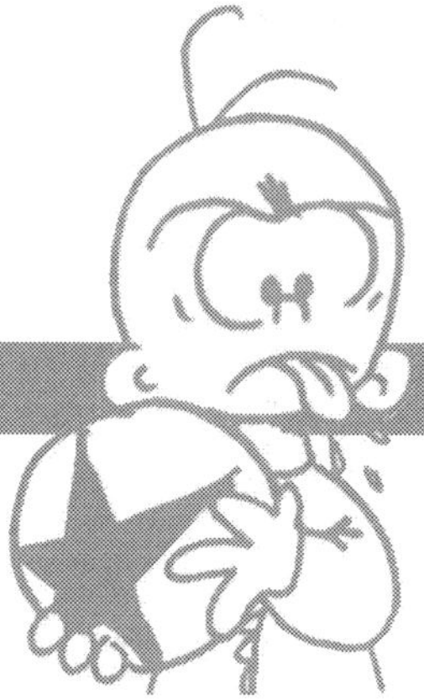

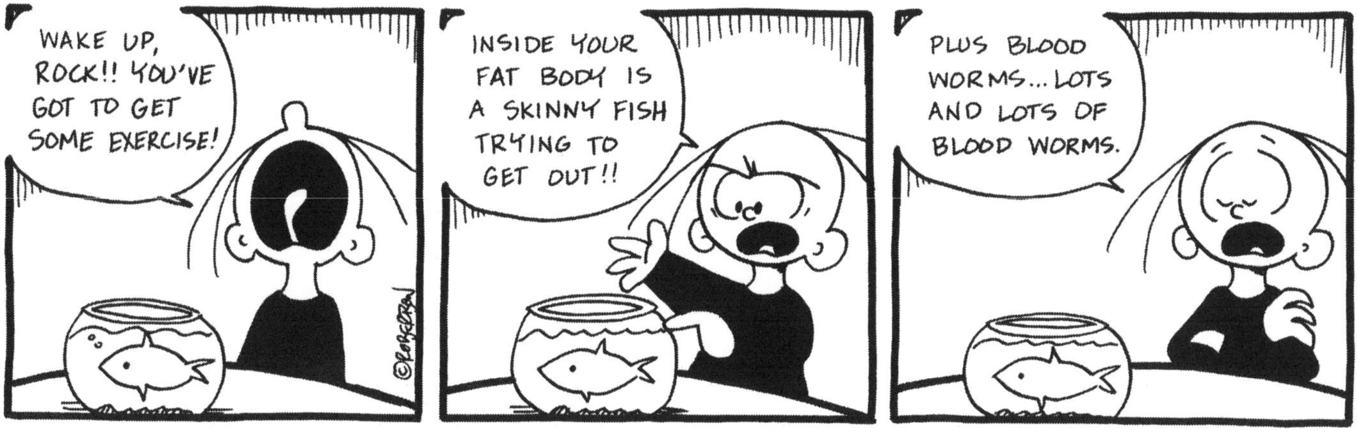
WAKE UP, ROCK!! YOU'VE GOT TO GET SOME EXERCISE!
INSIDE YOUR FAT BODY IS A SKINNY FISH TRYING TO GET OUT!!
PLUS BLOOD WORMS... LOTS AND LOTS OF BLOOD WORMS.

I DON'T KNOW IF YOUR DIET IS WORKING, ROCK.
THE SCALE SAYS FIVE POUNDS...
BUT I'M GUESSING A LOT OF IT IS WATER WEIGHT!!

WHAT ARE YOU DOING?
WE'RE GOING FOR A LONG WALK...
ROCK'S TRYING TO GET SKINNY.
IS HE HOPING TO FIT INTO A NEW SWIM SUIT?
WHY DOES EVERYONE KEEP ASKING ME THAT?!

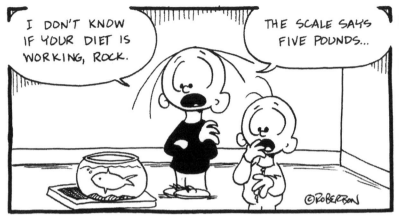

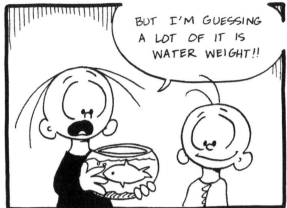

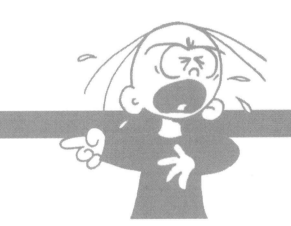

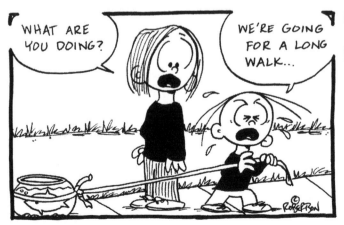

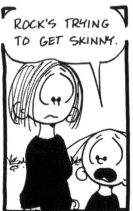

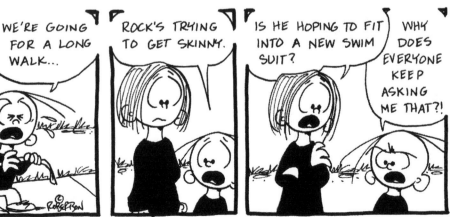

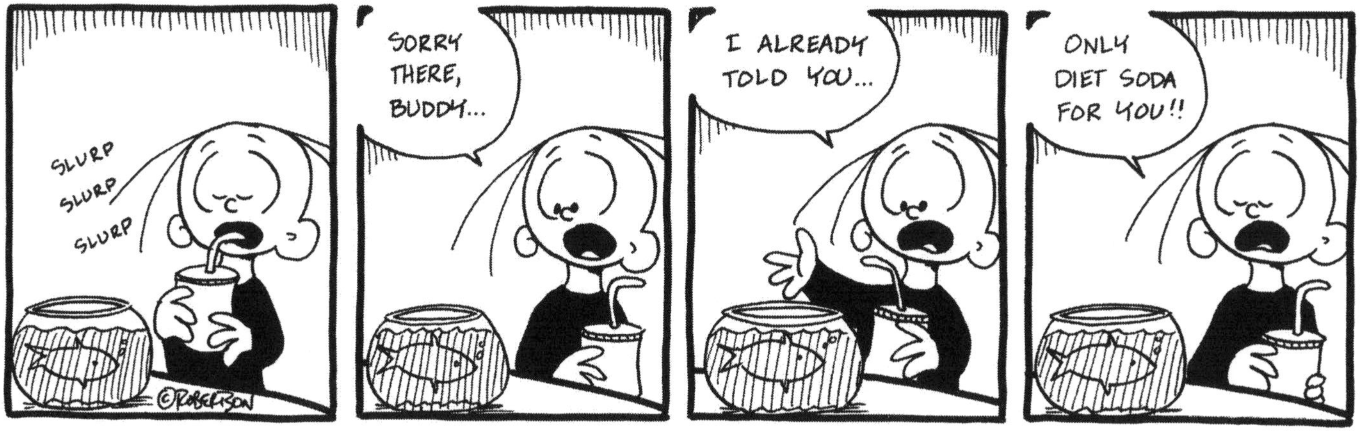
SLURP
SLURP
SLURP
©ROBERTSON
SORRY THERE, BUDDY...
I ALREADY TOLD YOU...
ONLY DIET SODA FOR YOU!!

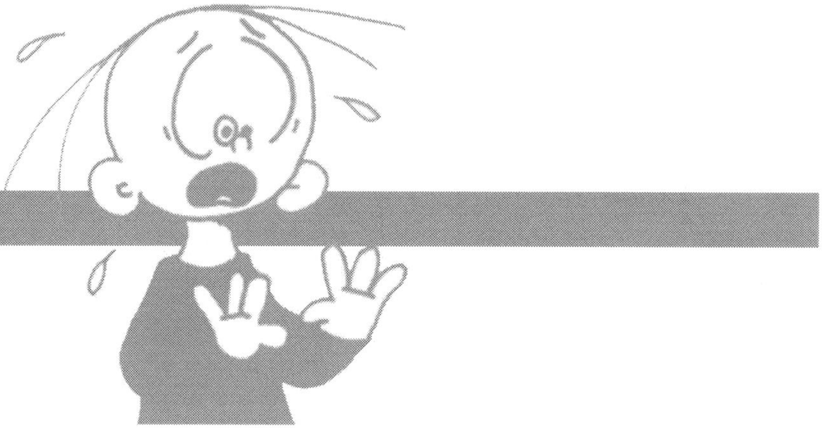

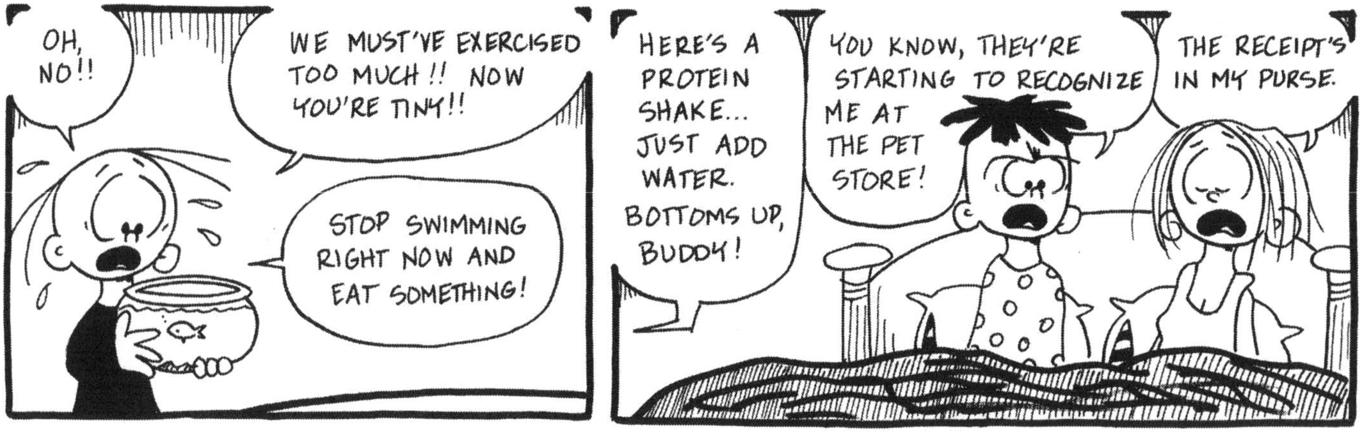
OH, NO!!
WE MUST'VE EXERCISED TOO MUCH!! NOW YOU'RE TINY!!
STOP SWIMMING RIGHT NOW AND EAT SOMETHING!
HERE'S A PROTEIN SHAKE... JUST ADD WATER. BOTTOMS UP, BUDDY!
YOU KNOW, THEY'RE STARTING TO RECOGNIZE ME AT THE PET STORE!
THE RECEIPT'S IN MY PURSE.

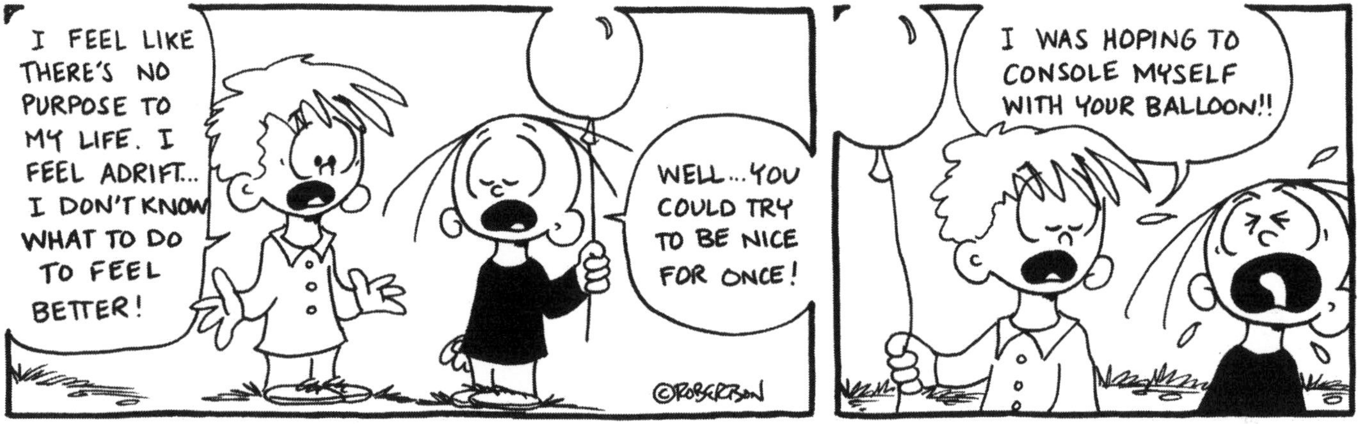
I FEEL LIKE THERE'S NO PURPOSE TO MY LIFE. I FEEL ADRIFT... I DON'T KNOW WHAT TO DO TO FEEL BETTER!
WELL... YOU COULD TRY TO BE NICE FOR ONCE!
©ROBERTSON
I WAS HOPING TO CONSOLE MYSELF WITH YOUR BALLOON!!

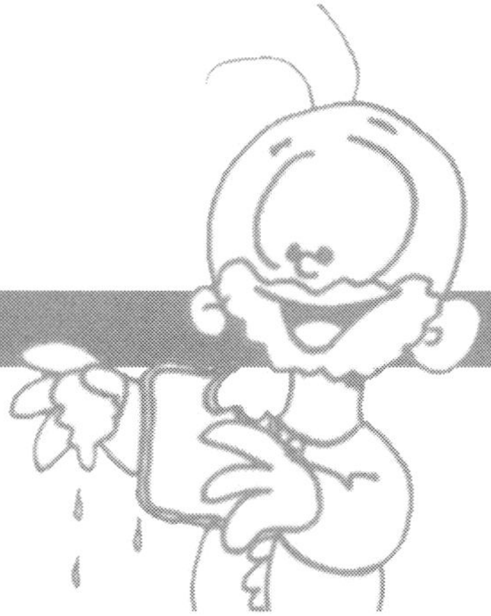

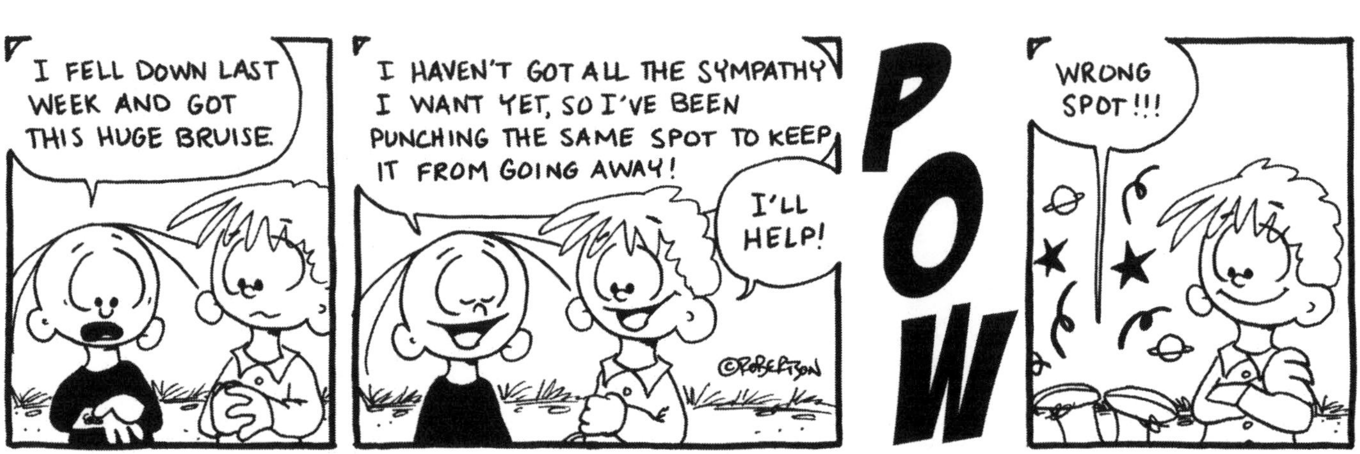
I FELL DOWN LAST WEEK AND GOT THIS HUGE BRUISE.
I HAVEN'T GOT ALL THE SYMPATHY I WANT YET, SO I'VE BEEN PUNCHING THE SAME SPOT TO KEEP IT FROM GOING AWAY!
I'LL HELP!
©ROBERTSON
POW
WRONG SPOT!!!

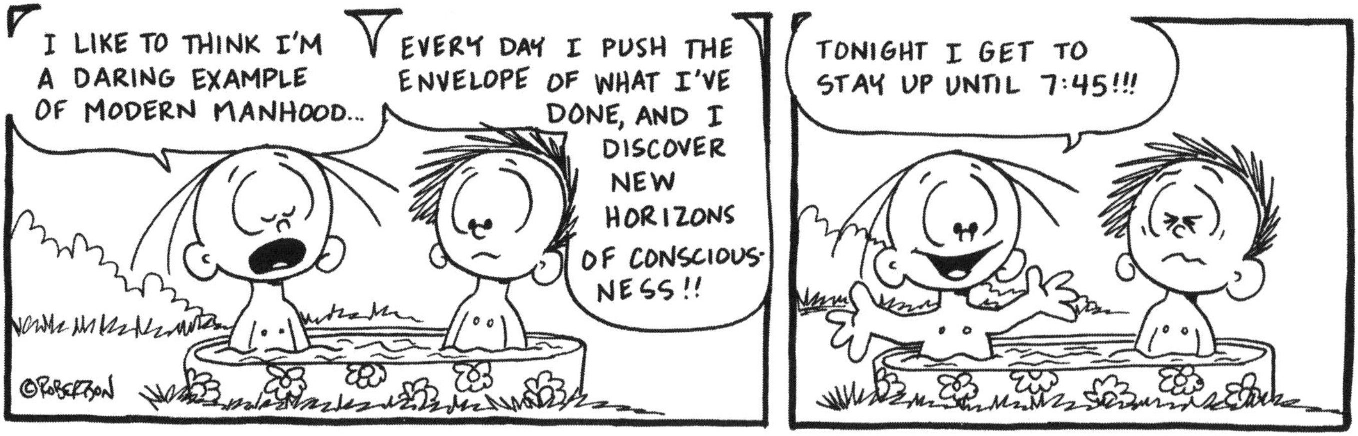
I LIKE TO THINK I'M A DARING EXAMPLE OF MODERN MANHOOD...
EVERY DAY I PUSH THE ENVELOPE OF WHAT I'VE DONE, AND I DISCOVER NEW HORIZONS OF CONSCIOUS-NESS!!
TONIGHT I GET TO STAY UP UNTIL 7:45!!!
©ROBERSON

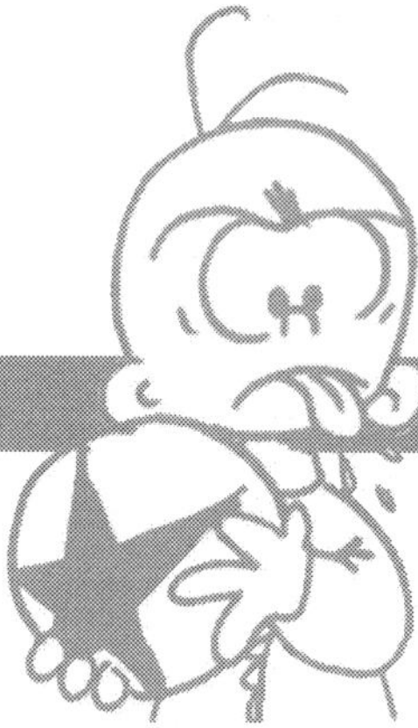

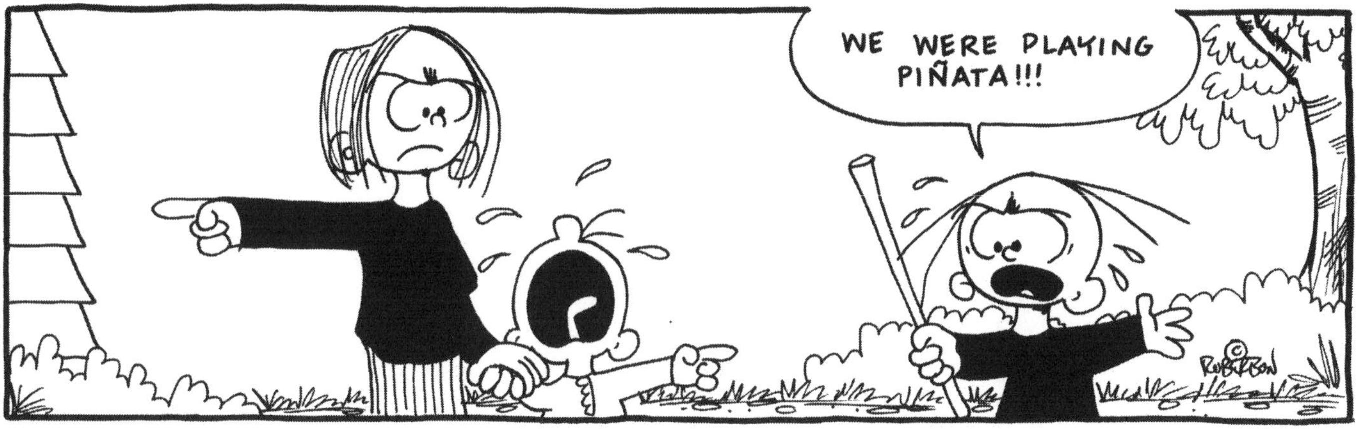
WE WERE PLAYING PIÑATA!!!
©ROBERSON

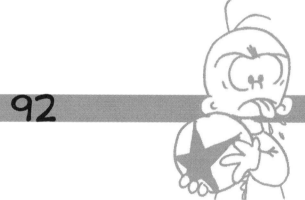

I THINK I'M READY FOR A REFILL!!
© ROBERTSON

DO YOU WANT TO SWITCH SIDES?
NO THANKS.
© ROBERTSON
I PREFER TO STAY IN THE SHALLOW END!

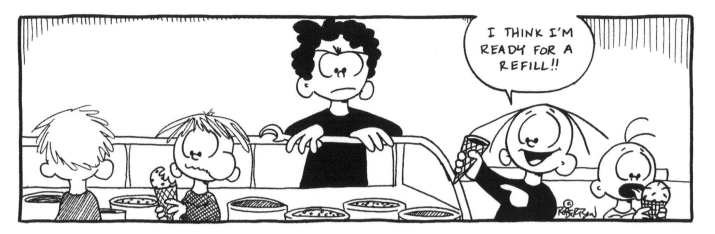

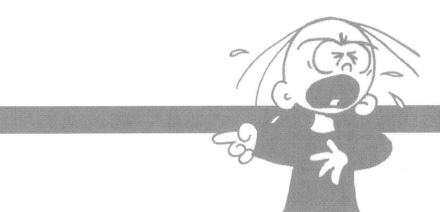

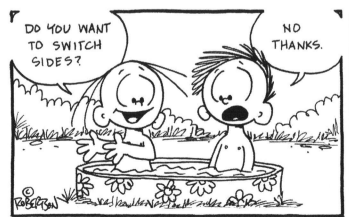

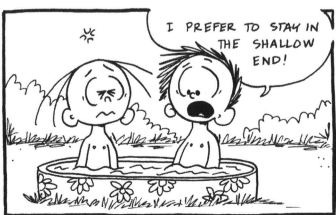

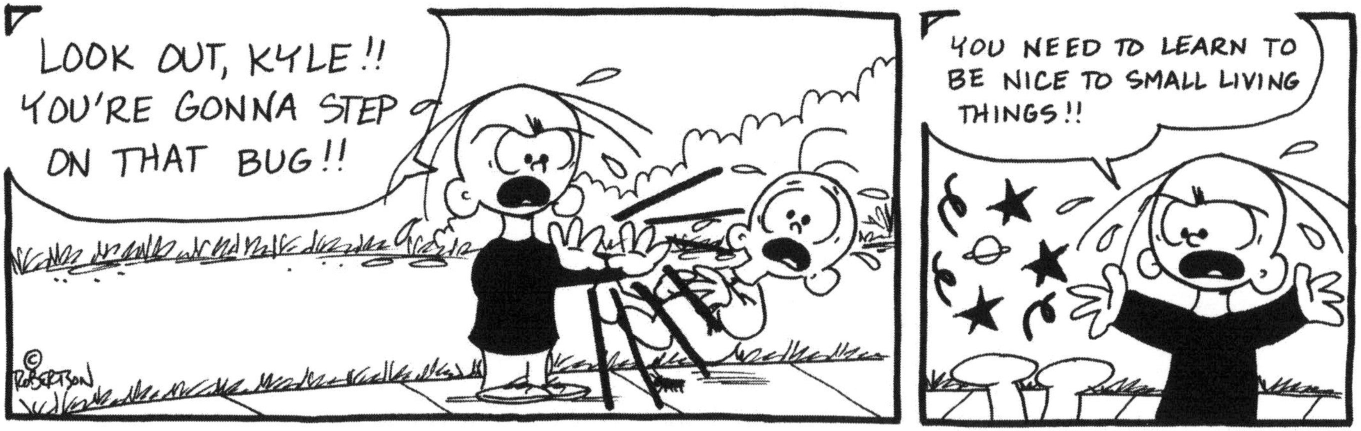
LOOK OUT, KYLE!! YOU'RE GONNA STEP ON THAT BUG!!
©ROBERTSON
YOU NEED TO LEARN TO BE NICE TO SMALL LIVING THINGS!!

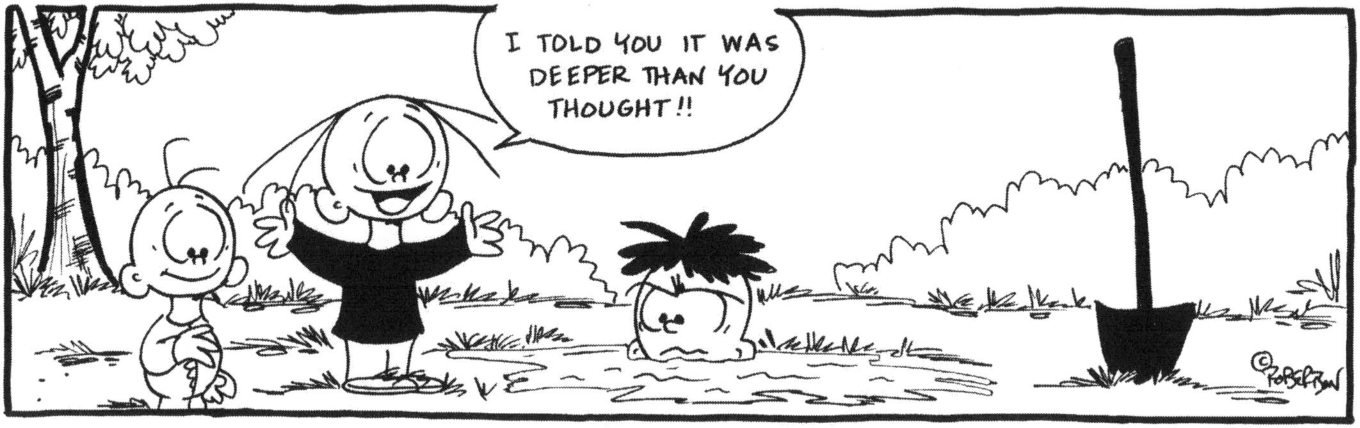
I TOLD YOU IT WAS DEEPER THAN YOU THOUGHT!!
©ROBERTSON

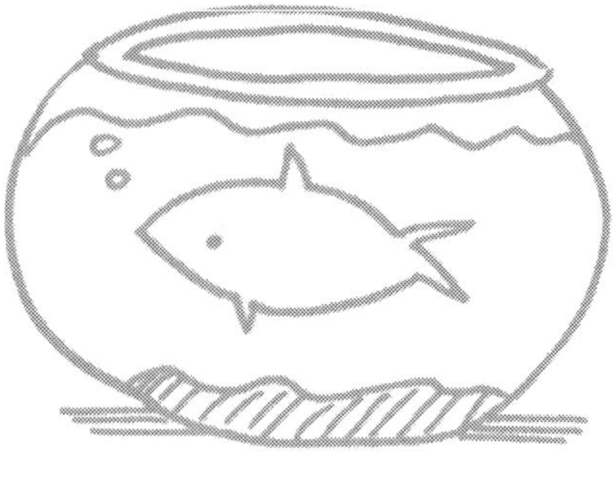

COLLECT THEM ALL!!!

AVAILABLE AT CASEYANDKYLECOMICS.COM

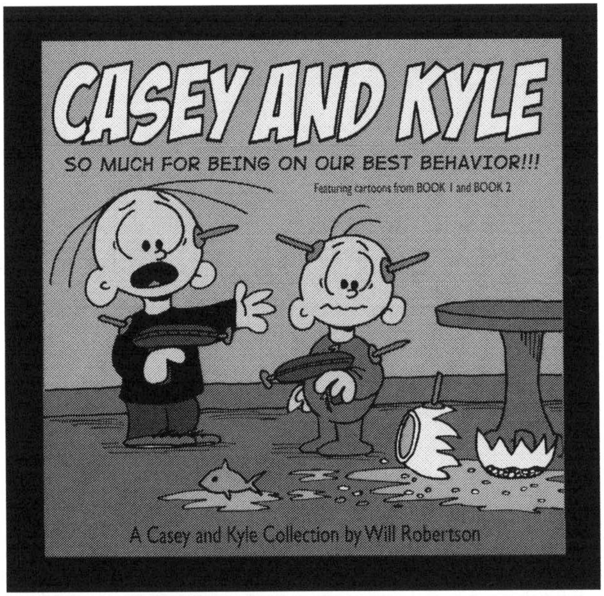
CASEY AND KYLE
SO MUCH FOR BEING ON OUR BEST BEHAVIOR!!!
Featuring cartoons from BOOK 1 and BOOK 2
A Casey and Kyle Collection by Will Robertson

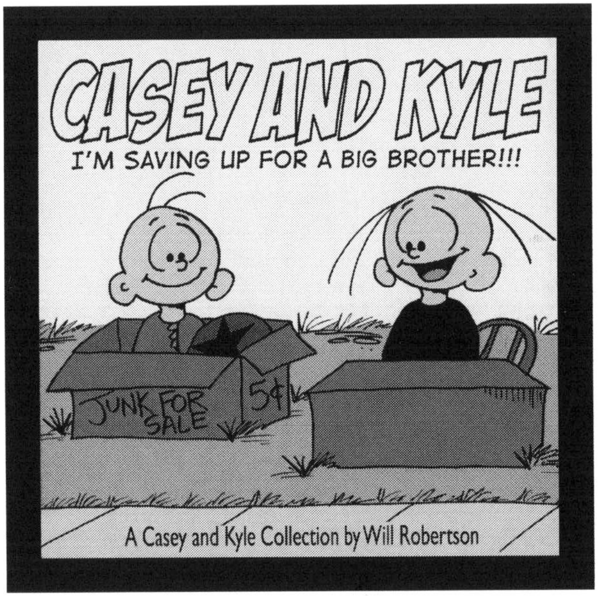
CASEY AND KYLE
I'M SAVING UP FOR A BIG BROTHER!!!
JUNK FOR SALE
5¢
A Casey and Kyle Collection by Will Robertson

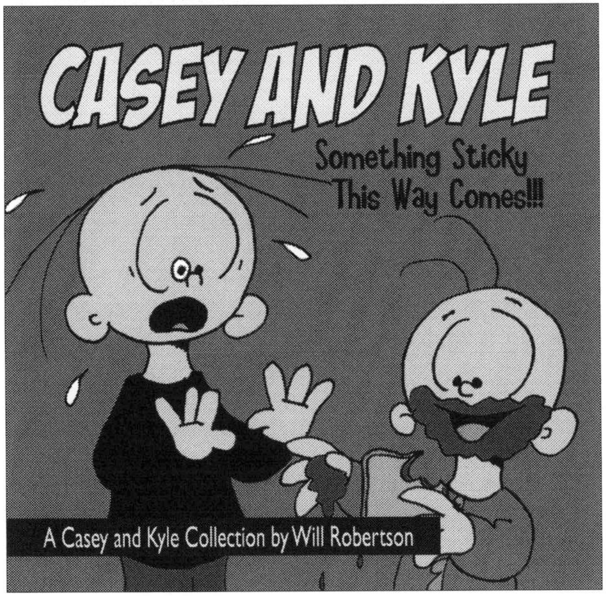
CASEY AND KYLE
Something Sticky This Way Comes!!!
A Casey and Kyle Collection by Will Robertson

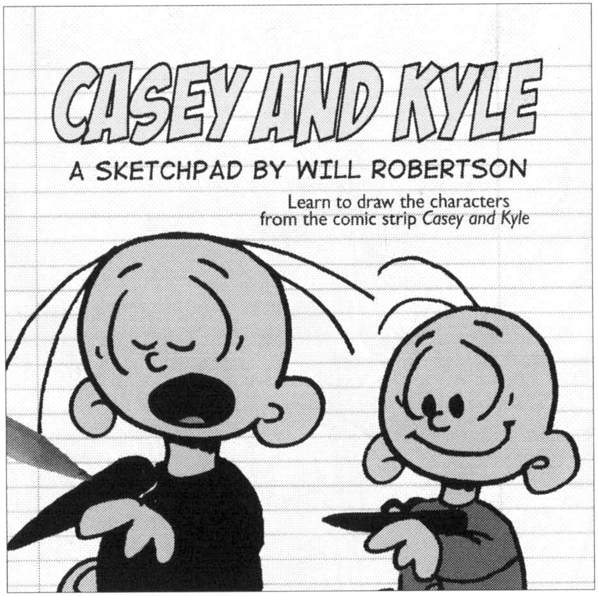
CASEY AND KYLE
A SKETCHPAD BY WILL ROBERTSON
Learn to draw the characters from the comic strip Casey and Kyle

ALSO BY WILL ROBERTSON

AVAILABLE AT CASEYANDKYLECOMICS.COM

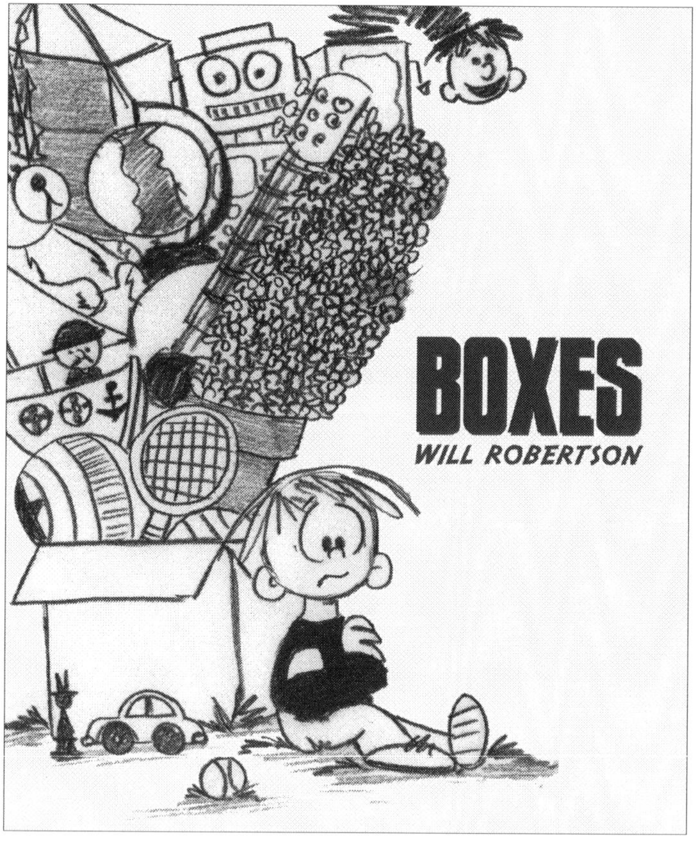
BOXES
WILL ROBERTSON

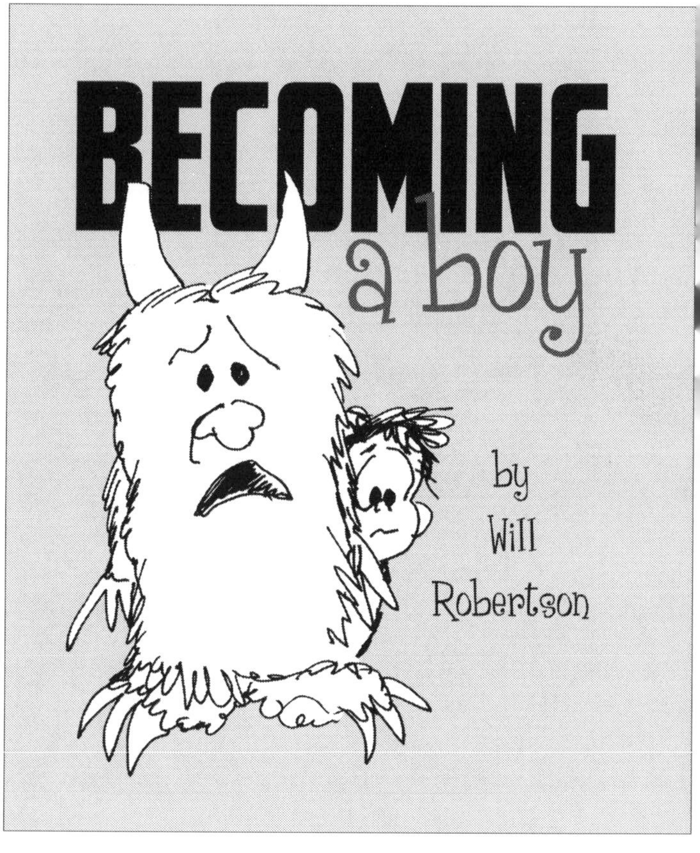
BECOMING
a boy
by
Will
Robertson